)3 by David Stout

erved

book may be reproduced in any form or by any electronic or mechanical
ing information storage and retrieval systems, without permission in writ-
publisher, except by a reviewer who may quote brief passages in a review.

red in the United States of America

)5 04 03

of Congress Cataloging-in-Publication Data

David.
t of the devil : the untold story of Thomas Trantino and the Angel Lounge
s / David Stout.
    p. cm.
BN 0-940159-70-8
Trantino, Thomas, 1938- 2. Murderers—New Jersey—Biography. 3. Police
ders—New Jersey—Lodi—Case studies. 4. Parole—New Jersey—Case studies.
itle.
HV6248.T72 S76 2002
364.15'23'092—dc21

2002001805

Cover and interior design: Jerilyn Kauffman

This book is available at a special discount on bulk purchases for promotional,
business, and educational use. For information write to:

Camino Books, Inc.
P.O. Box 59026
Philadelphia, PA 19102

www.caminobooks.com

NIGH...
THE D...

THE UNTOLD STORY OF T...
AND THE ANGEL LOUN...

DAVID STOU...

Camino Books, Inc.
Philadelphia

IN MEMORY OF PETER VOTO
AND GARY TEDESCO,
AND FOR THOSE WHO MISS THEM STILL

CONTENTS

Acknowledgments   vii

Introduction   ix

PART I

CHAPTER 1   AN OLD COP WITH A MISSION   3
CHAPTER 2   THIS PLACE CALLED LODI   6
CHAPTER 3   A FAMILY IN BROOKLYN   11
CHAPTER 4   THE BULLY   16
CHAPTER 5   NOT CUT OUT FOR MARRIAGE   18
CHAPTER 6   GARY AND ADRIENNE   23
CHAPTER 7   NOT A DAY TO REST   25
CHAPTER 8   FOREBODINGS   28
CHAPTER 9   A CELEBRATION TURNS DEADLY   32
CHAPTER 10   CRAZY FLIGHT   37
CHAPTER 11   BEFORE AND AFTER   41
CHAPTER 12   MANHUNT   45
CHAPTER 13   RAGE AND LEGEND   50
CHAPTER 14   ACROSS THE RIVER AGAIN   54
CHAPTER 15   THE ADVERSARIES   57
CHAPTER 16   THE TRIAL BEGINS   62
CHAPTER 17   FIRST ON THE SCENE   66
CHAPTER 18   THE SILENT PENITENT   69
CHAPTER 19   WHAT THE BULLETS TOLD   71
CHAPTER 20   TRANTINO ON A TIGHTROPE   74
CHAPTER 21   CHAOS, TERROR, AND DEATH   78
CHAPTER 22   TRANTINO'S MEMORY GAPS   87
CHAPTER 23   TWO PSYCHIATRISTS, TWO PERSPECTIVES   93
CHAPTER 24   DRIVING HER BOYFRIEND   100

CHAPTER 25   A LIFE IN THE BALANCE   102
CHAPTER 26   KALEIDOSCOPE   108
CHAPTER 27   A VERDICT AND AN "OBITUARY"   116

PART II
CHAPTER 28   "MAY GOD HAVE MERCY . . ."   121
CHAPTER 29   FROM LIMBO TO LIFE   127
CHAPTER 30   GETTING USED TO PRISON   132
CHAPTER 31   THE OTHER VICTIMS   139
CHAPTER 32   HOW CAN THIS BE?   143
CHAPTER 33   HELD HOSTAGE   149
CHAPTER 34   FEELING CLOSE TO FREEDOM   154
CHAPTER 35   A FEDERAL CASE   160
CHAPTER 36   ANDY VOTO'S EVENING   163
CHAPTER 37   TOO LATE TO BE SORRY   165
CHAPTER 38   SO MUCH TIME   170
CHAPTER 39   SPEAKING TO THE WIND   173
CHAPTER 40   AN ELOQUENT DISSENT   177
CHAPTER 41   WHAT'S TO LOSE?   181
CHAPTER 42   A TASTE OF TRANQUILITY   186

PART III
CHAPTER 43   "SORRY BEYOND ALL MEASURE"   191
CHAPTER 44   THE EYEBROWS GO UP   197
CHAPTER 45   HOPE FOR THE DEFENSE   201
CHAPTER 46   HALFWAY TO FREEDOM   205
CHAPTER 47   WINTER IN LODI   212
CHAPTER 48   RIP VAN WINKLE   219

Index   223

ACKNOWLEDGMENTS

I have pored over stacks of newspaper articles in my research for this book. While I detected errors and contradictions that crept into print over the years, I know that the journalists were doing the best they could at the time. Their collective work has been indispensable.

I have also read hundreds of pages of legal documents, including the trial transcript, correspondence to parole authorities, and various briefs filed by prosecutors and defense lawyers. I have done many interviews, by telephone and in person.

At no point have I invented dialogue. The dialogue is taken, in some instances, directly from stenographic records of the trial or hearings. On some occasions, I used dialogue as it was rendered in newspaper accounts. In other instances, the dialogue is based on what people told me—in other words, their best memories of what they recall saying.

The images and dialogue from Thomas Trantino's childhood, the events leading up to the crime and the crime itself, his time on death row—all are based in large part on his own recollections, as described in his book, *Lock the Lock* (Alfred A. Knopf, 1974).

I have spent a lot of time driving around Lodi, trying to know the community as well as one can if he is not from Lodi and of Lodi. Most important, I have spent many, many hours with some of the people whose lives were altered forever because of what happened on August 26, 1963. I am grateful to them for sharing their painful memories and unfulfilled dreams.

So I thank Andrew Voto and his wife, Matilda, for their time and hospitality on numerous occasions. And I thank Sadie Tedesco for sharing memories of her son, and Elaine Harvey and Patricia Tedesco for telling me about their brother. I thank the former Adrienne Peraino for telling me about her old boyfriend, Gary Tedesco.

Ron Calissi was generous with his time, on the telephone and in his home, in helping me to understand his father, prosecutor Guy Calissi. Michael Gross and Paul Gross were kind to share memories of their father, Albert Gross, who defended Thomas Trantino so vigorously. I thank other defense lawyers, including Stuart Pierson, Jeffrey Fogel, Ted Takvorian, and especially Roger

Lowenstein, who plumbed their memories and guided me through the thickets of the law.

The defendant's brother, Richard Trantino, was more than generous with his time. Without once betraying his brother's confidence, Richard Trantino gave me insights into their family. My thanks, too, to Joseph Delaney for setting aside a Saturday afternoon for me, and to Glenn Arterbridge for providing a glimpse of life as a corrections officer supervising Thomas Trantino. Susan Sciacca of the Bergen County Prosecutor's Office helped me obtain a copy of the trial transcript, which was invaluable.

The children of Peter Voto declined to be interviewed by me. That was their right, and in no way lessened my obligation to respect their father's memory. I have.

I thank the people I know from my newspaper days in New Jersey. They include Rod Leith, who helped me get acquainted with Andrew Voto and shared his insights of Lodi, Clint Taplin, David Corcoran, and Vivian Waixel. My thanks to Marc Watrel and the researcher Nick Maltezos.

I thank Edward Jutkowitz of Camino Books for believing in this book, and his tireless copy editor, Michelle Scolnick, whose conscientiousness made this book better.

Finally, I thank my wife, Margarita, who was endlessly supportive.

I have no financial arrangements, no deals of any kind, with anyone mentioned herein. My only commitment to them was a promise to be as fair and truthful as I could be. Any errors of fact or perception are mine. The people who talked to me have enriched this book, and my experience in writing it.

INTRODUCTION

I was twenty-one years old in the summer of 1963, living hundreds of miles from the scene of the crime. I remember that a chill came over me when I read what had happened.

A pair of hoodlums had overpowered two policemen in a bar in a place called Lodi, New Jersey. The hoodlums had taunted and humiliated the officers at gunpoint for up to a half-hour, forcing them to undress and beg on their knees for their lives. But that wasn't enough sport.

No, when the officers were in their worst terror, when they were most afraid of what was coming, they were shot to death.

At least, that is what I read in the newspapers that long-ago summer. The crime was so sensational that it made headlines in my hometown, Erie, Pennsylvania, where I was working odd jobs before my senior year in college.

I had never heard of Lodi and could not have pointed it out on a map. But I thought about the killings for days. I tried to imagine the fear of the victims, and how their relatives must have felt later. I wondered whether they would even want to go on living.

If there were any justice on this earth, I thought, the killers would be caught, given a quick trial, and sentenced to death. I hoped to read one day how they were dragged screaming to their own appointments with the Big Forever, voiding their bowels before being strapped into the chair whose electric current would boil their blood and send them to hell.

Then I forgot about the case. That summer and fall were momentous, after all. Martin Luther King Jr. gave his "I Have a Dream" speech, and four black girls were killed in a church bombing in Alabama, and the thirty-fifth president of the United States was assassinated in Dallas.

And early in 1964 I had a more personal experience with violent death. One of my mother's sisters (my godmother) was strangled by a man she had been dating. Her body was found in a snowbank along a highway on the edge of town. The crime was big news in Erie, fodder for the pulp magazines and barbershop gossip.

My mother had been in poor health for some time, and her sister's death was more than she could bear. Not just her death, but the way she died. That was the burden my mother could not carry. Within a year, she too was dead. And I had learned a lesson I have never forgotten: murder isn't just death. It's a wound that doesn't go away. Some of the living are victims, too.

I suppose what happened to my aunt and my family in 1964 helped to harden my attitudes about crime and punishment. So let me put my biases on the table.

Most people in prison are there because they did bad things. The laments about recidivism — the fact that so many people who get out of prison commit new crimes and go back to prison — are laughably naive.

Of course, a lot of people who get out of prison commit new crimes. They do that because they were criminals in the first place. This is not as complicated as some people try to make it. What *is* complicated is trying to change people for the better. Why should we expect a prison to turn a bad person into a good person when parents, teachers, counselors, or drill sergeants can't do it?

For what it is worth, I have read serious books about criminal justice and have talked to people who have made it their life's work. I have seen hearings and trials, been to jails and prisons, interviewed many judges, prosecutors, defense lawyers, police officers. I know that crime is spawned by poverty, parental abuse, parental neglect, racial prejudice, alcoholism, mental illness, and all the other suffering that people are heir to. I also know that many people endure those things and don't become criminals. They slog through life like most of us, striving for decency.

I believe in the death penalty for the worst killers. I want them to suffer as they await their fate. I want their victims' relatives, and society in general, to have revenge.

I witnessed an execution in Texas in 1995, and I respected the condemned man for giving up his life with courage and grace for what he had done: raped and killed his ex-wife and her niece. I saw this man die, and I still believe in capital punishment. If I am wrong to feel this way, then God will judge me.

I have said all this so the reader will know how I feel, and what I believe in. And I have said it because the case I describe in this book has made me question my beliefs more than I would have thought possible.

But this story is not mine. If it belongs to anyone, it belongs to Lodi, and especially to two families in Lodi.

§

In 1977, my newspaper career took me to Bergen County, New Jersey, just across the Hudson River from New York City, and a paper called the *Record,* situated in Hackensack.

Bergen County was entirely new to me. It was a baffling patchwork of communities, more than seventy all told. One of these is the clannish little borough called Lodi. The name sounded vaguely familiar. Early on, I heard my colleagues talking about a man named Thomas Trantino, how his very name was reviled in Lodi for killing two police officers a long time ago.

For goodness' sake, I thought. *It really is a small world. This is the case that so bothered me when I read about it years ago.*

I got to know Lodi a little. Mostly, I knew the slightly tacky stretch of Route 46 that cut through the borough. The road was, is, lined with fast-food places and used-car lots. I knew the terrible crime had taken place in a bar called the Angel Lounge, just off Route 46.

Every so often, Trantino's name would be in the news, either on the anniversary of his crime, August 26, or when he got some publicity for the drawings and paintings he did behind bars, or when he tried to win parole. I remember thinking, *Let him rot behind bars; I'm sorry they didn't fry the bastard.*

Parole denied, Trantino would sink from view for a while.

§

After five years, I left the *Record* to join the *New York Times.* And early in 1999, when I was working in Washington, D.C., I was offered a chance to do a book on the case that had made Thomas Trantino a household name in northern New Jersey. The crime had been committed so many years ago, yet it was still news. Trantino was still trying to get out of prison, for God's sake!

I thought I might not be the right guy for this project, given my personal feelings and what had happened in my family in 1964, but I was intrigued.

No one had written a book about the case. There had been so many rumors and myths. And so much time had gone by. Maybe, it was suggested, I could peel away the years to find out what had *really* happened.

So I decided to try. I knew that the truth would be elusive, that it might slip away just as I was trying to grasp it. I knew that one person's "truth" is another's lie, and that memories fade.

I knew I had to go back to Lodi. There were things I had to see and people I hoped to talk to, if they were still alive.

And before I saw anyone else, I had to see one man.

PART I

CHAPTER 1

An Old Cop
with a Mission

A late-winter rain is lashing the house as the old cop sits in an easy chair. He wears a flannel shirt, heavy slacks, and thick white socks to guard against a chill. A pillow is plumped under his left arm. It takes him a while to get comfortable; even the little things are a chore since the stroke.

The cop, whose name is Andrew Voto, can use a little help whenever he rises from the chair, and he leans on a cane. Though he goes out regularly for lunch with friends, he is most comfortable in this house at 56 Christopher Street in the Borough of Lodi, New Jersey. Lodi is a very Italian, very close-knit community just across the Hudson River from New York City.

This Saturday in March 1999 is a perfect day for staying home, talking on the phone with friends, reminiscing. Not so long ago, Andy Voto was the police chief of Lodi, so he knows a lot of people.

He has a lot of memories, too. Sometimes he has trouble making his words keep up with what he's trying to say. He blames the stroke for that and isn't a bit defensive. The memories are there, all right, and clear, each one of them. It's just that they run together or bounce off each other in odd ways. He has so many memories, now that he's closing in on seventy-three.

A couple of his mother's relatives were professional boxers a long time ago. Andy Voto knew Rocky Graziano, knew him well enough that the fighter came to see him in the hospital after the stroke, gave him a dollar bill for good luck. He knew the other Rocky too, the great heavyweight Marciano.

"He came to my mom's house for pasta," Andy Voto says. "I used to pick him up at Idlewild Airport. It was called Idlewild back then."

Andy Voto is at the place in life where a little thing can jog his memory and the years will just fall away, taking him back to a time where he wants both to laugh and to cry. It doesn't take much at all: a visitor asks about the photographs of two dogs, schnauzers of show quality, lovingly coiffed and primped. With no little pride and nostalgia, Andy says the dogs were his.

And then his mind brakes and does a hard right. Andy starts talking about his brother, and his brother's dog. "Pete had this Chihuahua that used to sleep on his shoulder when Pete was on the sofa," Andy recalls. He laughs at the image: Pete Voto, his older brother, also a cop, built like a bull (though with an oddly cherubic face), and just as strong. He'd been a wrestler in high school.

And what kind of dog did he have? A Chihuahua, for God's sake!

The really funny thing is that Pete, for all his good qualities, wasn't much of a dog lover. But he sure cared about that Chihuahua. Chico! That was his name.

"The dog died a few weeks after Pete did," Andy says. He doesn't say the dog died of a broken heart; he doesn't have to.

Andy has a hard time imagining his brother as anything but a big, intimidating man. He wasn't that tall, only about five ten, but he weighed close to 240 pounds. He had a neck like a fire hydrant and thick, beefy muscles. What would he be like if he had lived? Well, he'd be going on seventy-six. He'd probably be a little stooped over with age, and not as strong. Maybe he'd have arthritis. He'd be complaining about that when he wasn't bragging about his children and grandchildren.

Pete served on the battleship *Alabama* in the Pacific in World War II. He got his nickname, "The Bull," in the navy.

Andy remembers the time Rocky Marciano and his manager were having dinner with the Voto family. The manager said, "Rocky, I'd never bet against you in a fight, but if you went up against The Bull here ... "

Pete was just about the best big brother any kid could have, always walking Andy home from school and making sure he had his rubbers on in the wintertime.

"My brother Pete, he always worried that *I'd* get hurt on the job," Andy says.

On this rainy afternoon, Andy talks just a little about what might have been. He doesn't dwell on the paradox that Pete, his older brother, is forever young in memory. Hell, forty isn't old at all. That's how old Pete was when he died.

Andy Voto stands up and looks out at the rain. The window faces onto a cross street. Out there, he says, *right out there* less than a block away, that's where Pete's killer was that summer morning a long time ago. Trying to get away by hitching a ride with a milkman. Hell, there aren't any milkmen anymore.

It's fitting, somehow, that Pete's killer was practically outside the window just after Andy got the phone call telling him his brother was dead. The killing took place not more than a half-mile away, after all. Lodi is such a small place, in every way.

Just for a minute, Andy Voto wonders out loud whether everything would have been better if the timing had been different that August morning—a minute one way or the other, say.

His eyes get a faraway look as he remembers. "Get my fucking gun!" he was shouting to his wife, Matty, just after the phone call. "Get my fucking gun! Someone killed my brother."

What if he had dashed from the house in rage and grief while the killer was still outside? If they had shot it out, a lot of people would have been spared everything that followed. Maybe things would have been better no matter which bullets had found their mark ...

But Andy Voto doesn't let himself think that way for long. What's the point? There are things he loves about his life, especially his family. He has a mission, too. The mission is all about one man.

When he's in the mood, Andy maneuvers a big cardboard box into the center of the room. It's full of letters, old newspaper clippings, old detective magazines. The magazines are more than thirty-five years old, and they have big write-ups about the awful thing that happened on August 26, 1963. That date is the dividing line in Andy Voto's life, and in a lot of other lives. From that day on, everything would be different for Andy Voto, for as long as he's on this earth.

Help yourself, he says. Look through the stuff all you want.

There's a picture of Pete Voto in his Lodi cop's uniform, big face, baby-like, lit up with a smile. And there's a picture of young Gary Tedesco, wearing a serious face and the short-cropped hair and thin tie that were in style way back then. It's hard to believe that Gary would be in his late fifties now; that's how much time has gone by.

And there's a picture of Andy Voto, so much younger, so much bigger. Andy was no pushover physically; anyone can tell that from the old picture. It shows his face all torn up with grief and rage on the day of his brother's funeral.

The magazines are not wrinkled. The pages are not torn, and there is very little yellowing, considering how old all the stuff is. That's because Andy doesn't look at it very often.

So why does he keep the old magazines in the house at all? Doesn't it hurt to have them around?

No, he says. It doesn't. He's been hurt as much as he can be hurt. "Why do I save them? My brother's part of history." The rain lashes the house some more, and for a moment his shoulders sag under the weight of years. "And maybe I'm not so far from being part of history."

CHAPTER 2

This Place
Called Lodi

There are still people who remember when the cliffs of northern New Jersey and the green flatlands that lay beyond were a world apart, separated from the teeming metropolis by the Hudson River.

The George Washington Bridge transformed northern New Jersey. From the moment the bridge opened, in 1931, Bergen County became almost a suburb of New York City. Yet the seventy-odd municipalities of Bergen are as diverse as the various enclaves of Manhattan, Queens, and Brooklyn. The blue-collar communities of North Arlington and Lyndhurst in south Bergen could hardly be more different from Alpine, which lies along the river in northern Bergen County, its huge estates home to more than a few Wall Street buccaneers and world-famous entertainers.

No place in Bergen County has more sense of self, more sense of family, than Lodi, a borough of just over two square miles that lies some ten miles west of the George Washington Bridge. Lodi is intensely, proudly Italian. How strange, then, that it got its very name because of a Frenchman.

In 1825, the Marquis de Lafayette visited the county seat of Hackensack. Memories of the American Revolution, when Lafayette helped to forge a ragtag band of colonists into an army that defeated Great Britain, were still fresh. In adoration and gratitude, the New Jersey legislature wanted to name a section of Bergen County in Lafayette's honor.

Lafayette told the lawmakers that the United States already had enough places named after him. Then he recalled a little town in the Milan province of Italy. It was where he had been imprisoned by the Austrians, and where he regained his freedom after Napoleon crossed the River Adda to retake the town in 1796. The little town was called Lodi. If you wish to honor me, Lafayette told the lawmakers, use the name *Lodi*.

And so they did.

Lodi (pronounced LOW-die) was a farming community at first. Its transformation into an industrial center began in 1829, when an enterprising young man from Scotland named James Rennie, who already ran a textile mill in nearby Clifton, stood next to the Saddle River and knew he had found the perfect spot to build a dyeing and printing plant.

Soon James's brother Robert sailed from Scotland to join him in prosperity. Alas, the dye mill burned to the ground in 1833. James Rennie was nearly ruined financially, and crushed emotionally. But Robert Rennie had all of his brother's business acumen, and perhaps a bit more iron in his spine. And he had shrewdly bought large tracts of nearby land.

Robert Rennie rebuilt, and soon had a thriving dye and calico-printing plant on the ashes of the first one. His plant attracted workers by the hundreds. Most were Irish and Dutch; they had rough hands and strong backs.

Soon, he started a general-merchandise store, the largest for miles around. It drew hordes of shoppers. By 1865, Robert Rennie was known around the world. He was, of course, the most powerful person in Lodi. The meetings of the newly formed Lodi council were held on the top floor of his store, and Rennie was not above throwing his weight around.

But Rennie could not block competition from the textile mills of New England. Though his personal wealth was secure, his plant closed in 1875. The exodus of the jobless and their families gave Lodi the nickname "Deserted Village." Despondent, Rennie died seven years later. In 1891, the ghost buildings of Rennie's empire were destroyed by fire.

Three years later, the geographical outlines of modern Lodi were drawn. Civic leaders from the heart of Lodi asked permission to form a borough separate from Little Ferry, Wood-Ridge, and Carlstadt, the communities that were part of what could loosely be called "Greater Lodi" before 1894.

The legislature approved the petition, and a new Lodi was born. Its first mayor was Daniel Cook. The borough council passed ordinances prohibiting goats, cattle, and swine from wandering loose. A pool hall that stayed open on Sundays was ordered closed on the Sabbath.

And a tradition was started: the mayor and council approved the hiring of enough policemen to patrol the entire borough by foot. So the police officers and the people they protected came to know each other, like neighbors. Often, they *were* neighbors. The people who kept law and order in Lodi were like family.

§

A new generation of hungry young industrialists came to Lodi to start mills of their own. In 1903, the mills were consolidated as the United Piece Dye

Works. Soon, more than 7,000 people worked in the brick buildings along the Saddle River.

By this time, the Dutch and Irish were being replaced by waves of Italians. They worked long hours, and though the term hadn't been invented yet, they were becoming part of the American Dream. Collectively, as their nostalgia for the old country and the old ways blended inextricably with the ways of their new country, they were defining the community of Lodi. They *were* Lodi.

It was common for several houses on the same block to be owned by different branches of the same family. Neighbors married neighbors, and their children married the neighbors' children. The world felt safe.

The closeness made for a lot of laughter and gossip on front lawns. People walking by would stop to talk when they heard friendly shouts from a window. In the summer, the most delicious smells in the world wafted from the open windows, smells of tomato sauces cooking all day long, the old way.

The people of Lodi knew they would never be rich. But if you were from Lodi, if you were *of* Lodi, you had a pretty good chance of landing a job there. Just go down to Borough Hall. Everyone knew everyone else, and patronage jobs were part of the way of life.

Which was a good thing, because as the years went by there was less work in the dye mills. World War II spurred new technologies that brought synthetic fibers. The Lodi dye business faded. In its place came chemical plants and small industries.

One of those "small industries" was centered not along the banks of the Saddle River but alongside Route 46, which snaked west from the George Washington Bridge through Bergen County. Lodi's stretch of the highway was a mile long, and in the post-war years it spawned saloons that drew a rough crowd, so rough that Route 46 in Lodi came to be called the Sin Strip.

Back then, the bars stayed open until five in the morning. They did not attract men and women who were shackled to humdrum office jobs or housework. No, many of the people who felt most welcome there were those who lived and toiled on the fringes of the law.

§

Lodi cops were human. They had grown up with some of the gamblers who frequented the Sin Strip, as well as their friends and their friends' friends. And what was the real harm, as long as the unsavory types stayed along Route 46? Someone who liked to bet on horses or humans or numbers could find company in Lodi, hang out all night if he wanted, then go home at dawn to shower and sleep until the late afternoon. Then he could get up and look forward to doing it all over again.

In the early 1950s, there were eight nightclubs along Route 46 in Lodi. Exactly which politicians in Lodi, or in the county, decided to tolerate the bars, and what they got in return—these questions cannot be answered all these years later.

The people of Lodi would pay a terrible price, one summer night, for the bars that were allowed to thrive in their borough. But until the unspeakable thing happened, the feeling was that if certain people were going to drink and carry on late at night, well, why shouldn't they leave some of their money in Lodi?

From the outside, at least, the bars had a certain glamour. Young men with greasy, duck-tailed haircuts drove up in high-finned cars that looked like firetrucks on steroids. Their girlfriends' smiles glowed with lipstick.

One of the better-known places along Route 46, sitting at an odd angle to the highway at the corner with Baldwin Avenue, was a long, narrow building of white stucco. It had a long bar with stools, a linoleum floor, a bandstand, and a tiny dance floor. The bar had been one of the charter members of the Sin Strip joints. It was called the Heights Inn in the 1940s. In the 1950s it was the Hi-De-Ho Club.

State liquor-control agents were familiar with the place. In March 1955, its license was suspended for thirty-five days for allowing women who worked at the place to accept drinks paid for by male customers. In 1961, the bar changed hands again. It was acquired by two men doing business as Two Tonys Incorporated.

§

The two Tonys were old friends who had grown up in Lodi. Tony Grasso (the birth certificate said *Tony*, not *Anthony*) and Anthony Perillo were born in the early 1920s. Both went away to war, Tony Grasso to fight with the 101st Airborne Division in Europe, Anthony Perillo to serve in the Army Air Corps in the Pacific.

The two Tonys came home eager to get on with their lives. Tony Grasso had gotten to know a jeweler while he was in the army. The jewelry business sounded interesting, so Grasso used money from the G.I. Bill to take a course in diamond-cutting. For a while, he sold jewels. He bought them in New York City and peddled them door-to-door in New Jersey. It was hard work, and he thought it would be better to have his own store so people could come to him. Eventually, he did start his own store. It became a fixture in Lodi.

But first he had to make some money. So did Tony Perillo. "I had no trade or anything," Perillo said many years later. But he did have an appetite for hard work, as did Tony Grasso. So the two Tonys scraped together a little money and opened a bar on South Main Street in Lodi.

Tony Grasso was a bit of a glad-hander and storyteller; Tony Perillo, more businesslike. Both sets of traits were good to have in the bar business. The two Tonys didn't get rich, but they made a living. Both married and started families.

They thought they might make more money in a busier location. They knew the Route 46 bars prospered because they offered live band music and late closing hours. There were rumors that some of them offered more than that, but Tony Grasso and Tony Perillo would say years later that they weren't interested in that kind of thing. They wanted to run a place where people would pay to drink and be entertained. The two Tonys would provide live music and basic food, pizza and stuff. Simple as that.

They heard that a place was available smack on the border between Hasbrouck Heights and Lodi. The address was 501 Baldwin Avenue, but the place fronted right onto Route 46. They didn't have enough money to buy it, so they turned to a friend for help. He lent them money, and before long the Tonys were proud owners of a new bar.

But what to call it? Naming the place was a fateful decision, in a way. Had a different name been chosen, writers of lurid headlines would have been deprived.

Hey, the Tonys thought. We couldn't have afforded this place without our friend, our financial "angel." And so they called their place the Angel Lounge.

CHAPTER 3

A Family
in Brooklyn

Theirs was an unusual love story for the 1930s. Nat Trantino was a Catholic from Little Italy. Blanche Stein was Jewish. For a serious Catholic to marry a non-Catholic back then was almost unthinkable. And if a Jewish boy or girl married outside the faith, the family might chant a song for the dead. So when Nat and Blanche wed, it was two years before they dared tell her parents.

By early 1938, they had settled in a lower-class section of Brooklyn. Their first child was Thomas, born on February 11 of that year. Another boy, Richard, and a girl, Barbara, followed.

Nat Trantino worked in a place that made women's hats. The Trantinos had just enough to get by, which made them like millions of families of their time. Years later, after Thomas's crimes made the family surname famous, the kind of doctors who ponder why people do bad things tried to understand the dynamic of the Trantino household—in particular, the relationship between husband and wife. There was conjecture that Thomas Trantino's antisocial behavior arose in part from a lack of self-esteem, perhaps from having seen his father dominated by his mother.

Maybe the past held an answer, some doctors suggested. And maybe it did. Or maybe the marriage of Nat and Blanche Trantino was simply marked by the kind of fault lines and borders and truces that define every relationship that lasts, as theirs did.

§

Life had taught Blanche Trantino that a woman had to be strong. Her mother had kept Blanche and her six brothers and sisters out of the poorhouse despite a husband who spent too much money and time drinking. And when Nat and Blanche had to decide whether to raise the children Catholic or Jewish, they chose the Jewish path. Thomas was bar-mitzvahed at thirteen, but the family meals reflected a mixed heritage. Chicken soup and pasta were staples.

Most of Tom's friends were Italian. Tom had terrific energy. He enjoyed being the center of attention, the entertainer.

His teachers thought something wasn't quite right with young Tommy. He was smart enough, but he didn't try very hard. And he had an attitude. He was the smartass in every class. Had he been born a few decades later, he might have been tested for, say, attention-deficit disorder.

Years later, in prison, he reminisced about the tyranny and boredom of the classroom.

One day in the first grade he had to go to the bathroom. He raised his hand. By the time the teacher saw him, he was frantic.

"Yes, Thomas," she said. "What is it?"

"May I go to the bathroom please?"

"Didn't you go to the bathroom yesterday, Thomas?"

"But I have to go again today . . . "

No, she said. It's almost time for the bell to go home. You can wait.

So Thomas sat at his desk as his bowels emptied. When the bell rang, he skulked out of the classroom and out of the school, hoping that the tight elastic on his knickers would keep the turd from falling out. It did, for the five blocks to the apartment.

When he got home, his mother was there. "You smell from shit!" she hollered. "Come here!"

There was nowhere to run, no way to explain. *Slap, slap* on the face. She hit hard, and her son bobbed and weaved to dodge her hands.

The boy was full of shame and rage. "Fuck you!" he screamed.

The mother gasped. "I'm going to tell your father!"

"Fuck him too!"

That night, Thomas lay awake in bed. He fantasized about taking the big knife from the kitchen to school and shoving it deep into the teacher who had made him shit his pants.

$

A teenage girl introduced him to sex when he was twelve. An older boy introduced him to heroin when he was fourteen. He flinched for a moment when the needle went into his right arm, just below the elbow, but the floating sensation right afterward . . . oh, Jesus Christ!

Soon he had to have the feeling back two or three times a week, and then every day. He bought heroin from the neighborhood pusher. He got the money by stealing.

He lasted about six months in Eastern District High School before being expelled for slugging a teacher. When he was sixteen, his parents found their son's drug kit: a hypodermic needle fashioned from an eyedropper, a bottle top, cotton, and a few grams of heroin.

Nat Trantino was furious. He confronted his son, who smashed some of the household's humble furniture in his rage and dark hunger. Then he fled to his real home, the streets. When he dared show his face to his parents again, the police were waiting with them. He was taken to a precinct house, charged with drug possession, and locked in a cell for the night. The next day, a judge sent him to Kings County Hospital for a month of mental observation and the cold-turkey treatment—two weeks of stomach-churning nausea, cramps, sweating, and hallucinations.

For the second half of his hospital stay, he felt a little better. His appetite came back. He got counseling.

"Tom is a lanky, good-looking, tall boy who tried to cover up his anxiety by being friendly, very polite, and cooperative," a psychologist wrote. Tom told the psychologist he wanted to join the navy "because in the navy you have a clean life, and I like to be on boats."

But he didn't know what he wanted to do in the navy, and he wanted to work with his hands before going to sea. "I do not like the idea of going back to school," he said. Intelligence tests put his IQ at 99, or average. "He is aware of social demands and knows what constitutes socially acceptable behavior," the doctor wrote. Yet achievement tests indicated that he had learned little or nothing in the classroom.

The teenager was asked to draw human figures. He drew the head of a girl.

Let's see the entire person, he was urged.

"What, a whole body?" he replied with seeming amazement.

Tom's figure drawings showed that he felt "very inadequate and unable to cope with his difficulties," the psychologist said. "He seems to be putting up a front of toughness as a defense behind which he attempts to hide, probably as much from himself as from others, the feeling of lack of inner strength and resources."

The anxiety probably arose from sexual fears, the psychologist speculated. "There is evidence of suspiciousness. The female figure is seen as stern, but also as seductive. She appears to be perceived as much stronger than the male." The psychologist speculated that something in the Trantino family situation was spawning these feelings of anger and anxiety.

§

When his parents put up bail for his release, Tom bade them a hasty goodbye outside the courthouse and went to buy another fix.

The next few months were a blur. He slept when he got tired, day or night, wherever he happened to be. Being on heroin was terrible, but he couldn't stand *not* being on it.

He sought help for his addiction and was admitted to Riverside Hospital in the Bronx. He went through the sickness and the sweats of withdrawal. He knew there were two ways to make the symptoms go away: get cured completely, or get back on drugs.

He didn't agonize for long. He talked himself out of the hospital after a month and was back on drugs before sunset. Soon, he was shooting up several times a day, spending fifteen dollars a day on heroin. In the mid-1950s, that was as much as many blue-collar workers took home for eight hours of hard work. Tom Trantino pulled one burglary after another to fuel his addiction. He was sixteen years old.

More months went by. In the rare moments when he could think clearly, he knew he might die if he didn't break the cycle. So he checked himself back into Riverside, for a stay of six months. This time, the withdrawal symptoms were far worse and lasted a lot longer. His mother and father visited often, trying to recapture the son they had lost.

This time, the doctors' findings were more ominous. The patient displayed "a strong sense of isolation and infantile and insatiable need for gratification," one doctor wrote. His figures of women contained dark slashes on the breasts, a sign of aggression.

"The father figure is seen with fear and contempt," the doctor continued. "On one hand, he sees this male authority as a frightening 'monster' and then he sees him as an empty and impotent 'scarecrow.' This fear of male authority may brake his antisocial activities and may be an element in the future control of his behavior."

The doctor noted that an earlier therapist had simply been unable to break through the barriers Tom had erected. Despite overwhelming evidence to the contrary, Tom had insisted to the earlier therapist that he got along fine with his parents and siblings. He said he was sure he would not go back to drugs.

Tom insisted he wanted to have steady employment, said his father had arranged a job for him at his own workplace. The doctor who had noted the fear and contempt for the father figure said Tom's prognosis was not good as long as he was unable to admit that he needed help.

When Tom Trantino got out of the hospital, he barely nodded to the parents he had professed to love. He disappeared until five o'clock the next morning. When he came home, his skin was yellow and his eyes were glassy. He slept most of the day, getting up only to drink water. He had no interest in food.

By the time he was seventeen, he had a bottomless hunger for heroin. He needed fifty dollars a day, and he stole it, in burglaries and street heists in Brooklyn and Manhattan. His skin was the color of brass, his eyes like those of a dead fish. He rarely ate and came home at all hours to flop into bed. He went back to Riverside for another futile stay and returned to his old life the moment he got out.

On February 16, 1956, he and a fellow addict set upon a woman who was carrying about $500—the payroll for a dentist's office. The woman was knocked down, badly beaten and bruised. Trantino and his friend were soon caught.

This time, there would be no second or third chance. Thomas Trantino was indicted on charges of first-degree robbery, first-degree grand larceny, and second-degree assault. These were serious felonies. If convicted, he would go to prison for a long, long time.

He pleaded guilty to a reduced charge of second-degree robbery. On June 18, 1956, he was sentenced to five to ten years in Great Meadow State Prison at Comstock, in upstate New York. At Great Meadow, he was given an IQ test. He scored 107, a bit higher than he had in school. He was no genius but he wasn't stupid, either.

At Great Meadow he would make new friends.

CHAPTER 4

The Bully

Little Frankie Falco was a mystery to his teachers. Early tests put his IQ at 115—not high enough to mark him as a future Rhodes scholar, perhaps, but more than good enough to succeed in school. His teachers had known many children no smarter than Frankie who excelled in the classroom.

But even in elementary school it was clear that the life of the mind was not for him. "Frankie Falco showed no effort, did no work, and failed," one teacher wrote in a typical evaluation.

But he was much more than the class wiseass. "He cannot be a friend of the students," wrote another elementary school teacher. "He must dominate them. . . . He forces students to do as he commands, and even when they do, he beats them."

Those words were written decades before it became fashionable to suggest therapy for every maladjustment, before childhood bullying and the fear of it were talked about as serious problems rather than as routine rites of passage.

Unlike many other bullies, he was not subjected to bullying himself at home. He came from a stable, working-class family. His two brothers and two sisters were nothing like him; they took the straight path and he did not, and no one knows why, really. In that sense, he had a lot in common with Thomas Trantino.

Frankie Falco was different from the other children almost from the moment he could walk. Growing up in the teeming, polyglot Brooklyn of the 1950s, he never lacked for confidence. He was vain, proud of his athletic body, the dark hair and eyes, the thick neck and full lips that made up his Latin good looks.

His vanity bordered on narcissism. At home or in a gym, he loved to stand shirtless in front of a mirror, flexing his chest and arm muscles, smiling at the sight of himself. His preening seemed a bit much even for a precocious lad filling up with hormones.

As he crossed from young boyhood to early adolescence, the vanity became more pronounced. No one kidded him about it, either. A photograph of Frankie Falco at fourteen, published in *Life* magazine after he became infamous, shows him smiling for the camera. "He is very proud of his body and feels that girls are attracted to him because of his manliness and his boldness," a teacher observed.

All these years later, the magazine photo is disturbing. The adolescent smile is arrogant—a sneer, really. Young Frank Falco seems not just full of himself but full of contempt for the world. Most unsettling of all are the eyes. They shine with meanness.

But some girls (and later, women) were drawn to him. There was something exhilarating about being with a tough male who inspired respect and fear. And Frankie showed leadership ability: he became head of a gang of junior high toughs. He took a dislike to a twelve-year-old Puerto Rican girl, so he ordered the girls' auxiliary to give her a vicious beating.

Eventually, Frankie's behavior became so antisocial that his parents and teachers steered him to a psychiatrist, an enormous step in an era when the mere suggestion of mental disorder carried a stigma. The doctor recommended that Frankie be put in an institution with a full-time psychiatrist. Children's Village in Dobbs Ferry, New York, agreed to take him.

Children's Village was more than a school, yet not quite a reformatory. Later, it became clear that it was Frankie's very last chance to live a life on the right side of the law, and society's very last chance to do something about him.

The social workers at Children's Village had dealt with problem boys before, but seldom with anyone like Frankie Falco. In a perverse sense, he thrived there. Thrown in with other young bullies, he dominated those around him with his snarls and his fists.

He ran away whenever he could, so frequently that the counselors at Children's Village felt powerless. They discharged him, finally, as a chronic runaway. Still a young teenager, he had earned a reputation as a vicious criminal-to-be. Already, he seemed beyond change.

"We knew, from what a brutal boy he was, that people were going to be hurt, and we just couldn't do anything," one social worker said years later, when Frank Falco had made his mark. "Until someone gets killed, you just can't stop it."

But Frank Falco was not without talent. His good looks and strength were perfect for a hobby he started as a teenager: pretending to be a male prostitute, tricking homosexuals to go with him, then robbing them.

In 1959, the year he turned twenty-one, he held up a grocery store. The heist netted him a paltry thirty cents, but it marked his graduation into the world of grown-up crime.

He was sent to Great Meadow State Prison.

CHAPTER 5

Not Cut Out
for Marriage

Tom Trantino and Frank Falco became friends in prison.

Years later, psychiatrists would speculate on Falco's influence over Trantino, the fact that Falco seemed to be the strong male figure Tom had never had when he was growing up. Maybe that was why Frankie Falco was the dominant one in the relationship, if he truly was.

Young Tom Trantino was no slouch physically, compared to Frankie Falco or anyone else. He grew to nearly six feet tall, put close to two hundred pounds on his frame, and marked out his own walking-around space in the prison exercise yard. If anyone walked into his space without asking, he'd have to fight Tom Trantino. Tom won a few fights and lost a few. But he was never afraid.

So, at an age when other young men were fitting in with college classmates or army buddies, Tom Trantino was fitting right in at Great Meadow. The other inmates respected him; some even liked him.

The guards, too, got a kick out of this cocky young man. And once they knew about his mixed blood, they couldn't resist needling him about it. On one occasion, a guard really got under his skin with an anti-Semitic gibe. Tom and the guard scuffled (the guard claimed Tom tried to hit him with a shovel), and Tom was "put in the box," placed in segregation, for several weeks.

He learned not to let things bother him so much. He learned to tamp his anger down.

"Hey, Rabbi!" a guard would shout across the yard, to accompanying laughter. And so Tom Trantino became Tom the Rabbi.

In the summer of 1960, he became eligible for parole consideration. A psychological evaluation noted "some excellent work reports" on his record, that he hadn't been in a fight for more than a year, and that he had been going to group therapy since the previous fall.

"He is not dangerous unless he should become addicted," a doctor wrote. "Most of the disciplinary troubles have been the type when he stood to gain nothing and would be certain of punishment."

Parole denied.

He had his second parole hearing on May 25, 1961. Much of it centered on his history of drug use.

"If you find yourself slipping, would you talk to a parole officer?" he was asked.

"Yes, sir. I would," he replied.

A few moments later, the board decided. "All we can do is give you a chance," one official said. "It is time you gave your folks a break after all of these years."

"Yes, sir."

"I think you owe them something."

"Yes, sir."

Tom "The Rabbi" Trantino was twenty-three years old when he came out of Great Meadow on June 27, 1961. He had been away for five years.

That summer, at a party in the Bronx, he met a girl his age named Helene Pierra. Immediately, he knew she was what he was looking for: young, innocent, someone who didn't drink. In 1962 they were married. They settled into an apartment in Brooklyn. They had a son and named him Guy. Tom got a job with a wrecking company, a second job working nights as an apprentice at a printing plant. He didn't stay there long.

The straight life, the married life, had its drawbacks. It tied a man down. Tom preferred to drink and stay out late. He dressed like a dandy, kept his short hair in place. When he rolled up his sleeves, the women could see the tattoos on his arm. One said "Tommy"; the other, "True Love."

Helene knew her husband didn't fight off the women who found him attractive. But she didn't suspect the worst of it. Tom had never been faithful to her, not when they were dating, not even when they were honeymooning. Years later, Trantino would admit to having had sex with a woman not his wife just hours after the wedding.

Tom Trantino lived like a bachelor, leaving the care of their infant son to Helene. She complained bitterly about his drinking and carousing. The arguments got ugly, and he slapped her. He seemed to be very sorry, but not long afterward, when another argument flared, he slapped her again. The arguments and the slaps became routine.

As 1963 began, he was seldom in the apartment. Nights were for drinking and carousing, days for wandering around. Staying home just meant listening to Helene's whining and complaining and the baby's crying.

One fine day in late spring, Tom was walking along the boardwalk at Coney Island when he saw someone who looked familiar. Could it be? It was! Frankie Falco!

Frank Falco also had a wife, Patricia. She was only seventeen, but they already had a baby girl. Frank didn't like staying at home any more than Tom did.

Tom and Frank had so much catching up to do that day. They found a bar and got drunk together.

They hung out that spring and summer. Very soon, they shared an amphetamine habit (Tom knew better than to go back to heroin), and they did what they knew best to support themselves. They stole.

Frank Falco wasn't cut out for a steady, nine-to-five job either. But Frank did have abilities that made it easy for him to find work. He was an excellent enforcer for loan sharks. (Those teachers of his had been wrong; Frankie *would* amount to something!)

One borrower who had the bad luck to run afoul of Frank Falco was Robert Munoz, a young apprentice printer at the *New York Times*. One night in early July 1963, Falco confronted Munoz in a bar called the Vivere Lounge on the Lower East Side of Manhattan. It was too late for gentle talk; Falco pulled a gun, began to beat Munoz with it, told him to take off his clothes. (Falco liked to take a victim's dignity as well as his money.)

This time, Falco got carried away. He shot Munoz in full view of more than a dozen bar customers, then waved his gun at them and warned that any tattle-tales would be killed. The last the bar patrons saw of him, Falco was dragging his victim outside. The next day, the body of Robert Munoz was found floating in the East River.

Frankie Falco had never been good at thinking a problem through: the bar in which he'd killed Munoz was in the same building as Falco's upstairs apartment. It was a bit optimistic for him to think no one in the bar would tell on him. Besides, his sometime employers in the gangster world were dismayed. Frank Falco didn't know the meaning of restraint, for God's sake! Professional gangsters weren't about to provide cover for him. Soon, all the police cars on the East Side had his picture taped to their dashboard, not that he was a stranger to the cops.

Frank knew he needed a place to stay, so he called Tom Trantino. Come on over, Tom said. Years later, Tom recalled that Helene made coffee while Tom and Frank talked in the living room.

Frank told his friend what he'd done the night before in the Vivere Lounge. "The heat is very bad," Frank said.

"Don't worry," Tom said. "You have a place to stay for as long as you want." Tom went into the kitchen to tell his wife they had a guest. Helene was aghast. She knew Frank Falco was trouble, that the police were looking for him. "Are you crazy or something?" she hissed at her husband. "What if they come here? What about our baby in that room there?"

Helene began to cry. Tom hugged her, told her everything would be all right. He asked her to fix some food.

When Tom went back to the living room, Frank was cleaning his gun. "Don't let Helene see that shit!" Tom said.

Frank stayed over, going out at night on business, coming back late to flop on the couch.

The Trantinos fought worse than ever, not that Falco noticed much. He had his own wife to worry about. If she got really pissed off at him, she might call the cops. Better to get her out of town.

One day, Falco brought another old pal from Great Meadow to the Trantino apartment. His name was Rocco Benedetto. Frank and Rocco got to talking about personal stuff. Frank needed a place to stow his wife and kid for a while. Come to think of it, he could use another woman to help out with business. Someone with a little class.

Rocco was willing to help out. Send the wife and kid over to Jersey, he told Frank. Rocco Benedetto lived in a room above the Angel Lounge.

§

If Frank Falco missed his wife, he soon found consolation in the arms of a new woman, Norma Jaconetta. She was seventeen that summer of 1963. She had married too young and was already separated from her husband.

Norma Jaconetta was dark-haired, dark-eyed, and drop-dead beautiful. She was adventurous, too, more than happy to drive Tommy and Frankie whenever they needed to pull off a robbery to get money for booze, pills, and food. She was ideal for knocking on the door of an apartment in a fashionable building after Tom and Frank had decided it might be a good target.

If someone answered the door, there was no cause for alarm. The lovely young woman with the friendly smile would ask directions, or say she was looking for so-and-so. Of course, Norma would take note of whether the apartment dweller was old enough, or small enough, to be easy prey. An older woman who lived alone and had expensive jewelry made an ideal target.

So Tom and Frank would stake out the apartment, break in when they thought no one was at home, and grab as much stuff as they could. If the person happened to be home and answered the door, they would shove their way inside, get whatever they could, and leave the victim cowering. Frank Falco hadn't lost his knack for bullying, and Thomas Trantino was no one to mess with either. They would load their booty into Norma's car for the drive to her apartment in Paterson, New Jersey. The apartment served as a storage depot, as well as a love nest for Frank and Norma.

§

One day, the phone rang in the Trantino apartment. Helene picked it up, said hello, and gave it to Tom with a dirty look.

Pat Falco was on the line. She asked Tom if he knew where Frank was.

No, Tom said.

"You fucking liar!" Pat screamed. Between sobs, she raged about being left with that creep Rocco and no money and no help with the baby. She said she had gone to live in Allendale with a woman who was separated and had little children.

"I have no money, and that kid needs clothes, and I ain't got nothing," Pat Falco wailed. "I can't go on living like this."

Tom called his wife to the phone and told Pat Falco to give Helene a list of baby clothes and other things she needed. All right, Pat said. Tom could tell that Pat felt a lot better. Tom told Pat to meet him at ten that night at Third Avenue and 47th Street. He picked that spot because he had a girlfriend who worked in a cocktail lounge a block away.

Helene went shopping and came back with a load of boxes and packages for Pat and her baby. Tom kissed Helene goodbye and got a cab to Third and 47th. He was self-conscious standing at the corner hugging the packages.

He heard a horn honk, saw Pat Falco's blond head sticking out of a car window. The car stopped and Pat got out. Tom asked the driver to open the trunk so he could put the packages in. The driver got out. Tom saw that she was tall and slender. Gorgeous. Pat Falco introduced her friend: Patricia MacPhail.

Reprieved from the tedium of child care, Pat Falco wanted to have a drink. The three of them went to the cocktail lounge where Tom's girlfriend worked. But all of a sudden, Tom wasn't thinking about his girlfriend (or his wife). He liked Pat MacPhail, liked her a lot.

Pat MacPhail had lived a lot in a short time. She was twenty years old that summer, already the mother of two children and divorced from her second husband. She would fill a void in Tom's life.

Soon, Tom Trantino, Pat MacPhail, Norma Jaconetta, and Frank Falco were spending a lot of time together. Pat Falco fit in some of the time, though not when Norma and Frank were together. Had this been a few years later, they might have passed for hippies, might have called their lifestyle "free love."

But they didn't wear flowers in their hair, and they were definitely not gentle people.

CHAPTER 6

Gary and Adrienne

In that summer of 1963, men were wearing colorful madras shirts, and Stan Musial was playing his last major-league season. President Kennedy visited Ireland. A twelve-year-old singer named Stevie Wonder was a sensation.

Adrienne Peraino was eighteen. She was a bright girl, bright enough to have skipped a grade. She was attending Montclair State University already and had been going out with the same guy for four years. But he was not someone she had met on campus. She was still dating her high school sweetheart.

She was fourteen the first time she saw him. It was in the cafeteria at Lodi High School. He was only about five eight, but he had a trim, athletic physique. Anyone could tell at a glance that he was in shape. He had thick hair, ice-blue eyes, and a serious face. His clothes were just so. When she got close to him, she could tell he used Old Spice cologne.

I have got to go out with that guy, she thought.

She found out he was Gary Tedesco, the son of Patrick Tedesco at the high school. Mr. Tedesco may have been the only wrestling coach in the universe who was also a world-class typist. He could type well over a hundred words a minute, faster than many professional secretaries. He taught business courses and did accounting on the side. Mr. Tedesco was also involved in local Democratic politics. He had campaigned for Robert Meyner for governor and knew Guy Calissi, the Bergen County prosecutor.

Adrienne's father, Vito, was a supervisor in the Lodi public works department. So Adrienne and Gary would have plenty of Lodi stuff to talk about if she could get him to ask her for a date.

Bright or not, the slender, dark-haired Adrienne was no more sure of her-self than most teenagers. When she looked in the mirror she saw a girl who was pretty, sort of. She could not see what anyone else of normal eyesight could see: she was lovely.

Gary Tedesco was not blind. He finally did ask her out. On May 22, 1959, they went to a drive-in movie. And that, she recalled many years later, was that: "There was no one else." She sat at the Tedesco dinner table many times. She was family.

Adrienne loved Gary's straight-arrow ways, and his gentleness. He was protective not just toward his little sister, Patty, but toward his other sister, Elaine, who was a couple of years younger than Gary. Guys who wanted to go out with Elaine could sense Gary giving them the once-over, in a friendly sort of way. And he was gentle to his mother, Sadie Tedesco, who made no secret of the fact that he was her favorite.

Gary looked good in a T-shirt, whether working on a car engine or fishing, but he *really* looked good dressed up. He just had a knack with clothes. He worked for a Lodi clothing store in one of his part-time jobs.

As a toddler, he had posed for photographs in sailor suits, but what he wanted to wear most was a cop's uniform. When the children in his kinder-garten class were asked to dress up as what they wanted to be when they grew up, Gary dressed like a police officer. He never outgrew the dream.

For the first decade or so of Gary's life, the Tedesco family lived not in Lodi but in neighboring Garfield. Then, in a decision that was more fateful than they could have dreamed, the Tedescos moved to the other side of Harri-son Avenue. Now they lived in Lodi.

When Gary talked about someday becoming a state trooper, Patrick Tedesco tried to steer his son's ambitions back home. Being a Lodi cop was a lot safer than being a state trooper, Pat thought.

Gary Tedesco turned twenty-two on August 11, 1963. He was going to be sworn in as a Lodi policeman on September 1. His maternal grandfather, Joseph Serpone, was a master tailor and had been busy putting the final touches on Gary's uniform. Patrick Tedesco was going to pin the badge on his son at the swearing-in ceremony.

The family was going to throw a party the next weekend in honor of the new police officer. Soda, snacks, and favors were being stockpiled.

CHAPTER 7

Not a Day
to Rest

It bothered Tom Trantino to see Frank Falco neglecting his wife and child. "That's some real bad shit you're doing," Tom said to Frank one day.

Frank laughed. "You're full of shit. What about *your* wife and kid? You're fucking around night and day."

"At least I fill Helene's belly. What more could she want?"

Helene wanted what her husband would not give her: a married life. Fed up at last with her husband's carousing, with the sick cycle of abuse and apologies and more abuse, she moved out in early August. She and her child went to her parents' home in Sullivan County in upstate New York. Tom consoled himself in the arms of Pat MacPhail.

As for Frank Falco, he clung to some traditional beliefs, despite his philandering. That was why he was so upset when he heard early in August that Rocco Benedetto had beaten up Pat Falco. If his supposed friend Rocco felt free to beat another man's wife, God only knew what else might be going on! No self-respecting man would allow his wife to be mistreated by a man to whom he had entrusted her.

So Frank decided to visit Rocco, and he took Tom Trantino along. Perhaps their mental faculties were not razor-sharp (it was three o'clock in the morning when they broke into the apartment of the startled Rocco), but Frank at least had a clear intent. He fired a few shots over the head of Benedetto, who had been watching television in bed. Frank and Tom punched him around a bit. Then Frank told Rocco that they were all going to take a ride.

It was never clear whether Rocco wanted to look like a gentleman when he died, or whether he was simply stalling for time. In any event, he asked for and was given some time to perform his toilet, coif his hair, and dress in his best silk suit. He took his rosary with him.

During the ride along Route 46, Rocco talked the good talk. Don't make a mess of it, he pleaded. Let me die like a man.

Perhaps Falco and Trantino were emotionally touched. For some reason, they changed their minds. They decided Rocco could live, after all. So they put him out of the car and let him walk home.

§

One day that summer, when Frank and Norma were in her apartment in Paterson, he got a call from his wife.

Check out the newspaper, Pat Falco said.

Norma was sent to the store to buy a paper. On an inside page, she found an article about the murder of a nineteen-year-old apprentice printer in a place called the Vivere Lounge in lower Manhattan. The article said the killer was still at large; it was accompanied by a picture of her beloved Frankie.

The article upset Falco. He and Norma decided to set up housekeeping at another apartment she kept, in Totowa, New Jersey. From then on, Norma told the landlord that Frank was "Mr. Jaconetta." Frank Falco had to be careful of situations in which his identity might be checked closely.

§

Sunday, August 25, was warm and sunny, and Norma Jaconetta didn't want to stay indoors. She and a friend, Sarah Jane Vander Fliet, better known as Sally, decided to go to Palisades Amusement Park in Cliffside Park.

Sally was nineteen that summer. She had been married and divorced and had a child. She listed her address as Fairfield, New Jersey, but she spent a lot of time in Lodi.

Tom and Frank were pulling a robbery that day, and Norma would normally have been with them. But on this day, Falco was with his wife, and Norma thought it would make for an awkward social situation if she went along too.

Later, Tom Trantino told how they picked their target. He and Frank had a buddy from prison, one Anthony "Tony Winks" Cassarino, who was twenty-four. Falco trusted Cassarino; after all, Tony Winks had helped him dump the body of Robert Munoz into the East River. The New York police had heard about that, and so they were looking for Cassarino as well as for Falco.

As Tom told it later, Tony Winks knew of this apartment in Brooklyn Heights. Some guy lived there; he was well connected and had a lot of money. Taking him off would be no problem. Tom and Frank were short of cash, so they had to do something. As they sat with Pat Falco and Pat MacPhail in Pat MacPhail's kitchen in Allendale, they decided it was a "go."

"Can you get a babysitter for tonight?" Frank asked Pat MacPhail.

"Yeah. Why?"

"Good," Frank said. "Then we can all go out tonight after we take care of business."

"Me too!" Pat Falco said, jumping into her husband's lap and splashing kisses all over him. "Me too! Right, Frankie?"

"Sure," Frank said, laughing. "You too."

To save time, Frank said, everyone would go along. That way, they could go right from the job to wherever they wanted to celebrate.

Tom was happy for Pat Falco; she deserved some joy in her life. But he felt uneasy. Norma usually went on jobs, not Pat MacPhail, and Tony Winks was a newcomer.

Besides, Tom wasn't at full strength. He missed Helene and his son, so Pat MacPhail had driven him up to Sullivan County the day before to look for them. (Tom Trantino had no driver's license.)

Tom thought he knew where Helene was, but he hadn't been able to find her. He didn't know it, but she had moved in with her aunt.

A four-hour round trip, wasted. Pat and Tom hadn't gotten back until almost four on Sunday morning. He was bone-tired, but he had slept fitfully. Then he had had several drinks on Sunday afternoon. He had eaten a sandwich, but his body craved more nourishment than that, and more rest.

CHAPTER 8

Forebodings

The sun was just coming up over the Nevada desert.

Patricia Tedesco wanted to sleep some more, but something had awakened her. For a second, the eleven-year-old didn't know where she was. Then she remembered: she was in a Las Vegas hotel room with her parents. It was Sunday, August 25, 1963.

Her parents had been making noises in their sleep. Could it be that they were both having nightmares at the same time? Or maybe just one had had a bad dream and the other was saying, "Hush, hush."

Patty listened to her parents whispering in the dim light of the hotel room. Patrick and Sadie Tedesco were both wide awake now, and they sounded upset.

"I had a bad dream," Sadie said to her husband. "I want to see Gary." Later, trying to put a shape to the dream, Sadie Tedesco said she saw herself in their house in Lodi. People were coming and going but not saying much. No one was smiling, so it didn't seem like there was a party. It was more like a . . . funeral.

Patty didn't know any of this Sunday morning. She just knew she wasn't going to get any more sleep. She got out of bed.

Her parents had come to Las Vegas for some kind of business. The train trip across the country had been full of wondrous sights. They had taken the train not for the scenery but because Patrick and Sadie Tedesco didn't like to fly. They were all supposed to be in Las Vegas for another few days, then go back by train. So Patty could hardly believe her ears when she heard her parents talking about flying home right away.

Patrick Tedesco threw on some clothes and went down to the front desk. The hotel people said they'd see what they could do about airline tickets.

You're in luck, Patrick was told in just a few minutes. An airline had just had three reservations canceled. Book us, Patrick said.

Patrick and Sadie Tedesco called Gary in Lodi. It was three hours later there. They said they had changed their plans and were coming right home. Gary said he wouldn't be able to see his folks for long. He and Adrienne were going to a wedding. They'd stop by the reception afterward, and then Gary would head for the police station. He was a probationary officer, getting on-the-job training. In a week, he was to be sworn in as a full-fledged policeman.

Patty Tedesco felt kind of mixed-up on this Sunday morning. The idea of going home early felt good. Patty looked forward to seeing her big brother again. Gary was ten years older than she was and always looked out for her. Sometimes he'd take her for rides in the bright red 1932 Ford he'd fixed up. Patty liked having the other kids see her in that car.

And Patty loved Gary's girlfriend. Adrienne was exactly seven years older than Patty (both were born on September 10), and Adrienne had been Patty's sponsor at her confirmation just three months before.

But Patty thought her parents were acting very strange. Something was bothering them, but they wouldn't say what. Patty sure didn't know what it was. Could it be that her parents didn't know either?

§

Gary and Adrienne went to the wedding of a cousin of Lodi's mayor, Frank Belli. Then they stopped at the reception. Gary had never been a big drinker at all. A beer or two now and then, that was enough. Besides, he had to go to work Sunday night.

Adrienne was sitting with Gary in his car in front of her house that evening when the feeling came to her. It was not exactly a premonition, just a—what?

"Don't go," she blurted out.

"What?"

"Don't leave."

Gary laughed. It was funny how people were worried about him all of a sudden. Just a little while ago, after his parents arrived home from their abbreviated trip to Las Vegas, his mother had stopped him as he was heading out.

"Don't dare go to the police station tonight," Sadie Tedesco said. She didn't know why she said it, except that she was still feeling the chill that had made her want to come home. "A mother's intuition," she called it years later.

Gary humored his mother as best he could. He couldn't stay home. He was about to become a full-time cop, for crying out loud! Besides, as he put it, "What could happen to me in Lodi?"

And so he said good night to her, and she closed the door on him.

And now, here he was with Adrienne, who had caught a case of the same heebie-jeebies.

He chuckled. "I love you," he said to Adrienne. "I'll see you tomorrow."

§

The shift started at eight in the evening, when it was still daylight. It was supposed to run until four in the morning. That Sunday evening, Sergeant Peter Voto was not planning to flop into bed at the end of his tour. He had something more important to do: he was going to go fishing with his nine-year-old, also named Peter. The weather was supposed to turn cooler on Monday; the fish should be biting.

Peter Voto was Gary Tedesco's mentor. In a way, Peter Voto was paying back a debt by teaching Gary everything he knew about Lodi and police work. Pete had been a wrestler at Lodi High School. His coach had been Gary's father.

The Voto-Tedesco connection didn't end there. Back in the 1940s, one of Patrick Tedesco's students was a sweet-natured girl named Matilda Babagnoli. In 1948, she married Pete's brother, Andy.

§

The atmosphere in the ramshackle police station (the building had once been a mansion) was as friendly as always that evening, almost like family. One Lodi officer, Michael Serpone, was Gary Tedesco's first cousin.

Gary rode in Peter Voto's car for part of the shift. As they started their routine patrols, Voto and his protégé no doubt went by the hulks of the old dye mills, standing like gravestones over an industry and the hopes of men long asleep in the ground. Peter, being eighteen years older than Gary, may have reflected on how quickly things could change, how one's life seemed to just fly by. Peter Voto sure as hell didn't feel like he was forty years old, but he had reached that milestone on August 5, six days before Gary's birthday.

Gary Tedesco's career had already begun triumphantly. Less than two weeks before, he and Pete Voto had responded to a call of a burglary in progress at an ice cream store on Route 46. The store was located practically across the street from the Angel Lounge. Sure enough, when they got to the Frosty Maid Ice Cream Company, there were intruders.

Peter sent Gary to the rear of the store while he himself covered the front. One of the burglars came out the back door, hoping to flee in the dark. When he saw the man, Gary Tedesco told him to freeze.

The burglar stopped in his tracks, submitting to a search. Within minutes, Peter Voto had a second suspect. It was not a bad night's work for the cops, and especially for Gary Tedesco. He didn't even carry a gun yet, and he had already made an arrest!

"Don't you ever do that again!" his sister Elaine said right afterward, for once delivering a stern lecture to her older brother instead of the other way around. "What's the matter with you? You could get killed!"

Gary just laughed. He had made the first collar of his career, and had been given a commendation for it, while armed with nothing more than a flashlight.

No, that wasn't quite true. Gary was learning, as Peter Voto already knew, that a good cop's first weapon is the air of confidence and authority he carries. Though he was far less physically impressive than Pete Voto, Gary was no pushover. He too was a wrestler, and he had recently taken up boxing. There were few men he would be afraid of, one on one, assuming no guns or knives were involved.

After graduating from Lodi High, Gary had attended Fairleigh Dickinson University in Bergen County for a while. But the life of a college student wasn't for him, at least not yet. Being a cop was.

But here he differed from Pete Voto. Gary didn't plan to spend his career on the Lodi force. One day, he would be a state trooper, or perhaps a federal agent.

CHAPTER 9

A Celebration
Turns Deadly

Tom Trantino would rather have spent the rest of Sunday getting his body and mind squared away. After all, he was still tired and melancholy from the futile trip to look for his wife. And he'd had a few drinks during the day. They didn't help his mood at all.

But work was work. You had to grab the chances that came your way. Tony Cassarino had gotten this tip about a guy in an apartment on Ocean Parkway in Brooklyn who was an easy mark. So, as Sunday afternoon was slipping into Sunday evening, five people got into a car for a trip from New Jersey across the George Washington Bridge and on to Brooklyn. Pat MacPhail was at the wheel. With her were Tom Trantino, Frank Falco and his wife, and Tony Cassarino.

It was getting dark as Pat MacPhail found a parking spot a discreet distance away from the apartment building. Tom and Frank left their friends in the car and went to conduct their business.

Up the stairs they went, with practiced stealth. When they found the right door, they drew their guns. They would scare the guy shitless so he wouldn't dream of putting up a fight.

Tom knocked. He wanted everything to be quick and easy. Get in, get the money, get out, and no one gets hurt. Get in, get the money—

When the door began to open, Tom threw his shoulder into it and barged in, holding his gun in front of him. To his surprise, the weapon was pointed right at the face of a middle-aged woman. She looked so petrified that for a second he thought she might drop dead.

In came Frank Falco, just as another, older woman appeared from the back of the apartment. She, too, looked deathly afraid.

Not right, not right, not right. "Nobody's gonna get hurt," Tom said. "Just shut up and keep shut."

"My mother has a bad heart," the younger woman said. "There's no money here. Please go."

No money? That was the last thing the two men wanted to hear. Could they be in the wrong place? They had come all this way . . .

"The money's gotta be here," Frank said. "It's just *gotta* be here even if the guy ain't . . . "

The older woman begged for her pills. Tom asked her where they were, then fetched them for her, along with some water. He wasn't a monster, after all. They had come for the money, not to hurt a couple of women.

Tom wanted to get out of there, but Frank was going crazy. He threw furniture against the walls, then pulled the drawers out of the bedroom dressers and smashed them to pieces. He clawed at the paneling on the cabinets. It came free in ear-splitting shrieks.

"Don't worry," Tom said to the women. "We'll be leaving soon."

"Please make him stop. Please go."

Frank ripped the shelves out of closets, hurled clothes onto the floor, went on smashing things.

We have to get out of here, Tom thought. *He's making so much noise, someone's bound to call the police.* "That guy isn't coming," Tom said. "You're waking up the dead."

Finally, Frank was ready to leave. He'd found some stuff after all.

"You go down first," Tom said. "I'll meet you in the car."

"Make sure you tie them up good," Frank said. Then he was gone.

Tom didn't want to tie up the women. "Please now, just don't scream. Go in that back room there."

"We won't scream," the older woman said. "Just get out. Go."

Back in the car, Tom was furious with Tony. "You no-good punk cocksucker, you gave us a bum tip!"

"I can't understand it," Tony said. "I just can't understand it . . . "

This time, Frank played the rare role of conciliator. "Look," he said, pulling cash and jewels out of his pocket. "There's some good bread and good ice here."

Frank dangled some sparklers in his wife's face.

"Whoopie!" Pat Falco said, kissing her husband.

So the job wasn't a total loss. They'd gotten more than two thousand in cash, and they could fence the jewels easily enough.

But Tom was tired and depressed. Worn out, really. He didn't feel like celebrating. But everyone else did.

So they drove across the George Washington Bridge, picked up Route 46, and headed toward Lodi.

§

Around that time, Norma Jaconetta and Sally Vander Fliet dropped by the Angel Lounge. The place was too quiet for their tastes, so they tried another nightclub about a quarter-mile away on Route 46.

Around midnight, they headed back to the Angel Lounge, which was becoming a good deal more lively. Tom, Frank, and the others were there. Tom was trying to get himself into a party spirit. The men slapped a couple of big bills on the bar (it sure felt great to have cash!) and told the bartender to keep the drinks coming.

A local band, the Dell-Aires, was performing that night. There was a jukebox, too, and a small dance floor. Tom, Frank, and Tony danced with the women (Norma Jaconetta and Pat Falco remaining cordial with each other in the presence of the man both slept with), and they shared some of the pills Frank had brought along.

Tony Cassarino told some jokes, and Frank Falco sang. As for his voice . . . well, he might have been well advised to keep his day job (if he had had a day job), but only a good friend of Frankie's would have dared tell him that, even in jest.

Then things started to get too lively, even for the Angel Lounge.

§

Noise complaints involving the bar, known in police shorthand as "the Angel," were routine, so neither Peter Voto nor Gary Tedesco was surprised when the first one came in sometime after ten o'clock.

Nor had they any reason to be alarmed. Even in plain clothes, which he wore that night, Peter Voto was an intimidating man whose very presence could quiet a drunk. And Gary Tedesco had done some bartending in his spare time while waiting for the opening on the police force. Shutting people off, handling drunks the right way, dealing with the always hazardous mixture of alcohol and testosterone—all that went with the territory, for a bartender and for a cop.

Besides, Lodi being Lodi, the Voto and Tedesco families knew the families of the Angel Lounge's owners. Patrick Tedesco had helped Tony Perillo with the books on occasion. And although Gary didn't know it, his father had approached Perillo about a part-time bartending job for his son at the Angel Lounge.

Perillo had said he didn't need another bartender. Actually, he thought it would be awkward if he hired Gary and wasn't satisfied with him. There might be hard feelings if he had to let Gary go.

On Sunday nights, Tony Perillo's brother-in-law usually tended bar. His name was Nicholas Kayal, and he lived next door to Adrienne Peraino's family when she was growing up. As a matter of fact, the building that housed the Angel Lounge was owned by Joseph Peraino, a cousin of Adrienne's father. Such was the smallness of Lodi.

§

Assuming that they sized up the clientele on their first visit, Pete Voto and Gary Tedesco noticed some girls acting older than their ages and some guys who looked like they spent a lot of time in bars. Nothing unusual about that.

Witnesses would recall that Voto talked to Nicholas Kayal, asking for a little less noise. Then the cops went back on routine patrol, probably driving by some of the same places they had looked at before, maybe going over some of the same conversation as they patrolled the dark, sleepy streets of Lodi. Maybe Peter Voto was starting to think about taking his son fishing.

They went back to the Angel Lounge later for more of the same: another noise complaint. And when they were summoned to the Angel Lounge a third time, they were probably annoyed. Didn't those assholes at the bar have anything better to do with their time? Probably not, or they wouldn't be spending Sunday night there.

No, not Sunday night. It was well into Monday by now, past 2:30 in the morning. For sure, this would be the last time they would go to the Angel Lounge. Closing time was three, after all. And just an hour after that, their shift was up.

Inside, they found three men and four women still celebrating in the dim light. There was the lone bartender, Nick Kayal. The three male customers seemed to be drunk. One of the men was dancing unsteadily with a woman on the tiny dance floor, trying futilely to follow the rhythm of the blaring jukebox.

Sally Vander Fliet ducked into the ladies' room as she saw Voto begin calling for identification. When she came out a few minutes later, she saw Pete Voto take Tony Cassarino into a cloakroom. They came out about two minutes later, and Tony Cassarino hastily exited the place. The rest of the group was huddled around the other cop.

"This is my wife," Frank Falco said, referring to a striking young woman with dark hair. He seemed pretty eager to pass her off as his wife.

Pete Voto spoke to Nick Kayal. Then Voto told Gary Tedesco to go outside and radio for another patrol car. It was time to clear out the joint.

Just about the time Gary Tedesco was outside, walking toward the patrol car, Peter Voto was walking toward the corner of the bar near the bandstand. He had spotted a towel.

§

"Send another car to the Angel," Gary Tedesco said over the radio. The call was logged in at 2:50 in the morning. No one at headquarters heard any urgency in his voice.

He decided to go back inside. Just as he approached the door, one of the women was coming out. Gary Tedesco looked past her, then pulled her out the door and stepped inside the Angel Lounge. The door closed behind him. He could hear cursing. In the gloom, he could make out Peter Voto coming toward him.

Something wasn't right. A man was walking behind Voto, twisting the sergeant's arm up behind his back. Did his mother's parting words echo in a distant reach of Gary's memory?

"Oh, my God," Gary Tedesco said.

CHAPTER 10

Crazy Flight

Sally Vander Fliet ran out of the Angel Lounge in terror, into the fresh-smelling August night. This could not be, could not be! She had not even been to the Angel Lounge since last March, when the place was closed for a month for serving minors, and now on her first night back, this terrible thing!

She was not even part of the group, not really. She'd only been there because she'd spent the day with her good friend Norma. Sally had been introduced to Tommy Trantino and Frankie Falco and Falco's real wife and Tony Cassarino and Pat MacPhail only a few hours before, and they had seemed all right. But things had turned wild, so wild . . .

She had had so much trouble in her nineteen years. Now something much worse than anything else had happened.

She had seen Tommy holding a silver gun to the back of the big cop's head, twisting his arm behind him, then beating him down to the floor. She had seen two flashes of fire from the silver gun. The noise of the shots rang in her ears. Then there were more shots, and she thought she heard a moan.

She couldn't believe her eyes and ears, just *couldn't believe* any of it, until Norma gave her a good slap to wake her up.

She ran to Norma's car, parked not far from a fire hydrant, and got in, sitting in the driver's seat. In the dark, she saw another car creeping by with its lights out. Oh, it was Pat MacPhail, in her red Valiant.

And here came Norma, running, running. Norma stopped first at the empty police car, opened the door and turned off the headlights, then slammed the door shut. Then she was standing in the glare of other headlights, and there was a police car with its red dome light flashing, and Norma got into her car on the driver's side, and Sally slid over to make room for her, and Norma fumbled with the keys and finally got the key into the ignition and—

Tommy opened the door and started to scramble into the front seat, with Frankie right behind him, but there wasn't enough room for *four* people in the front seat, for God's sake, so Sally had to do a half-dive, half-somersault, ass-over-tincup maneuver into the back seat to make room.

"Come on, Norma, get the car started."

Sally was so scared, she couldn't tell if it was Tommy or Frankie who said that.

"I can't get it started," Norma said.

"Come on," Frankie said. "Get out of here. Get it started!"

By this time, Pat Falco had climbed into the back seat with Sally. "Frankie!" Pat said. She was in tears. The night had turned so crazy, with her having to stand there and listen to her husband tell a cop that *Norma Jaconetta* was his wife!

Sally Vander Fliet turned to see another cop car, its red dome light spinning crazily in the dark. Two uniformed cops were standing near the door of the Angel Lounge.

"Run, Frankie!" Norma screamed. "Run, if you want! If you don't want to get caught, get out of here. Run!"

Tom Trantino and Frank Falco didn't wait. They got out of the car and disappeared between the Angel Lounge and another building into a patch of woods.

Finally, Norma realized that she had the wrong set of keys in her hand. An eternity later, she found the right set and got the engine started. She peeled out, onto Route 46, went just a stone's throw, took the first right, drove on this street and that street.

As she drove, Norma gave advice: "Just say you don't know nothing and you just came here tonight, 'We met these two guys, we don't know them or nothing,' and we don't have to worry." She didn't sound very convincing.

Pat Falco wondered if someone would come and take her child away.

Norma saw a flashing red light in her rear-view mirror. She wasn't about to slow down. "Remember," Norma said, "if I get stopped, you don't know anything."

Norma drove through part of Hasbrouck Heights and into a factory area of Hackensack and stopped in a gas station lot to figure out where to go next.

And that was it; there was a police car. There was no running away anymore.

§

Tom Trantino's world was spinning from whiskey and pills and terror. He fell, got up, fell again, and got up again. He ran, fell, got up and ran. His sweat stank in his nose.

Milk truck! He saw it in the dark, saw the driver moving quietly from house to truck and back again.

The milkman lived in Lodi and was used to seeing its quiet streets in the dark. As he was making his rounds on Pasadena Avenue, several blocks from Route 46, he was startled when a man emerged from the darkness and hopped onto his truck.

"Some woman's husband is after me," Tom Trantino said. "I'll give you ten dollars to take me to Orange."

The request was absurd; Orange was miles away, in another county.

"I've got to deliver milk."

"Be good and take me there."

"I have to do my route. I can't take you anywhere." The driver was scared. He couldn't see very clearly in the dark, but the man who had just climbed aboard his truck stank of booze and sweat. The driver was afraid to try to throw the stranger off the truck, afraid to have him on the truck.

The milkman decided to return to the garage for help. He knew his boss would be loading milk there.

Tom Trantino had noticed that the driver had a speech impediment. It was crazy, what a man picked up when his blood was rushing. At least the truck was moving, moving, moving.

The driver stopped at a garage. What . . . ?

Through the open garage door, Tom saw a man loading milk. The driver got off and walked toward the garage. *He's going for help,* Tom realized. *Jesus Christ! I'm only a couple hundred yards from the Angel Lounge . . .*

He jumped off and ran. Soon he was in a big open space, running and falling and running and falling. Then he saw streets again. Oh! There was a bus stop! Several people saw him coming, saw that his sport jacket was torn and rumpled and wet. They recoiled when they saw his face. But he found a man willing to give him a ride up to Allendale, where Pat MacPhail lived.

§

Pat MacPhail left the Angel Lounge just before the killings—that much is not in dispute. But exactly what she did, and what she saw and heard, and when, will never be known with certainty.

All we have is the testimony she gave at Thomas Trantino's trial.

She told the court that the two cops had looked at her driver's license, had seen that she was too young to be drinking in the Angel Lounge, and had told her to leave—which was just fine with her, because things were starting to get really wild.

As Pat MacPhail recalled things later, Tommy started fighting with the big, strong cop while the younger cop was outside. As she headed for the door, she heard a scuffle.

"You rat-bastard motherfucker!" Tommy shouted. "Keep your hand out of your pocket . . . "

Pat was afraid. God only knew what bad things would happen, with Tommy talking that way to a cop!

She was at the door now. There, she saw the younger cop, on his way in. He blocked her way—just for a moment, she recalled. Then he peered inside and said, "Oh, my God!" And then he pulled her outside.

Thus delivered from the madness, she walked to her car. She recalled pulling her car up near the front of the Angel Lounge. She told of seeing Norma Jaconetta come out of the bar, then dash back inside the Angel Lounge. Then she saw another police car pull up to the Angel Lounge, and saw an officer get out, look inside the bar, then get back into his car and speed off.

She recalled hearing three shots *after the police car sped off.*

Pat MacPhail testified that she then did a U-turn and repositioned her car on the street. She decided to see what was what inside the Angel Lounge. She knocked. The door opened, and she peered inside, just long enough to see two bodies on the floor.

"Get the hell out of here," the bartender said, pushing her away and slamming the door.

She left as fast as she could and drove home to Allendale. The night was a sick blur.

§

Pat knew an Allendale police lieutenant, Frank Parenti, and she called him at home around four o'clock. She told him she had heard some terrible noises at the Angel Lounge.

That woke Parenti up in a hurry, and he raced over to Pat's house at 90 East Allendale Avenue. Alert by now to what had happened at the Angel Lounge, he listened to her story, then left about five o'clock to plug his knowledge into a manhunt that was taking on its own life. Anyone driving around at such an hour might be a suspect; cars were being pulled over all across central Bergen County.

The light of a new day was breaking through as Pat MacPhail gave her account again to another police officer, this time by telephone. The doorbell rang. Pat went to let in Frank Parenti, who had said he might be back.

"Open up and let me in," a man said. It didn't sound like Frank Parenti . . .

She opened the door. Tom Trantino was standing there.

CHAPTER 11

Before
and After

Telephone calls in the middle of the night were nothing new to Andy Voto. He was a lieutenant on the Lodi police force, after all. So when the phone rang around 3:30 in the morning of August 26, 1963, he woke up with no dread.

He was almost relieved to open his eyes. He had been dreaming again about his daughter Maryanne, gone from his life for two years. She had been born with a bad heart and died at the age of seven.

The windows of the house at 56 Christopher Street were open. Crickets sang in the grass, as though welcoming the cooler weather that had sneaked in. Andy Voto turned on the light in the downstairs sitting room and picked up the phone.

"Your brother's had it," said a cop at headquarters. "He's gone."

"Get my fucking gun!" Andy Voto shouted to his wife in rage and disbelief. "Get my fucking gun! Someone killed my brother."

Matilda thought at first that Andy was not quite awake, and was shouting his grief over Maryanne. Then she knew. Matty fetched his gun as Andy threw on clothes. In no more than a minute or so, he was ready to leave the house. "Don't you dare open the door for me!" he said to Matty. He had just lost a brother—a reality that he still could not wrap his mind around—and he didn't want to lose his wife.

Only steps from the Voto house, only minutes before Andy stepped outside, a young man in filthy clothes and with the stench of booze on his breath was bothering a milkman on his rounds. He wanted the milkman to give him a ride far away. No, the milkman said. And so the man finally took off on foot.

Andy Voto drove to headquarters to see what he could do, and because it was where he had to be. Grief filled his heart with a pain that was almost physical.

At headquarters, he saw his father, Jerry Voto. The cop who had called the elder Voto, who was sixty-three that summer, had been more gentle. Come to headquarters right away, he said. When Jerry Voto got there, a cop said, "There's been a bad accident."

"Stop kidding me," the older man said.

"Your son has been killed."

So Jerry Voto stood with his surviving son in the parking lot as they cried together. Andy was four weeks past his thirty-seventh birthday, not quite as strong as Pete, but still tough in a fight. When the anger started to overpower his sorrow, he was held in check by two Lodi cops. He wanted to go and kill . . . kill . . .

But there was no target for Andy Voto's rage. Not yet.

Andy had to see for himself, had to see where his big brother had just been killed. So finally he got a patrolman to drive him over to the Angel Lounge. The parking lot was crowded with police cars. Cops in uniform, cops in plain clothes went into and came out of the bar. They recognized Andy and cleared a path for him.

Andy stepped inside. The place stank of smoke and death. He felt one foot slip, looked down, and saw blood all over the floor. His brother's blood, some of it.

"Aw, Pete," he said, looking at the ceiling. "What have they done to you?"

§

It was about four in the morning when the phone rang in the Tedesco home. Gary's sister, Elaine, picked it up. This was the moment that divided the life of Elaine Tedesco, twenty years old that summer, into Before and After.

The caller said he was a police officer. "Is your mother there?" he asked.

"What do you need her for at this hour?" Elaine said. She wasn't stupid, after all.

Elaine didn't have to get her mother. Her father was right there, having just gotten out of bed for a trip to the bathroom. He took the phone.

Come down to police headquarters right away, the caller said. Then he said something about Gary's having been hurt in a bar fight.

§

Adrienne went from half-asleep to wide awake in an instant when Elaine told her over the phone that something bad had happened. But Elaine didn't know how bad, only that Gary had been hurt. Something about a bar fight. *God,* Adrienne thought, rubbing the sleep from her eyes. *I hope he wasn't cut up bad.*

Adrienne's father, Vito, was awake by this time. He decided to call police headquarters. The people there knew who he was. The Lodi public works boss ought to be able to find out what the hell was going on.

"I can't talk right now," an officer said. "The switchboard is lit up like a Christmas tree."

God, Adrienne thought. *Maybe he's hurt bad . . .*

She got in her car and drove to the police station. The building was all lit up. Cops were rushing in and out with crazy looks on their faces. She just couldn't believe the commotion. And it was Sunday night!

She spotted Gary's car, saw the tie he had worn earlier dangling from the mirror. That was his habit, hanging his tie from the mirror.

She went into the station and saw a couple of ambulance attendants go by. The fronts of their white uniforms were smeared with blood. *No,* she thought. *This cannot be. Don't let this be.*

She went up to the counter. "I'm here to find out about Gary Tedesco," she said.

"Where's your father?" an officer asked.

Where's your father? Then she understood. "I'm not Gary's sister," Adrienne said. "I'm his girlfriend."

"He passed away."

Adrienne's legs went weak. A second later she heard a terrible scream. Again, the awful scream. *Who's making that noise?* she wondered.

Just before fainting, she knew. The screams were her own.

§

Patrick Tedesco and his wife and their daughters went to police headquarters in the middle of the night. The place had an urgency never felt before, and the Tedescos felt a deep foreboding. Elaine said the Hail Mary to herself over and over and over as they walked in.

Some officers had them sit down. They saw Adrienne sobbing. Patty climbed into Adrienne's lap. "Don't worry, Adrienne," the young girl said, staring at the gold slippers she had put on before the dash from the house. "Everything's going to be all right."

But nothing Patty said seemed to help. Adrienne went on crying. She had been asked not to tell the Tedesco family Gary was gone. No one in the Lodi police department had any practice with this kind of thing.

Finally, a cop came to the Tedesco family. "I'm sorry," he said to the parents. "Your son is dead."

Then everyone cried.

Around five in the morning, Adrienne called one of her best friends, told her what had happened, and said she'd like to come over. Leaving the police station, she passed by Gary's car. She reached in and took his necktie. She draped it around her neck. It smelled of Old Spice.

§

At the home Peter Voto had left only hours before, Constance Voto, suddenly
a widow, collapsed in great heaving sobs as relatives and neighbors gathered.
Her daughter, Carolyn, stood next to her mother and cried. She was sixteen.
The older boy, Jerry, cried. He was twelve.

And then there was nine-year-old Peter, who was supposed to have gone
fishing with his strong, gentle father that morning. He, too, stood next to his
mother and cried.

The sun was rising on a new day.

CHAPTER 12

Manhunt

Well before sunrise, a manhunt was under way across northern New Jersey. The Lodi killers were being hunted by hundreds of cops. Dozens of cars were stopped and checked, to no avail.

The earliest newspaper accounts identified the suspects as "Tom Tarrantino" of Brooklyn and "Frank Ferraro," who was believed to live in Queens. Early reports said "Ferraro" had forced a bus driver to take him to Orange, New Jersey, where he had an apartment. Ferraro, it soon became clear, was one of Frank Falco's aliases. Pat MacPhail knew him by that name, in fact.

The police were getting information, sketchy and contradictory as it was, from the young women who had been at the Angel Lounge with Tom Trantino, Frank Falco, and Anthony Cassarino. And they were getting some information from Cassarino himself.

Cassarino was picked up not far from the scene of the killings, near Lodi's border with Hasbrouck Heights. "That guy ought to be a detective," Cassarino said, paying a compliment to Hasbrouck Heights patrolman William Hale, who nabbed him.

The Bergen County prosecutor, Guy W. Calissi, said that Cassarino readily acknowledged being wanted in New York City for questioning in the death of Robert Munoz, whom Falco had dispatched in full view of patrons in the Vivere Lounge.

The two-tone green car carrying Norma Jaconetta, Pat Falco, and Sally Vander Fliet was pulled over on Polify Road in Hackensack by a Hackensack detective, Frank Fusco. The detective had spotted the license plate number radioed in by Michael Serpone, Gary's cousin, who had pulled up to the Angel Lounge just in time to see the women drive off.

Norma Jaconetta, Pat Falco, and Sally Vander Fliet were all jailed as material witnesses. So was Pat MacPhail, upon returning to her Allendale home after driving Tom Trantino across the George Washington Bridge after he showed up on her doorstep.

Nicholas Kayal was also grilled as night turned to dawn on Monday. Guy Calissi said the bartender claimed at first that he had left the Angel Lounge just before the shootings. But it soon developed that he hadn't left the Angel Lounge; he had hidden under the bar during the bloodshed.

Anthony Cassarino, too, was held as a material witness. Calissi said that Cassarino professed to be eager to help in the investigation, but not without being assigned a lawyer. It was not immediately clear whether Cassarino could afford his own counsel: though he had $485 in his pocket when he was arrested, he claimed to be unemployed.

By the following day, Tuesday, more details of the crime were being disclosed, and others were being talked about in the stationhouses. Both men had been ordered to take their clothes off, then they were pistol-whipped. But that wasn't all. Very soon, there were rumors that the victims had been forced to kneel and beg for their lives and . . . God only knew what else.

§

Tuesday's newspapers gave readers their first look at Frank Falco and Tom Trantino. Falco's picture showed a sullen face atop a thick, powerful neck. Trantino's picture, cropped from an old mug shot taken when he was at Great Meadow, showed him in suit coat, dress shirt, and tie. His face was oddly asymmetrical, with the left side more rounded than the right. Or perhaps that impression was the result of simple adolescent awkwardness; his expression was not unlike that of a high school senior posing for the yearbook.

The law moved swiftly that Tuesday. A Bergen County grand jury indicted Trantino and Falco on charges of first-degree murder. And Rocco Benedetto (or was it really Carlo Benedetto, or Rocco Bennett?) was arrested for selling a revolver to Trantino and Falco.

A search of Norma Jaconetta's apartment in Paterson was most fruitful. It turned up jewelry and a mink stole, neither belonging to Norma; a rifle, a shotgun, and ammunition; and a power drill, two chisels, and a rubber mallet. Since Norma Jaconetta was not known as a carpenter or a sculptor, the police concluded that the tools had been used for burglaries.

Most significantly, the apartment search turned up a holster that had held a gun found at the Angel Lounge. The serial number on the weapon matched that of a gun stolen just days earlier from the home of a doctor in nearby Monmouth County, according to the deputy Bergen County prosecutor, Fred Galda.

By Tuesday evening, more than a thousand lawmen in New Jersey and New York City were looking for Tom Trantino and Frank Falco. They concentrated on Manhattan, Brooklyn, and Queens, canvassing bars and hotels in those boroughs.

§

It was still broad daylight around eight o'clock Tuesday night when a traveler checked into the Hotel Manhattan on Eighth Avenue, between 44th and 45th Streets. He signed as "J. Bello" and gave his address as Newport, Rhode Island. He carried no luggage. Mr. Bello was given a room on the twenty-fifth floor.

The hotel was just two blocks from the headquarters of the *New York Times* on West 43rd Street and was on the edge of the theater district. It was also not far from the shabby glitter of Times Square, where Tom Trantino had been wandering in his waking hours and sleeping in movie houses.

Late that night, the police got a tip: Mr. J. Bello was really Mr. F. Falco.

Lieutenant Thomas Quinn, a fifty-three-year-old New York detective with more than two decades on the force, was assigned to lead a contingent of a half-dozen officers to the hotel. Quinn was balding and wore glasses, making him look more like an insurance salesman than a cop.

The lawmen went to the twenty-fifth floor around 2:30 on Wednesday morning. With a passkey, Quinn carefully entered Room 2503. It was empty.

The cops went downstairs, checked with the clerk to be sure they had the right room number for Mr. Bello (they did), and set up surveillance. They waited for about forty-five minutes. Nothing.

When it was getting close to 3:30 a.m., Quinn decided that another visit to Room 2503 was called for. Back to the twenty-fifth floor they went. Again, the detectives quietly entered Room 2503. The light was on. Four empty beer bottles stood on the dresser.

Frank Falco lay on the bed in his underwear, fast asleep.

What happened in the next several seconds has been debated ever since. In the official version of events, Quinn held his revolver to Falco's throat, woke him up, and told him he was under arrest. Falco awoke kicking and screaming, grabbed an empty beer bottle, and hit Quinn with it, all the while trying to wrest the gun from Quinn. At least one other cop grappled with Falco, who was fighting with the desperation of a cornered animal.

Quinn emptied his revolver into Falco. Another cop fired three shots at him. Frank Falco fell dead onto his back, blood oozing from six bullet holes, red stains spreading through his underwear.

Although Falco's physical strength and viciousness were never in doubt and broken furniture attested to the ferocity of the death struggle, questions have persisted over the years. They boil down, really, to *one* question: Did the police simply blow Falco away as he awoke with a start?

There has been speculation, too, about who tipped off the police to Falco's whereabouts: a mobster eager to get rid of a loose cannon, or an ex-girlfriend, or perhaps Tony Cassarino, eager to cut a deal. No one knows for sure.

This much is certain: Frank Falco left very few mourners, and hardly anyone felt like asking whether the police had given him enough time to surrender. The headline over a *Life* magazine account of his life and death read "Requiem for a Punk."

"All Bergen County is proud of you," deputy Bergen County prosecutor Fred Galda told Detective Quinn.

The hunt continued for Tom Trantino, believed to be hiding somewhere in New York City. And while he never said so publicly, prosecutor Guy Calissi did not share in the elation over the death of Frank Falco.

§

On Wednesday morning, Trantino's parents pleaded for their son to give up. The police had been to the Trantino home to fetch his bloodstained clothes. The parents' entreaties were broadcast on radio and television and carried in the newspapers. By midday Wednesday, the world knew that Frank Falco was dead.

That day, August 28, 1963, was a memorable one: in Washington, more than 200,000 people heard Martin Luther King Jr.'s "I Have a Dream" speech in the name of civil rights.

That Wednesday evening, a Manhattan lawyer named Enid Gerling got a call from Tom Trantino, whom she knew through a mutual acquaintance. He wanted to turn himself in, and he wanted to be sure he wouldn't have a bad accident in a police station. The lawyer agreed to meet him in the Village Bar, on First Avenue between 21st and 22nd Streets.

§

Tom Trantino, clean-shaven, clad in a gray plaid suit and fresh white shirt and wearing dark glasses, drank a double martini. His lawyer encouraged him to have another; he might need it, she said.

A reporter and a photographer from the Associated Press got a tip and came by to see the celebrity suspect. Enid Gerling was pleasant to them and explained that her client had wanted to surrender early on, but he was afraid of Frank Falco. Now that Falco was gone, there was no problem. And perhaps the lawyer wanted witnesses to recall what Tom Trantino looked like *before* surrendering to the police.

Just after nine o'clock, Trantino and his lawyer, accompanied by the news people, walked into a precinct house on East 22nd Street.

"You're looking for this man," Enid Gerling told the desk lieutenant, Frank Brill.

"What for?" the lieutenant asked.

"Homicide," she said.

Turning to the young man in the gray plaid suit, the lieutenant said, "What's your name?"

"Trantino."

Recovering from his amazement, the lieutenant escorted Thomas Trantino to a cage and called for detectives.

Through the bars, Enid Gerling passed her client a candy bar and a cigarette. As she did so, her purse dropped to the floor, and the contents scattered every which way.

"We love you, Tommy!" a young woman shouted. "Don't worry!" That was Trantino's sister, Barbara, who had come to the stationhouse with her parents. The suspect's mother cried and dabbed at her eyes with a handkerchief.

Guy Calissi, Fred Galda, and some of their assistants interviewed Trantino that night (prosecutors had easier access to suspects in that pre-Miranda era), but without the confession they had hoped for.

Outside, Enid Gerling faced newsreel cameras. "He claims absolute innocence," she said of her client.

At one point, Trantino was led briefly before a throng of reporters. "I want you to know I'm being treated like a gentleman," he said.

The reporters fired unfriendly questions at him, and Trantino's blue eyes flashed. "My mother and father are over there," he said. "Don't you have any sense of decency?"

"Don't you?" someone retorted.

Trantino looked at the floor.

CHAPTER 13

Rage and
Legend

Around the time Tom Trantino was comforting himself with double martinis, the families of Peter Voto and Gary Tedesco were being comforted by New Jersey's governor, Richard J. Hughes.

The governor was a man of deep feeling, and a tough law-and-order man as well. His father had been at various times the mayor of Burlington, a state civil service commissioner, and the warden of Trenton State Prison, where the family lived for a while. Before being elected governor in 1961, Hughes had been an assistant United States attorney and a state judge. He would later serve as chief justice of the New Jersey Supreme Court.

There was an old story about Richard Hughes and his days on the bench. It went something like this:

A defendant well into middle age appeared before him for sentencing on a serious felony rap. Judge Hughes knew that the defendant was a habitual criminal not interested in going straight. "I hereby sentence you to thirty years in prison," Judge Hughes said.

"Your Honor," said the crestfallen defendant, "I'm getting old. I can't *do* thirty years!"

Whereupon Judge Hughes looked down at the man and said, "Just do the best you can."

§

Hughes went to the Santangelo Funeral Home on Lodi's Main Street, where Gary Tedesco lay in state, and to the Alesso Funeral Home on Union Street, where Peter Voto lay. Several hundred police officers from across the state also called. They were among the thousands of mourners whose cars jammed the streets of Lodi.

The governor shook hands and gently embraced the heartbroken. Peter Voto's wife, Connie, smiled briefly as Hughes spoke to her. But a moment later her eyes filled again with tears.

Then word came that Thomas Trantino had surrendered. Peter Voto's mother, Mary, could only sob.

"What does she know?" Andy Voto said. "All she knows is, her boy is dead."

Sagging with grief, Andy Voto was carrying a second burden, laid on his shoulders by his father. The son of immigrants, Genarro Voto was born on the docks of New York City. It was a fitting beginning for a man who would never quite lose the ways of the Old World; his first name had been Americanized to Jerry, but he was still Genarro in his heart.

And so Genarro came to Andy and spoke words that were both plea and command. You must kill the man who killed your brother, Genarro told his surviving son. You must take revenge for the family.

No, Papa. I'm a police officer. I can't do that, no matter how much you want me to, no matter how much I want to. I can't.

You must.

I can't.

Looking into Genarro's eyes, the surviving son knew that his father could never forgive him, knew that something else had died in the Angel Lounge.

For a moment in the funeral home, Andy Voto the police officer yielded to Andy Voto the man, son of Genarro. "You can bet one thing," Andy said of Trantino. "He won't live long."

Even as he spoke, a length of heavy rope dangled in the shadows of the Lodi police department's locker room. It had a loop like a hangman's noose.

§

Tony Grasso and Anthony Perillo went to both wakes. They could see from the eyes that some people blamed them for what had happened. Grasso and his family had been vacationing in Atlantic City when the call came in the early morning. Tony Perillo had been awakened by his brother-in-law, Nick Kayal. Perillo had arrived at the bar while the bodies were on the floor. He had looked away in revulsion and sorrow.

At the funeral home, feeling the eyes on him, afraid he would be tarred with the old "Sin Strip" image, Tony Perillo couldn't say out loud what he was telling himself over and over, what he would say years later: "This could have happened anyplace. Whoever comes through the door of the bar, I don't know who they are."

§

As he was carried to his grave on Thursday, August 29, Gary Tedesco wore the perfectly tailored uniform he would have put on in life just a few days later.

Shops and factories emptied that Thursday as the people of Lodi jammed the sidewalks beneath a gray sky. Hundreds of police officers marched on foot. Some two hundred police cars and forty motorcycles, their lights flashing in a gentle rain, escorted a motorcade of cars bearing flowers.

A Mass for Peter Voto was offered at Saint Joseph's Church in Lodi. Gary Tedesco's Mass was celebrated at Mount Virgin Church in Garfield. Police officers served as pallbearers at each. Then the two coffins were taken to St. Nicholas Cemetery in Lodi and buried not far apart.

Guy Calissi, Fred Galda, and their top aides arrived at St. Joseph's just in time to pray for the soul of Peter Voto. They had spent the first part of their day in court in New York City, where Thomas Trantino was arraigned. The defendant was ordered held without bail, and an extradition hearing was set for September 17. Calissi said he would get the extradition documents to Governor Hughes as soon as possible, and Governor Hughes was expected to forward them immediately to New York's governor, Nelson A. Rockefeller.

The four young women who had been at the Angel Lounge had been questioned extensively. So had Tony Cassarino. And Rocco Benedetto was behind bars for selling a gun to Trantino and Falco.

Noting that more than 150 complaints about the Route 46 dives had been logged since January 1962, a newspaper editorial said: "One wonders why something more has not been done to control Lodi's Sin Strip."

Asked whether the prosecutor's office was planning to investigate the Sin Strip situation, Guy Calissi said it was not. Though he did not say so, he doubtless felt that he had enough work to do in preparing a case in which he would seek the death penalty.

Besides, a grand jury had looked into the Sin Strip problem a decade earlier and had handed up a presentment containing a half-dozen recommendations for cleaning up the stretch of highway. Only one had been adopted: now the bars had to close not at five o'clock in the morning but at the slightly more sensible three o'clock. Soon after the Angel Lounge slaughter, closing time was changed to two o'clock.

On September 3, eight days after the Angel Lounge slayings, Lodi mayor Frank Belli said the borough council would discuss ways to make the Route 46 tavern owners adhere more strictly to state and local law.

The next day, Gary Tedesco's father, Patrick, filed a suit in New Jersey Superior Court against the Angel Lounge and the bartender, Nicholas Kayal. Legal experts said they believed the suit was the first in New Jersey history to base its claim for damages on a bar's allowing customers to have weapons, failing to warn others that such weapons were present, and serving drinks to those having weapons.

Governor Rockefeller of New York signed the documents for Thomas Trantino's extradition to New Jersey, but the defendant's lawyer resisted. Enid

Gerling said she wanted Lodi police kept away from her client. The lawyer had heard about the hangman's noose.

On the night of Monday, September 16, more than 1,400 people flocked to the Lodi High School auditorium for a show to raise money for the victims' families. Sponsored by the South Bergen County Licensed Beverage Association, a trade group for bar and tavern owners, the show featured some of the biggest entertainment names of the day: Tony Bennett, Kitty Kallen, Les Paul, the Four Seasons.

A week later, a New York appellate court judge issued an order delaying Trantino's extradition to New Jersey. Enid Gerling said Trantino's mother had raised doubts about whether her son really was in New Jersey on August 25 and 26. Blanche Trantino testified that her son had called her on August 25 and said he was at his apartment. The suspect's brother, Richard, testified that Tom had also told him he was at home all day Sunday.

§

Walter Winchell was an aging anachronism of journalism even in 1963, his staccato radio voice becoming a laughable self-parody, his column carried in fewer and fewer newspapers.

But he still had his following. In a column published on September 11, 1963, he wrote about the Angel Lounge: "In that recent cop killing in Lodi, N.J., the gangsters ordered both cops to strip, which has been printed. Before slaying the policemen, they tried to perform an unprintable act."

Winchell's syntax ran off the rails, typically, and his language was veiled. But its message was unmistakable. My God, readers thought. These men were forced to beg for their lives, then made to do *that* before being shot in cold blood?

What Winchell had hinted at was picked up by United Press International and the Associated Press and repeated in newspapers and on television, and a terrible legend was born. Many people accepted it as truth. Many still do.

CHAPTER 14

Across the
River Again

On September 25, exactly a month after the Brooklyn robbery that preceded the fatal night at the Angel Lounge, Thomas Trantino lost his fight to avoid extradition to New Jersey. A New York State appellate court ruled against Enid Gerling's attempt to have her client's arrest declared invalid.

Trantino was immediately taken from New York City to New Jersey under heavy guard. Clad in slacks, an open-collared white shirt, and a suit jacket, he was led into the Bergen County Courthouse in Hackensack for arraignment before county judge Joseph W. Marini. There he stood, head bowed, in handcuffs and leg irons. The defendant appeared dazed as the first assistant prosecutor, Fred Galda, read the indictment accusing him of taking the lives of Peter Voto and Gary Tedesco.

Finally, the judge asked him if he understood what the prosecutor had read.

"I wasn't listening," Trantino replied. He said he wanted his lawyer.

At Galda's suggestion, Judge Marini postponed arraignment to allow the defendant time to obtain counsel. Trantino was taken to the nearby Bergen County Jail, where at Galda's urging he was given a medical examination.

Trantino's legal representation was, in fact, becoming a subject of some uncertainty. The defendant's mother had asked a Hackensack lawyer to defend her son. The lawyer could not: he was already representing Peter Voto's widow, Connie, who had sued the owners of the Angel Lounge and the bartender, Nicholas Kayal. The grounds were virtually the same as those in the suit lodged by the Tedescos a few weeks earlier.

On October 15, a Hackensack lawyer, James A. Major Sr., was assigned as temporary counsel, clearing the way at last for Trantino's arraignment. The next day, Major entered a not-guilty plea on behalf of his client. The lawyer also relayed Trantino's complaints that jail guards had taunted him about his Jewish background, told him he would be better off if he cut his own throat, and made him sleep in a straitjacket one night.

Trantino's jailers denied making any ethnic taunts or threats but confirmed that the prisoner had been placed in a straitjacket. They said that was done after he took a swing at a guard.

On October 31, an experienced criminal-defense attorney named Albert Gross was assigned to defend Trantino at his trial. A younger lawyer, Herbert Koransky, was named to assist in the defense. The defense enlisted two young lawyers-to-be to help with the research. One was Michael Gross, one of Albert's sons. Years later, Michael Gross remembered the burden his father took up. "No lawyer wanted to take the case," Michael recalled. "Not if they had any practice in Bergen County."

But someone had to defend Thomas Trantino, and Albert Gross needed help. Besides Koransky and his son, Gross had the services of Ted Takvorian, then a student at Seton Hall Law School.

Takvorian was about Trantino's age, but years behind him in terms of "street savvy." Takvorian realized this from his first chat with Trantino in the Bergen County Jail. When he was able to mentally separate Trantino from the crime at the Angel Lounge, Takvorian found him likable.

Suddenly immersed in an emotion-filled murder trial, Takvorian had felt almost pathetically naive when he visited the man whose life he was trying to save. He had hoped Trantino wouldn't see through him.

But Takvorian was becoming a whole lot less naive, and very quickly. In the late-night sessions in Albert Gross's office near the Bergen County Courthouse, he was learning a lot about being a lawyer. Ambivalence, for instance. Though Albert Gross was throwing himself into the case, it was plain to everyone around him that he felt deep compassion for the families of the victims.

So did Takvorian. The whole weight of the case, or something as simple as an extra glance at the autopsy photographs, was a lot to take home and think about before falling asleep.

One night, after a late session in Gross's office, Takvorian went to his car and found it splattered with eggs.

§

Another legal battle was being fought around that time. It concerned the liquor license of the Angel Lounge. The day after the killings, the Lodi Borough Council had suspended the bar's license for eighty days. In mid-October, the owners, Tony Grasso and Anthony Perillo, sued to get it back. After all, the two Tonys argued, the maximum state penalty for serving minors was twenty-five days.

Borough officials resisted under pressure from local residents, but the owners had a point. The two Tonys pleaded no contest to charges of serving minors, and Lodi officials decreed that the eighty-day suspension could not be extended.

On Saturday, November 16, 1963, the Angel Lounge reopened. Business was slow.

§

"I remember on that night there were a number of people in the Angel Lounge who I am certain have vital information concerning the slayings," Tom Trantino declared in the autumn of 1963. The words appeared in an affidavit in which he said ballistics tests would help prove his innocence. The words infuriated the people of Lodi. Here was the killer (the people of Lodi had long since convicted him in their minds), talking like a truth-seeker. What Trantino remembered, or what he *said* he remembered, would be at the heart of the case for decades to come. It would stoke the bottomless hatred the people of Lodi felt for him, and still feel.

That autumn, the court granted a defense request for the appointment of two psychiatrists, a private investigator, and a ballistics expert to assist in the defense. The psychiatrists would be paid up to $550 each, the private investigator up to $500, and the ballistics expert $250.

On Friday, November 22, 1963, the day after a judge granted the defense requests to appoint experts, President John F. Kennedy was assassinated. For a few days, at least, Thomas Trantino's fate seemed irrelevant.

§

Albert Gross and Herbert Koransky had considered but later decided against seeking a change of venue, declaring that they believed Trantino could still get a fair trial in Bergen County. The trial was supposed to begin on December 2, but Gross said he needed more time. Thomas Trantino's trial was then scheduled to begin on February 3, 1964.

CHAPTER 15

The Adversaries

Guy Calissi knew he would need plenty of soup.

As the trial drew near, the Bergen County prosecutor often retreated to a second living room in the comfortable family home in Ridgewood. Deep into the night, he pored over the grand jury testimony and other evidence spread out on a table. He took notes in longhand (Guy Calissi never learned to type, not even using the hunt-and-peck method) and, as often as not, didn't have to look at them again. It was as though in putting his thoughts on paper he had imprinted them on his brain as well.

"Don't bother your father," Ethel, his wife of twenty-nine years, admonished the five children. When any of them dared to peek in, they might have seen him spooning down the thick pea soup he loved to make for his all-nighters. He was also fortified with a big mug of coffee, cigars, and antacid tablets.

The prosecutor was a vigorous fifty-four that winter. He had been appointed a decade earlier by Governor Robert Meyner, for whom he had campaigned tirelessly. As 1964 began, he prepared to seek the death penalty for the second time in his career. Several years before, he had won a conviction and death sentence against Edgar Smith, a twenty-two-year-old married man, for the 1957 sex-slaying of a fifteen-year-old girl in a gravel pit.

Guy Calissi's stamina and single-mindedness were legendary. He could go days with little food or sleep, wearing out assistants decades younger. It was a way of life he had learned early. The son of poor Tuscan immigrants, Guy William Calissi was one of seven children. Three died in childhood. When he entered grade school in Hoboken, New Jersey, he spoke little English. His family was so poor that his father went back to Europe. Unable to feed the children, Guy Calissi's mother placed him and a brother in an orphanage.

His father came back when Guy was ten years old, and the reunited family moved to Wood-Ridge, New Jersey. By then, Guy's English was much better. He was a pretty fair athlete, able to run a half-mile in just over two minutes, excellent time for his era. He studied hard and was offered a scholarship to Saint Lawrence University after graduating from high school. He turned it down. He had to stay home to help support the family.

In 1936, a year after his marriage, he enrolled in John Marshall College (now Seton Hall University) in New Jersey. He was twenty-seven years old. He got his law degree (summa cum laude) in 1941, clerked for a law firm during the day, toiled as a watchman at night.

In 1942, he started his own law practice. But clients were not plentiful in that pre-litigious time, and he worked at a shipyard in Kearny, New Jersey, to make ends meet. After a year and a half in the army, he tried to jump-start his law practice, moving his office to Hackensack. He worked in a soap factory at night.

The poverty of childhood and the grinding work of young adulthood did not embitter him. He never lost his natural friendliness. He remembered names, and the people he met remembered him. He was a natural for politics, and the Democratic Party was the natural one for him.

His political friendships led to jobs representing the Bergen County municipalities of Moonachie, Dumont, and Saddle River. He lost in his first two political races, for the Wood-Ridge Borough Council, but Guy Calissi was not a man to be discouraged. He tried again, and was elected mayor of Wood-Ridge. He served three terms, then managed Robert Meyner's successful campaign for governor in 1953.

As a boss, he could be driving and demanding. In a courtroom, he was relentless in pursuit of drug dealers, burglars and robbers, rapists and killers.

Criminals were his enemies, because they preyed upon decent and God-fearing people. A good and just society had a duty to put such criminals behind bars, to exterminate them, if necessary. It was as simple as that.

And yet, Guy Calissi was not all business, nor was he a prude. He loved baseball and liked the occasional ribald joke, told man-to-man. And he was anything but heartless. He sometimes urged leniency for a first-time offender in whom he saw true remorse. In or out of court, he was a notorious soft touch for people in trouble not of their own making, people in whom he saw good.

The children who played near his Ridgewood home flocked to a nearby pond for fishing in the summer, ice-skating in the winter. Calissi's Pond, the children called it. To get there, they cut across the Calissi property without fear. Guy Calissi loved their shouts and laughter, loved to see them enjoying the childhood he had been denied.

This, then, was the complex, compassionate man who stayed up late that winter, preparing for the trial he hoped would send Thomas Trantino to the electric chair. But as opening day neared, Calissi seemed especially intense.

"Two people were going on trial," his son Ron Calissi recalled many years later. "Tom Trantino and my father."

The slayings of Peter Voto and Gary Tedesco offended Guy Calissi in an almost personal way. Trantino (and his dead partner, Falco) had struck at the very embodiment of law and order. For the state to obtain anything less than a conviction for first-degree murder and a death sentence would be a defeat.

Although he never said so publicly, Calissi had been troubled by the death of Frank Falco. When the prosecutor got word that the police had been tipped off as to Falco's whereabouts, he dearly wanted him captured alive. That way, Calissi thought, he could play Trantino and Falco against each other, building an ironclad case against both.

So while cops chortled after Falco was blown away, guffawed at the photographs of him lying dead in his bloodstained underwear, Calissi took no pleasure.

§

Albert Gross was a formidable adversary. Gross had graduated from Harvard College, class of 1928, and from Harvard Law School in 1931. He lived in a big house on a hill in an exclusive section of Englewood, and he wore expensive suits.

His face often seemed to sag in fatigue or puzzlement. "Just a simple country lawyer," he called himself. That description was a joke to anyone who knew him. The eyes behind the glasses that rode low on his nose were laser bright, like the mind.

He had not been born to the silver spoon. His father was a brushmaker in Brooklyn. The family moved to Cambridge, Massachusetts, during Albert's childhood. He grew up thinking he wanted to be a doctor and was admitted to Tufts University as a pre-medical student. But he came down with scarlet fever just as he was to start classes and was home sick for a year.

If nothing else, his illness gave him time to reflect. Perhaps he wasn't meant to be a doctor after all. So he went to Harvard (on a scholarship) and trained for the law.

Struggling to get his practice going in the depths of the Great Depression, he sometimes accepted groceries from clients who could not pay him in cash. He persisted. He worked long hours. Eventually he prospered, and by the time he was selected to defend Thomas Trantino, he had been a lawyer for three decades.

Albert Gross had known adversity. He had succeeded through intelligence and hard work. In those ways, he was not unlike Guy Calissi.

The trial judge, Joseph W. Marini, could identify with both lawyers. Like Calissi, Marini came from a big Italian family; he had a brother and four sisters. Joseph Marini was born in Cosenza and came to the United States when he was seven years old. The judge was sixty-four that winter. He had a quiet, easy demeanor with litigators, witnesses, and juries. He was a patient man, but smart lawyers knew not to push him too far. There was a streak of iron in Marini's spine, and if a lawyer didn't like some of his rulings, that was just too bad: the higher courts liked the judge's rulings just fine. Judge Marini was proud that very few verdicts in his trials were ever overturned.

Clearly, the judge had a mind for the law. That had been obvious since 1920, when he graduated from Fordham Law School, where he showed so much promise that he was admitted to the bar before graduation.

Like Gross, the judge was a loyal Republican. He had been in politics since his early twenties, when he was elected to the Cliffside Park Council and then to three terms as mayor. He served briefly in the New Jersey General Assembly, quit early in 1930 to become first assistant Bergen County prosecutor, then ran for Congress in 1932. Despite the landslide for Franklin D. Roosevelt, Joseph Marini lost to his Democratic opponent by a mere 800 votes.

He was named to a district court seat in 1947, began filling in at county court in 1956, and was appointed to county court in 1960.

§

Jury selection began on Monday, February 3. From a pool of about one hundred men and women, twelve jurors and two alternates were to be selected. Trantino, who had lost close to twenty pounds during his jail stay, listened peacefully and attentively.

Security was tight as the selection took place in a third-floor room of the new courthouse annex. People were searched before entering. Whenever Trantino was led to or from the courtroom in handcuffs, the corridor was cleared beforehand. The atmosphere was tense, hushed.

"How would you feel if your verdict sent a man to the electric chair?" Calissi asked a prospective juror. That brought sobs from Trantino's mother, who sat in the rear with her husband. She was escorted out by a courtroom attendant and returned a few minutes later, teary but composed.

Then as now, it was standard practice for lawyers in a criminal case to ask prospective jurors if they had any relatives in law enforcement. Two men said they did. One said a detective in the prosecutor's office was a brother of his sister-in-law; the other said his wife's brother-in-law was a New York City detective.

No matter, the defense said.

Four days later, the task was complete. Eight men and six women were seated. They were salesmen, mechanics, clerks, housewives — all in all, a typical cross-section of their community. For a case of such magnitude, the selection went fairly smoothly, except for one bizarre incident.

Calissi's trusted first assistant, Fred Galda, learned that one of the fourteen panel members had just pleaded guilty to a crime herself. Her husband owned a liquor store, and back in December she had sold a bottle to a minor. The woman was excused and replaced by another woman.

As he prepared his opening statement, Calissi was bothered by the persistent rumors, now accepted in some circles as truth, that Peter Voto and Gary Tedesco had been forced to perform sexual acts on each other. As far as the prosecutor was concerned, what had really happened in the Angel Lounge was bad enough.

The facts would speak for themselves—damningly, Calissi was sure.

CHAPTER 16

The Trial Begins

"The state will prove that Thomas Trantino did kill and murder Gary Tedesco and Peter Voto willfully, deliberately, with premeditation," Guy Calissi said as the trial got under way. It was the early afternoon of Friday, February 7, 1964.

"Thomas Trantino grabbed Peter Voto, overpowered him, held the gun to his head, marched him towards the front of the Angel Lounge . . . And Thomas Trantino asked him to disrobe, and used filthy language that you will hear, holding the gun to his head . . . Gary Tedesco came in while this was going on. Gary Tedesco immediately was asked to disrobe, and he did it quickly. He was down to his shorts and he just had on his shorts and his socks and his shoes."

Then he came to the heart of the matter. "Thomas Trantino, the state will prove, put two bullets in the head of Peter Voto," the prosecutor said, "and then put a bullet into the boy, Gary Tedesco."

That last was something new; early on, investigators had said Trantino killed Voto and Falco killed Tedesco. Did the prosecution now have evidence linking Trantino to both deaths?

Seated at the defense table, Trantino listened intently. He was dressed in a coat, a dress shirt, and a fashionably narrow tie. He might have passed for a vacuum cleaner salesman or a graduate student, though he was pale from his months in a cell.

His bald head bobbing, now and then reflecting the light from the high ceiling, Guy Calissi strode before the jury box. "We all have a burden, a very heavy burden, in this type of case," he said. "If we prove to you that this man Trantino shot Peter Voto and shot Gary Tedesco to death in the manner that I have stated, then I ask you to bring back a verdict of guilty in the first degree without a recommendation of mercy."

Herbert Koransky delivered a brief opening statement for the defense. Parts of it sounded very much like Guy Calissi's opener.

"This is probably the most serious decision any human being can be called upon to make, the fate of another human being," he said. "There can be no more important decision in our lifetimes."

Keep an open mind, he urged the jurors. Turning to the pale-faced young defendant, Koransky said, "I ask you to give him your earnest and honest attention and to render your oath as jurors, to give him the fairest possible trial that you can."

Guy Calissi had not known until that moment whether Thomas Trantino would testify in his own defense. Now he did know, and he relished the prospect of cross-examining him.

But there was no high drama in the early going. The early prosecution witnesses were a civil engineer, hired to give the dimensions of the Angel Lounge, and two photographers who had taken pictures of the rough chalk outlines where Peter Voto and Gary Tedesco had fallen, mortally wounded, and of the victims during the autopsies.

Then came Captain Robert Facella of the Lodi police. He told of watching the autopsies. The postmortem on Tedesco was performed at the Santangelo Funeral Home in Lodi starting around 10:20 on Monday morning; Voto's autopsy took place an hour and a half later at the Alesso Funeral Home.

Facella testified that only one bullet was removed from Tedesco, from the left shoulder area. As for Voto, two slugs were removed from his head and one from his abdomen. The main purpose of Facella's testimony was to establish that the bullets had been properly tagged and placed in envelopes for safekeeping during the autopsies. What was actually discovered during the autopsies would be brought out by Bergen County's medical examiner, Dr. Raphael Gilady.

Licensed to practice medicine since 1917, Raphael Gilady became the Bergen County physician in 1927 and served until the name of the post was changed to medical examiner around 1940. He had been the medical examiner since that time and had performed some 3,500 postmortems.

Among them were the autopsies on Peter Voto and Gary Tedesco, whom the doctor had pronounced dead in Hackensack Hospital around 4:30 on the morning of Monday, August 26.

"The one performed on Peter Voto, which was in the Alesso Funeral Home, was performed at about eight hours after death," the doctor explained.

"What about the other one?" Calissi asked.

"The other one, performed on Tedesco, was performed in the Santangelo Funeral Home, also in Lodi. That was performed about nine hours after death. They were performed in succession. I did one, then did the other one."

A trial is like a minefield for a lawyer. Sometimes he thinks he is on safe terrain, only to find out suddenly that there is danger underfoot. But the lawyer must not stumble. So Guy Calissi went on smoothly, even though a contradiction in his case had just emerged.

A police photographer and Captain Facella had testified that Tedesco's autopsy had been performed first, starting around 10:20 in the morning, with Voto's beginning some ninety minutes later. Yet the medical examiner had just recalled performing the autopsy on Voto *eight* hours after the victim's death, and that on Tedesco *nine* hours after death.

"Doctor, could you please direct your attention to the first autopsy," the prosecutor continued. "Which one was that?"

"The first autopsy was done on the body of Voto."

There. The contradiction was out in the open, at least to anyone listening closely enough. Would the defense pick up on it? If so, could it plant any seeds of doubt about the rest of the state's case?

"He was about forty years of age, quite obese," the doctor said of Voto, using *obese* in the technical sense and saying nothing of the bull-like strength that went with the 240 pounds on Voto's frame.

The medical examiner told of initially finding three wounds on the body of Peter Voto—one on the left side, another on the abdomen just to the right of the navel, and a third on the left jaw. The bullet into the victim's left side had slashed through the liver, causing terrible bleeding. The bullet that entered the left jaw area had traveled upward and lodged in the brain.

"Then there was a bullet in the back of the head a few centimeters below the hairline," the doctor went on. "That bullet entered into the brain and embedded itself there."

The doctor said that any of the wounds could have been fatal. Asked whether he had found any other injuries, the medical examiner said he had. "Mr. Voto had a bruise across the bridge of his nose, exactly over here," the doctor said, pointing to his own face, "and over his right eyebrow."

That question, of course, was meant to buttress the state's contention that Voto had been pistol-whipped. Calissi had gotten the answer he wanted.

And what of the other autopsy? Physically, of course, the victims could hardly have been more different. "This was a very young boy," the doctor said of Gary Tedesco. "Twenty-two years old, very slim."

The young victim had been shot twice in the chest, with one bullet tearing through his heart and the other ripping through his liver. Both bullets had come out his back and ended up somewhere in the Angel Lounge, either intact or in pieces.

Those who loved Gary Tedesco could draw only small comfort from what came next. "The bullet that went through the heart caused instantaneous death," the doctor said. "It created a tremendous rupture, a tremendous tear in the heart, but the other bullet as well could have caused death because it created a tunnel through the liver, with a great deal of tearing and injury to the liver with hemorrhage."

A third bullet had been fired into Gary Tedesco's right side, coming to rest in the muscle around the left shoulder blade. That slug was the only one recovered from his body.

Finally, there was a furrow on Tedesco's midsection, apparently made by a fourth bullet, which grazed him.

"Also a bruise over the forehead on the left side," Dr. Gilady added.

As for the discrepancy in the time of the autopsies and the order in which they were performed, the defense never mentioned it.

§

Lodi's police chief, Phillip Wagenti, said he had known Gary Tedesco since he was a boy of twelve or so. Testifying about Tedesco's preparation for joining the police force, the chief depicted a small-town informality to the whole process. "I told him to come around and get acquainted," Chief Wagenti said. "I told the superiors these new men would be around the headquarters and teach them some of the routine police work . . . "

The last witness of that first day was a Bergen County police photographer who had been assigned to take pictures of the Angel Lounge interior on Monday, August 26. His pictures showed shoes and a small pile of clothing, a piece of a gun butt lying in front of the women's bathroom next to a cigarette machine, and bullet holes in the walls.

The trial was adjourned for the weekend.

CHAPTER 17

First on
the Scene

The rules did not allow Guy Calissi to say to the jury, "Pay attention to every detail now, because we are getting to the real nuts and bolts." But that is probably what he wanted to say.

On Monday morning, he put on the stand a young intern at Hackensack Hospital who had pronounced the victims dead (he showed X-rays revealing metal fragments in the bodies). Then Calissi took testimony from yet another police photographer who had taken pictures of the Angel Lounge.

And then the prosecutor called the two Lodi police officers who had answered the call for help at the Angel Lounge, first Robert W. Oetting and then Michael Serpone, Gary Tedesco's first cousin.

Both Oetting and Serpone had been on the force about five years. Both were assigned to the eight-to-four shift on August 25 and 26.

A bit nervously, Oetting recounted the radio calls that came over that night.

"At three-fifteen a.m., approximately, Detective Peter Voto called . . . about . . . "

"What time?" Calissi asked helpfully.

"Quarter to three," Oetting corrected himself. The call was from the Angel Lounge. "Another call was received approximately at ten minutes to three." This time, Oetting recognized the voice as Gary Tedesco's.

A hush fell over the courtroom as Oetting and then Serpone recounted the terrible night.

§

Serpone drove. As the two cops pulled into the parking lot of the Angel Lounge, they saw the car used by Voto and Tedesco. A young woman was standing by its open door.

As Serpone pulled his car to a stop, he and Oetting saw the woman walk toward a car near the curb, on Baldwin Avenue. They also saw a man walking toward that car. Serpone saw silhouettes inside the car. The cops didn't know what to make of the situation.

Serpone and Oetting got out and walked to the door of the Angel Lounge. Oetting banged on the door. "This is the police! Open up!"

The door swung open, and a young blond woman in a blue jumper emerged. "Excuse me," she said, slipping past the two officers and going toward the car by the curb.

Serpone and Oetting had no reason to want to stop the woman who had opened the door and slipped by them. They did not know that her name was Pat Falco, and that at that very moment she was holding a gun by her side.

The cops went inside. The gloom smelled of stale booze, cigarette smoke, and . . . something else.

A man was walking toward them from the rear.

"What's going on?" Oetting asked.

"Thank God!" Nick Kayal said. "There's been a killing here."

Then Serpone and Oetting saw the bodies on the floor, amid great spreading pools of blood. There was a big man in trousers and T-shirt, a smaller man in his underwear. For a moment, the cops didn't recognize the forms on the floor. Then they did.

The two cops rushed outside. Serpone had the presence of mind to get the license number (HNF-569) just as the car was speeding off.

Oetting and Serpone faced a split-second decision: to go back inside and try to help their fallen friends, or to chase the car.

"Hurry up!" Serpone told his partner. "Let's get that car. That's Pete and Gary lying there." Though neither Oetting nor Serpone wanted to say it, their two comrades looked to be beyond help.

"We chased the car," Oetting recalled. "It turned right into Savoie Street. Towards the end of Savoie Street the road forks off into the right and to the left. There is a triangle in the middle of the road there."

When Oetting and Serpone came to the fork, the car was no longer in sight. Knowing that the right fork led to a busy street that fed into Route 46 and Route 17, the major north–south artery in the area, they turned right. But the car had vanished into the night.

The cops headed back to the Angel Lounge. Oetting estimated that the futile chase had taken no more than two minutes.

Peter Voto was lying on his back. Gary Tedesco was on his side. Some of the clothing they had taken off was strewn about like dirty laundry.

"Leave everything alone," Oetting commanded the bartender. Serpone, meanwhile, rushed back to Lodi police headquarters to fetch an ambulance.

He sped back to the Angel Lounge, helped load Peter Voto into the vehicle, then drove as fast as he could to Hackensack Hospital, knowing that another ambulance was right behind him, carrying his cousin Gary Tedesco.

Serpone was at the hospital no more than ten minutes, he said. Long enough to know that two Lodi cops, one a member of his family, were dead.

Michael Serpone kept his composure on the stand, answering questions matter-of-factly. What he did not say, could not say, was that the really important questions were running through his mind, day and night.

Serpone recalled working an early part of the shift with Peter Voto, then switching over to partner with Robert Oetting. That meant that he, the seasoned Michael Serpone, rather than the inexperienced Gary Tedesco, might have been Voto's partner on the three visits to the Angel Lounge.

Serpone knew that some people in the Tedesco-Serpone family were whispering those questions. How would things have turned out if Serpone had ridden with Voto? *Should* he have been there?

The questions had been eating at Michael Serpone since the previous August. They would never go away. Michael Serpone's life would never be the same.

CHAPTER 18

The Silent
Penitent

The jurors deserved some comic relief. Tony Cassarino provided it, though perhaps unintentionally. He was called as a prosecution witness on February 12.

"Mr. Cassarino, where do you reside?" Guy Calissi asked.

"New York City," the witness replied. "Forty-four Downing Street."

"On August twenty-fifth, nineteen sixty-three, were you in the borough of Lodi, New Jersey?" Calissi asked.

"I refuse to testify on the grounds that I might tend to incriminate myself," Cassarino said, his New York City lawyer, Joseph Schwartz, standing supportively by his side.

Had he been with Thomas Trantino, Frank Falco, and the others in the Angel Lounge the night of August 25?

"I refuse to answer on the grounds that I may tend to incriminate myself."

Did he know Tom Trantino and Frank Falco? Same answer.

To move things along, Judge Marini broke in. "Are you refusing to answer because of things that happened in the state of New York in which you and Frank Falco were either associated or connected?"

"I refuse to answer," Cassarino said.

"Speak up loud," the judge commanded.

It didn't really matter how loudly Cassarino talked. "I refuse to answer, Your Honor," he said.

Anthony Cassarino, who was twenty-four at the time, was under indictment in New York City on a charge of accessory to a homicide for helping Frank Falco dispose of the hapless Robert Munoz. Thus, Cassarino's invoking his constitutional right against self-incrimination was understandable, as well as eminently sensible.

But there was more. Tony Cassarino had come to the courthouse girded spiritually as well as legally. On his forehead was a gray smudge: the ashes of a penitent.

February 12 was Ash Wednesday, after all.

CHAPTER 19

What the
Bullets Told

In thirteen years of police work, August O. Hoppe had fired thousands of guns and studied their bullets under a microscope. Before beginning his police career, he had worked as a machinist, making him that much more familiar with the markings left on a bullet in its millisecond-long passage through a gun's barrel. The markings thus imparted are as individual as fingerprints.

August Hoppe held the rank of sergeant in the New Jersey State Police. He was the head of the force's firearms-identification laboratory.

His testimony would be technical, and at times hard to follow, given the number of shots fired inside the Angel Lounge and the resting places of the bullets and bullet fragments. So the prosecution had to explain Hoppe's arcane science in plain English.

Hoppe was questioned by Guy Calissi's deputy, Fred Galda. "Sir, in these various comparison tests, just what do you do with the gun in the testing of bullets?"

"The bullets are fired into cotton," Hoppe explained. "The bullets are recovered and placed under the comparison microscope. The comparison microscope consists of two metallurgical scopes that are joined by a bridged eyepiece. The eyepiece enables the examiner to look at the two bullets as one but have control, separate control, over each bullet. We will take the bullet and match up the tool marks that are left on the bullet after it has passed through the bore of a gun."

"Then with this method are you able to determine as to whether or not a particular bullet came from a particular gun?"

"Yes, I am."

Three days after the killings in the Angel Lounge, Hoppe had received three handguns, plus assorted bullets, bullet fragments, live cartridges, and empty cartridge casings. The guns had been found in or near the Angel Lounge.

One by one, Galda handed these guns to Hoppe and asked him to identify them. The deputy prosecutor did the same with bullets and fragments that had been found at the scene and tagged as evidence.

One weapon was a six-shot .38-caliber Colt police revolver. The hand grip had been broken, suggesting that this was the weapon Thomas Trantino had used to club Peter Voto. Hoppe identified pieces found at the scene as having come from the grip. Three live rounds were found in the cylinder, and there were three spent cartridges. One bullet from the gun was found embedded in a side wall of the Angel Lounge, another just above the rear door. This was the gun that had been stolen from a doctor's home; the police charged Rocco Benedetto with selling it to Trantino and Falco.

The second weapon was a .38-caliber Harrington and Richardson hammerless revolver. It was nickel-plated, or silver in appearance. (Several witnesses had seen a silver gun in Tom Trantino's hand.) There was one discharged cartridge in the weapon, and two live rounds.

But, Hoppe testified, his tests determined that the gun did not work properly. The barrel was so full of rust when he received it that he concluded it had not been fired in some time — certainly not in the Angel Lounge.

The third gun was a .38-caliber Smith and Wesson with a five-shot capacity. This was Peter Voto's gun. It had been fired five times.

One bullet from this gun was found in Voto's abdomen, another in Gary Tedesco's left shoulder. Since the bartender was sure he saw Frank Falco grab Voto's gun while the big cop was struggling with Trantino, Hoppe's testimony indicated that Falco had fired at both victims. A third bullet from Voto's gun was found in the floor of the Angel Lounge, near the footrest along the bar. Hoppe said numerous bullet fragments had been found in pieces too small to be matched with a particular gun.

And most intriguingly, Hoppe identified two .38-caliber bullets that had been recovered from Peter Voto's skull. They had been fired from the same gun — but not from any of the three guns in evidence.

Thus, there were *four* guns in the Angel Lounge that night, but only three were recovered. Guy Calissi was sure Trantino killed Peter Voto with that fourth gun, then disposed of it.

Albert Gross's cross-examination was brief and nonconfrontational. He was happy to have Hoppe say again that the silver revolver hadn't been fired in a long time.

The witness was excused.

"The state rests," Guy Calissi said.

This was a surprise. The state had wrapped up its case on the fifth day of testimony; there had been speculation that the prosecution would take much, much longer, that the trial could go on for several weeks.

After the jury was excused, defense counsel Herbert Koransky moved for a judgment of acquittal. He argued that the young women, whose accounts Calissi relied upon to portray the horror in the Angel Lounge, were unreliable and untrustworthy. Nor was Nicholas Kayal a good witness, Koransky asserted, since the bartender had ducked and hidden once the shooting started.

The defense seized upon Hoppe's testimony that the silver gun was inoperable and the fact that two bullets recovered from Voto's body came from a gun that was never found.

"This man cannot be convicted on speculative evidence as to the existence of another gun," Koransky asserted.

Judge Marini seemed almost scornful. "Are you serious in that argument that this is speculation, with the testimony we have had here in court?" he asked.

"I am most serious."

There had been testimony that, amid the drunken horseplay before the confrontation with Voto and Tedesco, Tony Cassarino had fired a gun in the Angel Lounge, apparently not meaning to hurt anyone. Where was *that* gun, Koransky wanted to know. "The defendant Trantino cannot be charged with anything concerning that gun, either the possession or firing of it or anything of the sort."

Then an earsplitting shriek ripped through the courtroom, echoing off the walls. It was followed by loud sobs as Trantino's mother crumpled to the floor. Four court officers rushed to her, lifting her and carrying her out of the room. Her wails continued from the corridor.

Resuming, the judge pointed out that before ducking down and hiding, Nicholas Kayal had observed Trantino holding a gun to Peter Voto's head and had seen Falco holding a gun.

"Although he ducked and went behind the bar, then he heard shots, and then you got two bodies on the floor dead," the judge said. "That is a pretty good circumstance that the jury can take into consideration."

Motion denied.

Apparently shaken by Blanche Trantino's outburst, Albert Gross asked for a recess. "One of my chief witnesses will be Mrs. Trantino, the wife of this defendant," he said. A moment later, he corrected himself; he had, of course, meant to refer to her as the *mother* of the defendant.

A recess was granted, and Gross met with Mrs. Trantino. She was better, but still in no shape to testify.

The judge called it a day.

CHAPTER **20**

Trantino on
a Tightrope

It was Friday, February 14, 1964. On this day, Gary Tedesco and Adrienne Peraino, their love still young and idealistic, might have exchanged valentines full of hope and dreams. Peter and Connie Voto, their older love strengthened by time, would have shared memories.

Thomas Trantino, the man who had dashed the dreams and added grief to the memories, was testifying in his own defense on this day. It was three days after his twenty-sixth birthday.

The trial was a half-hour late getting started, and spectators filled every seat. The people were searched before being allowed in; the hatred toward the defendant was still almost palpable. Emotions were so high that relatives of the defendant and the victims were not allowed inside the courtroom.

And yet, feelings aside, there was no doubt that some people crowded into the courtroom out of nothing more than curiosity. What was he like, this notorious Angel Lounge killer? In truth, he was rather ordinary-looking in jacket and tie, neither ugly nor particularly handsome. The voice that had not cowed Peter Voto, the voice that was one of the last things Gary Tedesco heard, was little more than a whisper.

"You have to talk a little louder, Mr. Trantino," Judge Marini said early on. "After all, this is your opportunity to tell your story."

So he told his story, speaking softly and sipping from paper cups of water handed to him by courtroom attendants. Guided by Albert Gross, he told of his upbringing by a Catholic and a Jew, his confirmation in the Jewish faith, the fact that he had a brother and a sister, that neither sibling was married. With the defendant's life at stake, the judge allowed Gross plenty of leeway.

Trantino told of sliding deeper into drug addiction, of stealing to support his habit, of finally being sent to Great Meadow State Prison at Comstock, where he became friendly with Frank Falco and Anthony Cassarino and acquired the nickname that would stay with him: Tom the Rabbi.

Trantino said he wasn't sure exactly when he got out of Great Meadow. He said he thought it was 1961, when he was twenty-three years old.

No doubt, Guy Calissi heard that with contempt. Most people remembered the dates of watershed events in their lives: graduating from high school or college, entering the army, getting out of the army, getting married. Walking out of prison should have been a big day in the life of Thomas Trantino. And he wanted the jury to believe he wasn't even sure of the year?

By mid-1963, Trantino continued, he had been out of prison for two years. He had held a couple of straight jobs, for a house-demolition company and in a printing plant. He and his wife, Helene, lived at 1983 East Seventh Street in Brooklyn, and soon a child was on the way. Tom Trantino was coming home nights. He was not doing drugs.

And then one day he ran into Frank Falco at Coney Island. That night, they got drunk at the Vivere Lounge in lower Manhattan. It was a handy place for Frank: he lived right upstairs. On another night soon afterward, Tom and Frank met their old friend Tony Cassarino at the Vivere. All three got sloshed.

"I hadn't used dope again," Trantino went on, "except for a few times Falco had Dexedrine pills." He got into the habit of using Dexedrine whenever he drank a lot, which was often. He left his job at the printing plant. He and Frank Falco began to steal things. Sometimes Norma Jaconetta would go along.

When Tom couldn't make it home to his wife and child, he would stay in New Jersey, at Patricia MacPhail's house in Allendale. Pat MacPhail had two young children who lived with her.

Trantino and Falco continued to steal. They continued to down whiskey and pop Dexedrine. "Sometimes I experienced hallucinations," Trantino said. "Sometimes it was just blank."

Gross was guiding the defendant across a tightrope, trying to show that his life was so surreal from the booze and pills that he might not have known what he was doing on the early morning of August 26, 1963. The lawyer was counting on psychiatric evidence to reinforce that notion. On the other hand, Gross had to worry that the jurors would be so repelled by Trantino's debauchery that they would loathe him. But it was a risk he had to take.

Gross was also counting on his client's account of the rather full day he had had on Sunday, August 25, 1963. Trantino had slept at Pat MacPhail's on Saturday night, after she drove him on the unsuccessful trip upstate to find his wife.

He didn't feel like eating breakfast on Sunday morning, but he did feel like having some whiskey. He also had a hunger for Dexedrine, which Frank Falco supplied when he dropped by with Tony Cassarino. That afternoon, Tom had a sandwich. By that time, he had drunk several whiskeys.

Then it was off to Brooklyn to rob the apartment "Tony Winks" had scouted out—and not well enough, as it turned out. Driving back to Jersey, his friends wanted to celebrate their haul. Tom didn't; he was feeling like a party pooper.

"Acute depression had set in," he testified, "and I was . . . I didn't even want to go to Jersey, but they kept saying to go, and I went."

To the Angel Lounge.

Tom recalled loosening up a little with double seven-and-sevens. By the time Norma Jaconetta and her friend, Sally Vander Fliet, came by, he was feeling a whole lot better. He had never met Sally until that night.

He had known the comely Norma for a couple of months, and he danced with her. "After a while I stopped dancing, and I was just drinking and drinking," he recalled.

How many drinks did he have? About ten, he thought.

Nicholas Kayal had already testified that Tom Trantino was "a good drinker," that he could hold his liquor, and that he was sober as Sunday night became Monday morning.

Sober by the standards of the Angel Lounge, maybe. But Albert Gross wanted the jurors to ask themselves this: Could any man who had drunk fourteen or fifteen whiskeys over the course of a day in which he ate only a sandwich really be called sober, especially if he'd been taking pills along with the booze?

He had lost track of time, Tom Trantino testified. "I was standing at the bar and there was a violent explosion, so I presume it to be—"

"Don't tell us what you presume," his lawyer broke in. "Just what you saw."

"A violent explosion right by the side of my ear and it was just like a blast, like a siren ringing inside my brain. Everything, all the lights—everything started to spin and spin and spin."

And then what?

"Before I knew it, there was somebody next to me. There was pushing, and I don't know if I was fighting with someone or what, and while the confusion all over—it was like a kaleidoscope of wildness, of sound and light."

"Did you see Falco?" Gross asked.

"I saw Falco, and he was standing. He had—he looked like a devil to me."

Like a devil?

"Well, the way like his eyebrows were arched and he looked . . . He had . . . I can't explain it, but it was just a look . . . All I can remember is there was a lot of yelling and screaming, and I was starting to feel sick and sicker."

The next thing he knew, Trantino said, he was running out the door. He didn't remember clubbing Peter Voto, didn't remember pulling the trigger, didn't recall any bodies on the floor of the Angel Lounge. He did remember running to Norma's car and sitting there with Frank Falco for a moment.

"When you left the Angel Lounge and went into Jaconetta's car, did you take with you a gun?" Gross asked his client.

"I don't remember having a gun, sir."

He did remember getting out of Norma's car and running away right after Falco fled. And he remembered going nowhere slowly on the milk truck, remembered "falling and running and falling and running and falling," then being "out in the open somewhere" before finding a guy who was willing to drive him to Pat MacPhail's house in Allendale for ten bucks.

"I asked her if she would take me to New York. I said, 'Take me, please.'"

She dropped him off "someplace uptown." At this time, he said, he was highly emotional and "still very drunk." He didn't know how he had gotten the injury on his wrist. He took a cab to his parents' home, where he collapsed into bed after his brother yelled at him. Hours later, his mother woke him with the news that the police had searched his apartment in Brooklyn. After two days of wandering, he turned himself in.

§

No doubt, Guy Calissi listened to Trantino's story with contempt, eager to rip it apart, certain that Trantino couldn't hide behind his flimsy shield of memory loss. As he took notes on a yellow legal pad, preparing to shred Trantino's story, the prosecutor counted on the jurors' sticking to the basic facts.

The most basic fact of all, of course, was that two police officers had walked into the Angel Lounge alive and had been carried out dead.

This was not a Rashomon-like tale in which the "truth" is forever elusive. By balancing one account against another, discarding some memory figments that just do not fit, it is possible to reconstruct what happened.

At least we can come close—perhaps as close as we want to.

CHAPTER 21

Chaos, Terror, and Death

The minutes were full of screaming and terror. They ended in fury and death. That much is certain from the accounts of the people who were there, even allowing for lies or hazy memories.

But how many minutes went by? Probably not as many as the dark legend has it, although no one knows for sure. And how much terror was there, especially in the minds of Peter Voto and Gary Tedesco? We can never know. Perhaps we don't want to know.

It all started with a slow Sunday evening in the Angel Lounge.

§

Nick Kayal's shift, like Peter Voto's and Gary Tedesco's, began at eight o'clock.

The most popular drink of that night was a seven-and-seven, or Seagram's 7 Crown whiskey and 7-Up. Too cloying for middle-age tastes, the libation was a popular one with young, unsophisticated drinkers of the time.

Nick Kayal poured a lot of them. Pat MacPhail, Pat Falco, and Norma Jaconetta were all drinking seven-and-sevens. So was Tony Cassarino, after warming up with a beer and a martini. And so was Tom Trantino, looking natty in light slacks and sport jacket. Before the night was over, he would have eight or ten drinks, maybe more.

Frank Falco was dressed to kill in a gray sharkskin suit and white shirt. Frank started with a beer and switched to scotch on the rocks. Sally Vander Fliet stuck to Coca-Cola.

Pat Falco and Pat MacPhail wore high heels, as though they were several years older than their true ages. Which, in some ways, they were.

The bar wasn't crowded; no more than eighteen or twenty customers at any one time. Then there was the band. As the music and the night droned on, Nick Kayal was getting a little annoyed with the musicians. They weren't really supposed to drink while they were playing, but they were sneaking straight shots bought by Falco, and not being very quiet about it. The booze didn't help the music any; a couple of times Nick had to tell the band guys to cool it.

Sally Vander Fliet and Norma Jaconetta had been in earlier, but had left when they saw hardly anyone they knew. They had gone to the Cottage Inn, another nightspot on Route 46.

"All in all, this was a much nicer kind of a place," Sally would later say of the Cottage Inn. "They have entertainment there every week, some known people. It was a cleaner place; nicer type of people went there."

Maybe the Cottage Inn was just too dull for Sally and Norma on the Sunday night of August 25, 1963. So back to the Angel Lounge they went, and this time they found Tommy and Frank and Tony. (Oops! Norma had to be careful how she acted: Pat Falco was with her husband.)

Between 10:30 and 11:00, Nick Kayal saw the two cops come in. Even if he hadn't recognized Peter Voto, he would have known they were cops, plain clothes or not. Nick Kayal wasn't surprised, not with the evening's noise output.

Voto and Tedesco stood at the end of the bar, near the door. They weren't smiling.

"Want a drink?" the bartender said, intending no disrespect.

"We're here on business," Voto said. "We've had a complaint. What's going on?"

"I don't know," Kayal said, realizing that didn't sound too smart.

"Let's go outside," Peter Voto said.

Outside the bar, in the fresh-smelling summer night away from the cigarette smoke, Peter Voto laid down the law in a quiet, firm way. Fun is fun and enough is enough.

Nick Kayal understood. Back inside he went, hoping for a little sanity amid the noise. But the $50 bill that Frank Falco had slapped on the bar wasn't used up yet, what with most drinks costing eighty cents to a buck each.

The four members of the Dell-Aires played on, more or less, though Nick Kayal had to tell Big Al, the drummer, to stop sneaking shots. He played like a two-year-old banging on a pail. And Bobby B., the singer, started slurring his words so badly that Nick sent him home. (It's a hell of a thing when a bartender has to shut off the *band*, for Christ's sake!)

The time dragged. Hearing the loud music and the stupid jokes, Nick Kayal thought what most bartenders probably think at one time or another: there were easier ways to make a living than watching people get shit-faced.

Norma and Sally danced with each other, and Tom Trantino danced with Norma for a few fast numbers.

The band took a break. Tony Cassarino and Sally were dancing to the jukebox when Sally thought she heard loud noises over the music. She also heard a noise on the floor, near her feet. Jesus, there was Tom Trantino standing there, holding a smoking gun and laughing and grinning like a horse's ass. His face was lit up from the colored lights of the jukebox.

The music ended. "Boy, Tom, that was close," Tony said good-naturedly. He left the dance floor, taking his place at the bar again, and Sally went back to her seat next to Norma.

Sally saw Nick Kayal wrap the gun in a towel and tuck it on a shelf behind the bar for safekeeping.

The bartender wasn't surprised when, around one o'clock, he got another visit from Voto and Tedesco. Gunshots qualified as loud noise, after all. Even on Route 46 in Lodi.

Again, the bartender went outside for a consultation. This isn't funny, Peter Voto said. We've got other things to do besides ride herd on the Angel Lounge.

Nick Kayal went back inside. Most of the other customers left. So did the remnants of the band, and not a minute too soon. Frank Falco had played the drums briefly, then tried to fill in as a vocalist. Frank sang his rendition of "You'll Never Walk Alone."

Frank wasn't the greatest singer in the world, but at least he was loud. Too loud, maybe. Especially for a night when the cops had been around twice already—

The firecracker sounds almost made Nick Kayal jump out of his shoes. The noise was like a couple of cherry bombs going off next to his head. That goddamned Tony Cassarino must have done it; he was standing next to Nick with that shit-eating grin on his face.

Sure enough, Tony had a gun in his hand.

Nick Kayal heard a funny noise above him, looked up, and saw the chandelier whirling around him. The dumb bastard had shot at the chandelier! A couple of seconds later, Nick felt something hard under his shoe: an empty shell casing.

"Don't worry," Frank Falco said, laughing and patting the bartender on the head. "We're just kidding."

Just kidding. This was all Nick needed, to have the cops come back a third time. Just kidding . . . How the hell do you kid around with a gun?

Finally, only Tom Trantino, Frank Falco, Tony Cassarino, and the girls were left. With any luck, they'd clear out pretty soon. Anyhow, it was past 2:30. Closing time was three.

Nick Kayal went around the bar and locked the door. Now he wouldn't have to deal with any new assholes; all he had to do was get rid of the ones already inside. He began to wipe down the bar and get rid of the dirty ashtrays, hoping the people would take the hint.

The gunplay seemed to be over, but the gang was still making plenty of noise. Now that the band was gone, the jukebox was going like a son of a bitch. Tom and Frank were still knocking down the booze pretty good.

There was a loud knock on the door.

"Who is it?" Nick Kayal shouted.

"Lodi police."

Shit. The bartender went around to unlock the door and let them in.

Peter Voto and Gary Tedesco walked down the length of the bar, stopping in front of the last of the celebrants. Anyone could tell from Voto's face that he was in no mood for nonsense. And Peter Voto was no one to mess with.

"What the hell happened?" Voto asked the bartender.

"Just some firecrackers."

The big cop thought that was bullshit; anyone could tell from his face. "All right," he said to the gathering. "Let's see some ID."

Voto braced Tony Cassarino first, taking him into the coatroom to check his paperwork.

Gary Tedesco came over to Frank Falco and Norma Jaconetta. Alarmed that Voto was checking Cassarino's paperwork, Frank pulled Norma close to him. "Tell him I'm your husband," he whispered.

"Oh, yes, I'm his wife," Norma told the young cop.

There was a good reason for this little charade. Frank Falco, who was being hunted for killing Robert Munoz, was carrying identification belonging to Norma's estranged husband, Joseph Jaconetta.

"All right, then, let's break this up," Gary Tedesco said. Something told him they might need reinforcements to get this bunch out of the place. He must have been glad when Pete told him to go to the car to radio for backup.

Pat MacPhail had shown her identification and had been told that she could leave. She was starting to think that that was a really good idea. The playful gunshots had been a little too much excitement.

In the coatroom, Cassarino was nervous; the New York City cops were looking for him and Falco in the killing of the apprentice printer who'd been dumped into the East River. There wasn't much chance that the Lodi cops would check with New York City tonight, but still . . .

After two minutes or so, Voto and Cassarino came out of the coatroom. Tony Cassarino left the Angel Lounge in a hurry.

§

Frank Falco and Norma Jaconetta stood side by side, watching Peter Voto talking to Tom Trantino. They couldn't hear what was being said.

Norma and Sally had met Voto a few weeks before. One night, they had heard a ruckus in the apartment downstairs from Sally's. The couple down there were having a bad fight, so bad that Sally called the police. Four Lodi cops showed up, Sergeant Pete Voto among them.

And earlier this very night in the Angel Lounge, Sally and Norma had exchanged greetings with Voto. Nothing special, just a friendly "Hi, how are you?"

Now, Peter Voto looked at the bartender. "Okay, Nick, where is it?"

"Where's what?"

There was a sudden quiet. Voto said nothing. Instead, he continued walking around to the end of the bar. He stopped when he saw the towel. Voto picked up the towel, no doubt feeling right away that there was something inside. He unfolded the towel, picked up the gun inside, then started folding the towel over it again.

"Norma," Voto said, not in an unfriendly way, "did you ever see this gun before?"

Norma looked straight at him. "No, I never saw that gun."

Norma smelled trouble. She knew that Frank and Tony didn't want to be taken in for questioning, not with all the heat they were still feeling for killing that printer in New York, not with the job they'd just pulled in Brooklyn. It wouldn't take the police very long to figure out that Frank's last name was Falco and not Jaconetta.

And Tom Trantino could be nasty, especially when he felt cornered. The situation was getting dangerous. So Norma sidled up to her friend Sally Vander Fliet. "Sally, let's get out of here. Rabbi is uncontrollable when he gets scared about anything."

And then it began. Trantino took out a gun and came up behind Voto. He grabbed the big sergeant in a headlock and held the gun to the back of his skull. "Everybody to the front of the room," he said. "Don't move, motherfucker, or you're dead."

The women screamed. "Don't let anything happen!" one woman shouted.

"All right," Trantino said, twisting Voto's arm up behind him, "everybody to the front of the room." No man could handle Peter Voto that way—unless he had a gun.

Bar stools scuffed and bumped.

"Get his gun!" Trantino shouted to Falco. "Get his gun!"

The women screamed some more.

Frank Falco took the towel and gun from Voto's hand and grabbed the sergeant's own service revolver.

"Don't move, motherfucker, or you're dead!" Trantino shouted again, trying to frisk Peter Voto even as he pushed him along.

There was more screaming. Some of the stools went *bump, bump, bump* against each other. The legs scraped on the floor.

"You son of a bitch, rat bastard, motherfucker, you are going to die!"

§

Pat MacPhail was almost at the door now. If she could just get through the door, she would be safe, safe, safe.

"Get your hand out of your pocket and drop it!" she heard Tom Trantino say.

Now Pat MacPhail was right there, at the door, and all she had to do was get through it—

And then her way was blocked by Gary Tedesco, heading back into the Angel Lounge.

Peering inside, Tedesco said, "Oh, my God!" Then he grabbed Pat MacPhail, pulled her out through the door to safety, and stepped inside.

The young man's face went white as he saw Peter Voto, the ex-wrestler who feared no one, helpless with his right arm twisted up behind him and Tom Trantino holding a gun to the back of his head. The silver gun gleamed in the dim saloon light.

Frank Falco was strong. He grabbed Tedesco and pulled him farther inside, spinning him around, effortlessly bouncing him off the bar.

Finally, Gary Tedesco was just standing there. Frank Falco was on top of the bar now, a gun in each hand. Except for his sharkskin suit, Falco looked like a crazy cowboy from the Wild West.

"Take your clothes off!" someone shouted to Peter Voto.

Voto did nothing at first. He was no coward, and he wasn't used to taking orders from punks.

Trantino struck him with the pistol. Voto winced; then he began to undress, but slowly.

"Take your clothes off!"

"I'm trying to. Where do you want me to put my tie?"

"Get down, you motherfucker!" Trantino shouted, swinging wildly at the big man's head. "Get down, you motherfucker! Get down on your knees . . . "

The women screamed some more. "Please don't hurt us. Please . . . "

Peter Voto got his suit coat, shirt, and tie off, but Trantino kept hitting him. More screams tore through the dim, smoky air.

"Take your clothes off!" This time, someone was shouting at Gary Tedesco, who was standing only five or six feet away and in front of Falco.

Gary did as he was told, getting out of his clothes as fast as he could, not bothering to unfasten his cuff links. As he fumbled with the buttons and kicked off his shoes, perhaps he dared to hope that the freaks who had gotten the best of them would leave after having their fun. Maybe the whole thing would make for a good ribbing in the stationhouse for him and Pete . . .

§

Norma Jaconetta darted outside and went to her car. Later, she recalled sitting in the dark for about a minute and a half.

No, she told herself. *No.* She couldn't leave her friend Sally Vander Fliet in the bar, where all the trouble was.

Norma got out of the car and ran back inside. "Sally!" she screamed.

Norma saw that Tom Trantino was still clubbing the big cop, again and again. Tommy had started hitting him even before she ran out.

"Sally!"

Through the din and the screams, Trantino went on pistol-whipping Peter Voto, so hard that the gun's plastic grip broke apart. Peter Voto sank to his knees.

What was going through Peter Voto's head as he reeled under the blows, finally driven to his knees long after a lesser man would have been knocked senseless? Perhaps he was thinking of his wife and children, asleep at home at that very moment, not far away.

Or maybe he was still thinking like the tough cop he was. He had been in tricky situations before. If he could just hold himself together a second or two or three longer there might be a chance to use his smarts and his quickness and his bull strength—

By this time, Nick Kayal was crouched down behind the bar. He closed his eyes and knelt in prayer. *Our Father, Who art in Heaven . . .*

Frank Falco looked at Gary Tedesco. "Where's your gun?" Falco demanded.

"I don't have a gun. I'm not a policeman yet." As he was standing in his underwear amid the chaos and the smells of tobacco and stale booze, Gary must have been beyond embarrassment.

Finally, Peter Voto must have known that the lunatic standing over him, hitting him with the gun, was not going to let him live. Maybe he was already slipping out of consciousness, out of this life, before the first bullet.

There was an explosion of noise and orange fire from the gun held by Tom Trantino, and Peter Voto fell face down.

"What are you doing?" Falco shouted above the screams of the women. "What are you doing?"

"We are going for broke!" Tom Trantino shouted. "We are burning all the way! We are going for broke!"

"You're crazy!" Falco said. "What are you doing? Rabbi, you're crazy!" But Falco was caught up in the insanity; he fired too.

Gary Tedesco had just watched Peter Voto die. Now he knew that his own moment had arrived, after twenty-two years, two weeks, and a few hours on this earth.

More shots, from one of Frank Falco's guns as well as Tom Trantino's, and Gary Tedesco fell down. His body shook for a moment. He groaned. He sobbed. He died.

"They're dead!" a woman screamed. "They're dead."

"Let's get out of here!" Frank Falco said. "Get out of here quick!"

"My gun's empty," Trantino said to Falco.

"Sally! Sally!" Norma went up to Sally Vander Fliet and grabbed her arm. "Sally!"

Sally's eyes were strange; she looked a thousand miles away.

Finally, Norma slapped her friend to break the spell.

§

Thomas Trantino, at age twenty-three, about to leave prison on June 27, 1961, after serving a term for robbery.
Courtesy of the Record

Thomas Trantino beams at his 1962 wedding.
Courtesy of the Record

An undated mug shot of
Frank Falco.
Courtesy of the Record

Andrew Voto, circa 1962.
Courtesy of the Record

Gary Tedesco
Courtesy of the Record

Peter Voto
Courtesy of the Record

The interior of the Angel Lounge hours after the killings.
Courtesy of the Bergen County Prosecutor's Office

Thomas Trantino returning to jail after postponement of his arraignment in
September 1963.
Courtesy of the Record

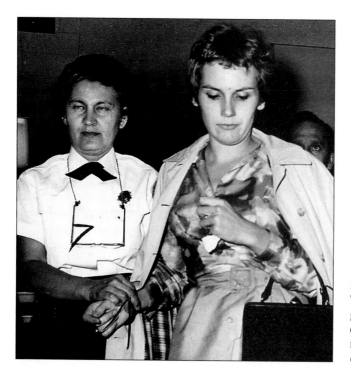

Pat MacPhail,
Thomas Trantino's
girlfriend, in
custody as a
material witness.
Courtesy of the Record

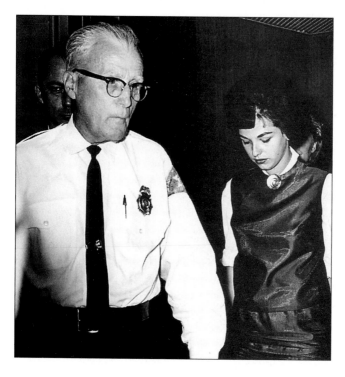

Norma Jaconetta,
Frank Falco's
girlfriend, in
custody as a
material witness.
Courtesy of the Record

Guy Calissi, the Bergen County
prosecutor, who sought the
death penalty.
Courtesy of the Record

Fred Galda, Guy Calissi's top
assistant. (This photo was
taken in 1982, when Galda
was a judge.)
Courtesy of the Record

Defense lawyer Albert Gross confers with his client, Thomas Trantino, during the trial in February 1964.
Courtesy of the Record

Judge Joseph W. Marini, who presided over Thomas Trantino's trial.
Courtesy of the Record

The shots had interrupted Nick Kayal's prayers. He heard feet scuffing and bumping, the sounds of people running toward the door.

But not all the footsteps were going toward the door. Some were coming around the end of the bar. When he dared to open his eyes and look up, he saw Frank Falco standing there. "Please," the bartender said. "Please, have mercy."

Frank Falco looked disgusted. He picked up his jacket, grabbed the loose change from the bar, and hurried away. Nick Kayal heard Falco's fading footsteps, heard the door close behind him.

Kayal stayed where he was, crouched down behind the bar. He let a minute go by. It was quiet, so quiet. He thought he was all alone. And alive, *alive!*

Finally, the bartender got to his feet.

§

Pat Falco didn't want to kill Nicky the bartender, didn't think she could. But Frankie had put a gun in her hand just before running out, and she was still his wife, no matter what.

Now Nicky was coming up from his hiding place. "Don't move or you are dead," Pat said.

Nick Kayal thought the little blonde looked a lot bigger with the gun in her hand. Maybe he fainted then, or maybe he just blacked out on his feet. The next thing he knew, Pat Falco was heading toward the door.

Just as Pat got to the door, she heard a knock on the outside. "Frankie?" she cried out.

"Police!" answered the man on the other side. It was Officer Robert Oetting.

She opened the door and saw two uniformed cops. Pat held the gun down by her side. "Excuse me," she said, walking right past them as she made her exit.

She ran to the car where her friends were, letting the gun fall out of her hand just before she got there.

§

As Nick Kayal told it later, he paced around in the dim light of the bar, a place so familiar to him but one that had just become a slaughterhouse, with blood spreading in great pools.

"I didn't know what to do," he testified. "I wanted to go to the phone. Then I heard a knock on the door . . . I opened the door a little bit and I saw it was Pat MacPhail . . . "

§

Pat MacPhail had pulled her car to near the front of the Angel Lounge. She had seen Norma Jaconetta come running out, then had seen her run back into the Angel Lounge.

It was all so crazy, the way the night was playing out. Pat wasn't exactly sober, and she couldn't see everything that was going on in the dark around her. But just after Norma went back inside, Pat thought she saw another police car pull up and a cop get out, peek inside the bar, then hurry back to his car and drive off.

Then Pat thought she heard three shots.

She just had to see what was going on. She parked her car on the street again, then walked to the bar entrance.

The door to the Angel Lounge was locked. She pounded on it.

Nick Kayal opened the door a crack and saw her.

"Get the hell out of here!" he said.

For just a moment, Pat MacPhail was able to peer inside. She saw Pete Voto lying dead on the floor. Her view was partly blocked, but she was able to see Gary Tedesco's feet.

Then Nick Kayal gave her a straight arm, hard enough that Pat MacPhail went down the steps of the entrance.

Nick Kayal pulled the door shut again. He thought he heard Gary Tedesco moan. He had to get to the phone, had to call his brother-in-law, Tony Perillo. Had to call the police . . .

Unbelievably, there was another knock on the door.

"Who is it?" the bartender shouted.

"Lodi police!"

Kayal opened the door and saw a uniformed cop (almost surely either Serpone or Oetting).

"Thank God!" Kayal said. "There's been a killing here."

The cop turned and ran outside. Kayal followed him outside, into the clean night.

The cop seemed to be having trouble raising headquarters on the radio. Nick Kayal went back inside, picked up the phone, and dialed the operator. Call the Lodi police, he stammered to her. Two cops have been shot. Then he let the phone dangle.

The Angel Lounge smelled of blood, smoke, and death.

CHAPTER **22**

Trantino's
Memory Gaps

Guy Calissi began his cross-examination of Thomas Trantino by taking him matter-of-factly over some of the same ground the defense lawyer had plowed: his schooling, his initiation into drugs, his parents' discovery that he was a user.

Trantino said that he was "about sixteen" when his parents found his drug paraphernalia, and that he was pretty sure the year was 1953. Something was wrong there, of course: Trantino turned fifteen on February 11, 1953. The prosecutor didn't point out the contradiction. Perhaps he thought it unimportant, or maybe he didn't want to portray the defendant as mentally confused. That was the defense's goal.

There was an odd, almost comic exchange that seemed meaningless—at first. Trantino recalled getting out of a juvenile center and resuming his drug use, only more often. The drugs made him feel "lethargic," he said.

"What does that mean?" Calissi pressed.

"It means real like lazy, sleepy."

"'Soporific,' does it mean?" Calissi asked.

"Yes."

Then Judge Marini turned to the defendant. "Where did you learn the word 'soporific'?" the judge asked.

"From reading," Trantino said.

"You have been doing a lot of reading?" the judge asked.

"Yes."

The judge's comments about big words opened a door for Calissi.

"And while we are on that," the prosecutor said, "you used the word 'kaleidoscope.' Do you remember using that word?"

"In what sense?" Trantino asked.

"When you were in the Angel Lounge and the shots—the noise at your ear—do you remember using that word?"

Trantino did. "A kaleidoscope is like sort of a telescope with all mixtures of colors."

That avenue led neatly into the subject of Trantino's hallucinations. Tell us more about them, Calissi said.

"I have had a lot where I thought I was in a cell," Trantino said obligingly. Pushed to be more specific, he said he had had hallucinations when he was in a hospital, trying to kick his drug habit, or waiting in a courtroom "bullpen."

"What was hallucinating about thinking you were in a cell when you were actually in a cell?" Calissi asked.

"You didn't let me finish, Mr. Calissi."

"I am sorry."

"I imagined that there were all sorts of rats and bugs crawling all over me and chewing on me."

The judge became confused about exactly when Trantino kicked his heroin habit and the accompanying hallucinations. Trantino said he hadn't used heroin since about 1956, before serving his stretch at Great Meadow, but that he had had some hallucinations since then anyhow.

The judge thought the defendant had previously said he *hadn't* had hallucinations since getting off heroin.

"I'm sorry," Trantino said. "I must have used the 'no' instead of the 'yes' then to the question."

Thus did Thomas Trantino further the impression that "the truth" was what he chose to remember, or what he improvised as he went along.

Calissi brought up Trantino's jobs with the house-wrecking company and the printing company early in his marriage. Did he have any other jobs?

"I don't recall," Trantino said.

Calissi had to have been pleased with that response. Here was a man of seemingly normal intelligence who said he couldn't remember his job history from less than three years before, when he was drug free. What Trantino was saying seemed to defy common sense.

Nor could Trantino remember much about his conversations with Frank Falco and Tony Cassarino after their reunion. And he was vague about how many times he got together with his old friends, and what they did.

Calissi glided right over the robbery in Brooklyn; he was interested only in what had happened west of the Hudson. "What time did you get to the Angel Lounge?" the prosecutor asked.

"I guess it was around ten o'clock."

"You don't know the exact time?"

"No, sir."

There were so many things Trantino said he didn't remember very well. Yes, he recalled dancing, but he didn't know how many times. He remembered

Falco singing and Cassarino telling jokes. He remembered the jukebox playing but not whether he dropped any coins in it.

"And when was the first time you saw the officers you spoke about before?" Calissi asked.

"All I remember is, sometime after the explosion by my ear." But Trantino insisted he didn't recall any other explosions, or whether he ever took out his gun, which Pat MacPhail had thoughtfully tucked into her purse. He said he knew there were two police officers in the Angel Lounge that night only because of what he'd found out later; if he had to rely on his memory, he wouldn't be able to say.

"All right," Calissi said. "Right after the explosion, what happened? Tell me."

"I told you, I heard this, like a siren."

"A siren?"

"Siren—what seemed inside my head—and the lights—everything was spinning, and I remember there was a great deal of confusion and yelling, and I was becoming ill. I didn't feel too well. I wanted to get out of there. The next thing I remember, I was running out the door."

"Just prior to this boom and the siren, did you see the police officers asking for identification of the group that you were with, Falco, et cetera?"

"No, sir."

"You didn't see that?"

"No."

But Trantino remembered running out the front door; Calissi drew that out of him. And he remembered running to a car.

"Which car?"

"I think it was Norma Jaconetta's car."

Was anyone in the car when he got there?

"I think so."

Well, then, Calissi asked, "Were there strangers in there other than the people you had gone with?"

"I was in such wild confusion, I don't know," Trantino said. He said he couldn't remember any conversation in the car, except someone saying it wouldn't start. But he was able to recall that Falco got out of the car and ran.

Calissi wanted to back up a little. He asked Trantino when Pat MacPhail had given him back his gun, the one she had carried in her purse for him. Trantino said he didn't know.

"Was it before or after the siren?" Calissi asked.

"I really can't really [sic] recall too much," Trantino said.

But he did remember running, running, running and seeing the milk truck.

"What were you running about?" Calissi asked.

"I don't know. I was sick. I was confused."

"Were you running because of anything that happened in the Angel Lounge?"

"I don't know."

He did recall finding some guy "at a gas station or a bus depot or something like that" who was willing to give him a ride. Trantino remembered asking the man to drive him to Allendale, recalled that the man knew the way, recalled giving him Pat MacPhail's address, 90 East Allendale Avenue, so the man could drop him off there. But he didn't recall whether the man was young or old, or what kind of car he drove.

And did he recall giving the man ten dollars? Well, he said, it might have been five dollars. Or maybe ten. But not more.

Trantino recalled that Pat MacPhail was crying, and that he asked her to take him to New York City. "Didn't you go to the bathroom and wash off your wounds where you were bleeding?"

"I don't recall doing it," Trantino said.

Nor did he recall the route Pat MacPhail took on the way to the city: "Whatever it was led right into the George Washington Bridge." But he did recall that there was almost no conversation in the car, and he was certain he had never threatened Pat MacPhail or shown her a gun.

Clearly, Guy Calissi was convinced that Trantino had still had a gun. "Are you positive that you didn't have a gun when you finally ended up at Mrs. MacPhail's house that particular morning?"

"I am pretty sure, yes sir."

"Pardon?"

"Yes, sir."

"Are you pretty sure, or are you sure?"

"I am pretty sure. I am pretty sure I would remember."

Around the time he took a cab to his parents' apartment he might have been a little drunk, he said.

"Did you have a gun then, when you got into the cab?" Calissi asked.

"No, sir."

"Did you discard a gun on the way to New York or when you got into New York City?"

"No, sir."

"You know that for sure?"

"I am pretty sure of that. I would know it."

Didn't you have a silver gun? Calissi pressed.

"No, not that I could recall."

In matter-of-fact language, Calissi led the defendant through his wanderings around Times Square, his decision to call a lawyer, and his surrender to the New York City police.

Then Calissi thought it would be good to back up again. "Well now," the prosecutor asked, "do you remember grabbing Sergeant Voto or the officer that you talked about before and telling him to walk or he is dead if he makes a move?"

"No, I don't."

"Do you remember putting a gun to his head, behind his head, and walking him toward the front . . . ?"

"No, I don't."

"Do you remember putting two bullets in his brain?"

"No, sir. I know I didn't do that."

"Do you remember shooting Tedesco?"

"No, I know I didn't do that."

Again, Judge Marini broke in. "How do you know you didn't do that?" the judge asked.

"Because I know I would never do anything like that."

"Oh," the judge said. "You wouldn't do anything like that?"

"I know I would never do anything like that," Trantino repeated.

The trial transcript, of course, offers no clue as to Judge Marini's tone. If he had sounded even a little sarcastic, could the jurors have been affected? Would they have been swayed just by the judge's breaking into the cross-examination at all, as though the judge himself were expressing skepticism?

On the other hand, was the defense just as happy to accept the opportunity, served up by the judge, for Tom Trantino to say twice that he knew he would never do anything like shoot Peter Voto and Gary Tedesco?

Calissi's next line of questioning hinted that the prosecution knew more than it had let on so far. "Didn't you talk to one of the band members that night and refer to the two men at the end of the bar as police officers?" Calissi asked.

"No, sir."

"And didn't you tell one of your friends you were with to put the gun away?"

"No."

None of the band members testified at the trial, and there is no indication of what they told investigators. As for Trantino's having told one of his friends to put the gun away, it seems likely that he would have said that to Tony Cassarino, who had playfully shot at the chandelier.

So, had Tony Cassarino given some information to the prosecution before showing up in court wearing his penitent's ashes and cloaked in the Fifth Amendment? Or was Guy Calissi using a little ruse to emphasize the amazing gaps in Trantino's memory?

"What were you running away from?" Calissi asked.

"I don't know," Trantino replied. "I just didn't feel good. I had to get out of there."

"You mean a siren noise made you run?"

"Yes, sir."

Cross-examination, even in a sensational murder trial, is seldom as dramatic as it is portrayed on a movie screen. Nor does it have to be. An effective cross-examiner needs to limit the witness's responses, and Calissi was doing just that. He was ensnaring the defendant with his own words: after first saying he didn't know what he was running from, Trantino said a "siren noise" had made him run. Perhaps Calissi wanted the jury to wonder if the siren had been a real one, from a police car or an ambulance, rather than the one buzzing in Trantino's head.

Trantino said under cross-examination that he didn't remember cursing Peter Voto, or telling Frank Falco to get Voto's gun, or saying, "We are burning all the way, we are going for broke," or anything like that. And he didn't recall giving the bartender a gun to wrap in a towel, although he did recall that he and Falco both had guns that night.

So, Calissi asked Trantino, when you got to New York City, why did you take a cab to your parents' place instead of your own?

"I don't know."

Well, was he running away from something?

"I wasn't running away. I was just going to my mother's house."

"At six o'clock in the morning?"

Then, once again, Calissi steered Trantino back to the events that occurred in the Angel Lounge and shortly after he left the bar. No, Trantino said, he didn't recall telling Peter Voto and Gary Tedesco to take their clothes off, and he didn't remember much at all about what he said to Pat MacPhail about taking him to New York.

Calissi was fairly confident the jury would see what he saw, plain as day: Trantino seemed to remember the things that showed him in a good light, and, conveniently, to forget the things that portrayed him as a killer.

CHAPTER 23

Two Psychiatrists, Two Perspectives

The defense put a psychiatrist on the stand to try to show that Thomas Trantino hadn't known what he was doing that night in the Angel Lounge, even assuming he had done what the prosecution said.

Samuel R. Kesselman had been a physician since 1940. His specialty was neuropsychiatry, or the prevention and treatment of nervous and mental diseases. In 1964, as is true today, the terrain where mental illness and the law came together was poorly mapped.

Dr. Kesselman knew that territory from the perspective of both prosecution and defense. He was a consulting psychiatrist for several New Jersey penal institutions, including the state prison at Rahway. He had served in the army and had testified in many courts-martial. He had also testified for defendants in homicide cases throughout New Jersey.

The doctor had examined Thomas Trantino on December 1, 1963, in the Bergen County Jail. "I then asked him to go into the details of the offense, and he responded: 'I know it was on a weekend in August. I think it was a Saturday.'"

Though he had gotten the day wrong, Trantino had recalled quite a bit about the events leading up to the shooting. He remembered committing the Brooklyn robbery, going to the Angel Lounge, and giving his gun to Pat MacPhail to stash in her purse.

And he remembered putting down a $20 bill for drinks and Frank Falco's saying, "Take your money off the bar," and Falco's slapping down a fifty.

Trantino told the doctor he remembered the drinking and dancing and joke-telling. And he remembered a gun going off while he was looking down at the dance floor. But he thought Cassarino had fired it, not himself. He re-

membered drinking the shots the bartender kept pouring, remembered someone asking him for identification.

"Then everything is like a kaleidoscope," Trantino had told the psychiatrist. "Falco had a gun out. Then I think I hit a man."

Trantino told the doctor that he had read newspaper accounts of the
crime, and that they had confused him. "I think I must have hit him with a gun.
I remember Falco's face. He had weird eyebrows, just like the devil. We forced
two guys to the front. I remember hitting one of the guys maybe twice, and
probably it was with a gun."

In his account to the psychiatrist, Trantino thought it was Falco who had
ordered the two men to strip. "As soon as I heard that, I saw that look on his
face. I ran out the door and Norma Jaconetta was sitting in the car and Falco's
wife was in the car."

He remembered the car not starting, remembered getting out and running. He recalled hopping aboard the milk truck to nowhere, recalled finally
getting a ride to Pat MacPhail's house in Allendale.

As Dr. Kesselman related what Trantino had told him, it seemed that
Trantino had remembered things a lot more clearly on December 1 than he
had during his own trial testimony.

In the jailhouse interview, the defendant said he had never seriously considered suicide, and had never thought of killing anyone else. The doctor
thought Trantino was "oriented as to time and place . . . Memory was fair on
remote or recent events with the exception of details of the offense itself."

Dr. Kesselman had concluded that Thomas Trantino had a "sociopathic
personality disturbance," coupled with a drug-and-alcohol addiction and emotional instability.

All right, Albert Gross said. Then the defense lawyer posed a question
that, in essence, asked: Given Trantino's childhood and earlier drug addiction
and the drinking and pill-popping of August 25 and August 26, and his wild
flight from the Angel Lounge after the bloodshed, did Trantino know that
what he had supposedly done was "morally wrong"?

Calissi immediately objected, and Judge Marini sided with him. "Morally
wrong, that is not the test," the judge said. What might be "moral" to one person would seem "immoral" to another.

Whereupon Calissi and Gross became embroiled in an argument about
what was permissible and what was not in the kind of hypothetical question
that Albert Gross had crafted. The judge decided to excuse the jury during the
lawyers' back-and-forth. But while the jurors were still in the courtroom, the
judge asked Gross to clarify just what he meant by "morally wrong" in his hy-
pothesis: Was Gross talking about using drugs "or are you talking about shooting two policemen?"

Gross moved for a mistrial, arguing that the judge's last remark was prejudicial.

Motion denied. But when the jurors returned, the judge told them he had not meant to imply that the defendant had admitted anything.

And finally, back to the question Gross had been asking in the first place.

"Assuming the facts in the question," the defense lawyer asked the doctor, "what is your opinion as to whether Thomas Trantino at the time of the alleged offense knew what he was doing was morally wrong or morally right?"

Again, Calissi objected. The judge, wanting by now to move things along, asked Gross if he was trying to establish insanity, or simply seeking "background evidence," in which case he might allow the question.

"I say, if Your Honor please," Gross responded, "in all sincerity and all candor that I am not sure at all what the doctor's answer to this question will be, so that—"

"Well, that isn't the point," the judge interjected.

"—so that my defense will have to be based on what is developed," Gross went on.

Coming from a seasoned trial lawyer, Gross's answer was remarkable. Was he being disingenuous in saying that he didn't really know how the doctor, his own witness, would answer? Or did his remarks suggest the desperate situation in which the defense found itself?

The answer would come a few minutes later. But first, the doctor answered Gross's question: "My professional opinion was that at the time of the alleged offense Thomas Trantino was not able to determine—well, what was morally right or wrong at the time of the offense."

The doctor said he thought Trantino had consumed enough alcohol and pills to affect his reasoning and judgment, and to unleash a rage stemming in part from his resentment of authority.

The judge sought clarification on the effects of Dexedrine and alcohol, and how a person who has taken far too much of both feels when the effects wear off. The back-and-forth between judge and witness went on for several minutes.

Then Gross showed where he was headed. "Doctor, in your opinion, in such a situation would Trantino be able to entertain the deliberation necessary for murder in the first degree?" the lawyer asked.

"Objection," Calissi said.

Objection sustained. The judge said it was up to the jury to answer that question, unless Gross laid a much better foundation for asking the doctor. Gross argued that he had laid a proper foundation, and that the jury was entitled to hear the doctor's opinion.

Judge Marini relented; the question would be allowed if the words *first degree* were omitted and the term *premeditation for murder* substituted. The first term implied too much of a legal conclusion, the judge said.

Finally, Gross got the doctor to say what he wanted him to: "My opinion is that Thomas Trantino was not able to create the intent to commit murder in the first degree at the time and place specified."

There. Albert Gross had been aware from the beginning that the tide of facts was running against his client, who had been seen and heard threatening and hitting Peter Voto and firing a pistol at him and Gary Tedesco. Gross couldn't blame it all on the dead Frank Falco, couldn't argue mistaken identity, couldn't deny that his client had been there.

Perhaps he could at least save him from the electric chair.

§

In his cross-examination, Guy Calissi easily made the point that many of Dr. Kesselman's conclusions came from his jailhouse interview with the defendant, which had lasted all of an hour and a half.

And speaking of the anger burning in Trantino, Calissi said, "Can you explain why, under the circumstances, this hostility wasn't expressed against lay people or ordinary citizens in the Angel Lounge?"

There is an axiom among trial lawyers that, especially in cross-examination, one should almost never ask "why" without knowing what the answer will be. But surely Guy Calissi felt safe, based on the doctor's direct testimony, in asking him that question. The answer must have delighted him.

Yes, the psychiatrist said, it was very understandable why Trantino would have been hostile to police officers and not to ordinary citizens. "Historically, we have a lad who has never been able to develop a favorable relationship with his father, and consequently he is closer to the mother image and not to the father image."

Trantino's troubles in school and his confinement at Great Meadow would have made him antagonistic to authority, the doctor went on. "Such an individual is, in the professional jargon, a cop-hater, and in a situation where all this hostility has been accumulated over the years within an individual, and he faces a provocation of someone telling him to do something in a commanding tone of voice, he is apt to release all of these feelings . . . and having released them would make one feel calm and good about it."

"Calm and good, did you say, Doctor?" Calissi asked.

"In such an individual, yes."

"Would that individual then keep running and running away? He would feel so good he would keep running?" Calissi asked.

"Are you referring to Thomas Trantino?"

"I think so."

"It is my professional opinion that Thomas Trantino was not escaping from the scene of the alleged crime, but his was a flight from premonition of impending disaster." This mental and emotional state was common to people in psychiatric wards who were plagued by delirium tremens, the doctor went on smoothly. And Trantino had been only a step away from the DTs.

But wait, Calissi said. Hadn't the doctor just testified that a man like Trantino would feel calm and good after releasing all that pent-up anger?

Again, the doctor maintained that Trantino had been running away from a "sense of impending disaster" rather than from a crime.

The prosecutor sought more clarification about the amnesia that Trantino claimed to have for the bloodshed in the Angel Lounge and about the fact that, as of the jailhouse examination of December 1, he had seemed perfectly capable of telling right from wrong.

The psychiatrist replied that when "the toxic state he was suffering from" began to wear off, Trantino had a better grasp of his situation.

So, Calissi pressed, was the doctor saying that the defendant had been temporarily insane that night?

"From my understanding of his behavior," the psychiatrist said, "I would say that he did suffer from an acute psychotic alcoholic psychosis."

"That is fine," Calissi said with a straight face. "What does that mean?"

"That he was temporarily ill due to the toxic effect of alcohol at the time of the alleged offense," the doctor said.

Judge Marini broke in: "If he ran out of the place, got into a car, recognized everybody, then ran away, what does that indicate to you in connection with this acute psychotic effect of alcohol? Is that consistent?"

"A person can be generally oriented as to who he is, what time it is, and still be quite disturbed on a psychotic level," the doctor said, going on to say that "after the commission of the act of violence there tends to be a neutralizing effect; the individual seems to slow down a bit."

Calissi must have sensed that the defense psychiatrist had done little, if any, damage to the state's case. The "lad" who resented authority, as Dr. Kesselman had described Trantino, had just turned twenty-six. In that winter of 1964, some of the jurors remembered living through the Great Depression, remembered relatives who had gone off to war. Did they really care if Tom Trantino had been closer to his mother than to his father?

And despite their oaths not to decide the case prematurely, they had to feel deep sympathy for the families of Peter Voto and Gary Tedesco. So how did the jurors feel when the doctor explained that "a cop-hater" like Trantino would feel "calm and good" after releasing his rage?

§

In rebuttal, the prosecution called its own psychiatrist, Laurence M. Collins. He had been a doctor for more than half a century.

On September 26, 1963, Dr. Collins had examined Trantino, telling him at the outset that anything he said could be used against him at the trial. Whereupon Trantino said he wouldn't talk about the night at the Angel Lounge unless he had a lawyer by his side.

"I asked him what was the name of the place where he was, which was the Bergen County Jail. He said, 'This is Comstock.' I said, 'You know this is not

Comstock,' because previous to that he asked me about a lawyer. He said he didn't want a Jersey lawyer, that he wanted a New York lawyer."

On the day he examined him, Dr. Collins said, Trantino was "not only sane but capable of comprehending his position, consulting with counsel in an intelligent manner, knew the nature and quality of his acts and could distinguish the difference between right and wrong."

But the doctor said he could give no opinion of Trantino's mental state when he was at the Angel Lounge. The defendant had refused to talk about that night.

Albert Gross's cross-examination brought a comic interlude. The defense lawyer asked if a person who had consumed fifteen or so stiff drinks throughout the day and evening, plus taken some Dexedrine, would be able to deliberate enough to commit first-degree murder.

"I would have to know what his tolerance was," the doctor said.

Well, Gross said, let's assume each drink contained three ounces of whiskey.

"You have no right to assume that," Judge Marini said. "There is no such testimony." The judge said he might allow Guy Calissi to recall Nicholas Kayal "to find out how much they serve over a bar of that kind."

Gross said that would be fine with him, but the judge said it really wasn't necessary to bring Kayal back. Most likely, the judge said, a double drink would contain an ounce and a half of whiskey.

Undaunted, Gross went on. Suppose, he asked the doctor, that "a normal man" had consumed, say, sixteen or seventeen double seven-and-sevens, plus a couple of Dexedrines, in one day.

The doctor said the man would "have a loss of contact with his environment" and be "out of the picture."

"Thank you very much, Doctor," Gross said. "That's all."

No, it wasn't. Judge Marini had a question: "Doctor, assuming though that the person who is alleged to have that many drinks is alleged to have grabbed a person and put a gun to his head and marches him and makes him undress and waits until he undresses, under those conditions, would that make any indication to you as to what your opinion would be?"

"Yes, sir," the doctor said.

"I object to the question, if Your Honor please," Gross interjected.

"I sustain the objection," the judge said. "Let the prosecutor ask the question."

It is not often that a judge sustains an objection to a question that he himself has asked. Judge Marini seemed to have realized that he had posed a question that would have been far more appropriate for the prosecutor to ask.

Calissi simply asked how long it would take a person to come to, assuming he had downed as many drinks and pills as Gross said his client had.

"It should take several hours before he becomes aware of his environment," Dr. Collins said.

Calissi didn't press the point. The judge's question (objection sustained, or not) had been most helpful. After all, Trantino had been aware enough to flee the scene.

And Calissi had a rebuttal witness who would tell of Trantino's mental state.

§

Albert Gross called the defendant's mother to the stand. Crying at times, she told of her son's addiction and alienation, of his inability to lead the straight life. Guy Calissi did not cross-examine her. He had no desire and no reason to grill the woman for whom he had so much sympathy, whose son he was trying to send to the electric chair.

CHAPTER 24

Driving Her Boyfriend

Pat MacPhail had known a lot of boozy nights and bleary mornings in her short life, but the story she told the jury made it seem as though nothing had prepared her for the early morning of Monday, August 26, 1963, when she opened her door and saw Tom Trantino standing there.

"What are you doing here?" she said. "I heard there were two cops killed in Lodi . . . "

"Frank shot them."

"How did you get here, Tommy?"

"I walked, ran, crawled over bushes, over fences. I cut myself . . . "

His clothes were filthy, his face streaked with blood and shiny with sweat. His face had a look she had never seen before on any man.

As Tom pushed his way in, his right arm was reaching over to the left side of his belt. Then she saw that his right hand was touching the handle of a re- volver stuck in his belt, as though ready to draw. She saw that his left wrist was bleeding badly from a deep cut.

He rushed by her, went into the bathroom, rummaged in the medicine chest, and found some hydrogen peroxide to wash out the wound.

"I need to get lost," Tom said. "Maybe upstate New York. Maybe New York City. I don't know where. I just have to get lost . . . "

"Why, Tommy?"

"You're going to drive me."

"I can't, Tommy. There's no one to baby-sit right now."

"We'll take the kids with us. I need you to drive me. I was helping Frank."

"We can't take ... What do you mean, 'helping Frank'?"

"You will probably hate me for this, but *I* shot the policemen."

"Oh, Tommy ... "

"The cops were going to get him. Take me to New York City."

§

She took Route 4 toward the George Washington Bridge, with Tom Trantino beside her in the front seat.

"I was just trying to help out Frank," Tom said. "Don't go too fast. Don't drive over the speed limit."

A lot was going through her mind right then. She was worried about her small children, sleeping with the bliss of the innocent back in Allendale but with no grown-up to protect them. She wanted to help Tom Trantino, but she was frightened, very frightened. Tom had started out by saying that *Frank* had killed the two cops. Then he said that he himself had done it. My God, could that be?

The George Washington Bridge loomed just ahead. "Go through the exact-change line," Tom commanded. "If anyone stops us, say I'm your husband."

At last, they were on the great bridge across the Hudson. Already, the span was busy with people on their way to Manhattan or the Bronx or somewhere. They were people with good jobs and good lives and nothing to fear from the law, and Pat MacPhail wished she could be like them.

How had her life turned out this way, to be twice-divorced already and with two little girls, ages two and one, asleep alone back home as their mother drove a crazy man smelling of sweat and whiskey and blood ... ?

Her eyes filled with tears.

"Don't go too fast," Tom reminded her.

She obeyed, letting the faster cars whiz by her.

"Okay, stop," her passenger said as they neared 178th Street.

She pulled over.

"The other girls know better than to tell on me," Tom said. "If anyone finds out where I was taken, I'll know who told them."

Tom Trantino leaped out. Pat MacPhail saw him run to a cab and get in. As quickly as she could, she turned around and headed home. *Oh, God,* she thought on the way. *The state might take away my children if someone finds out I helped a murderer get away. Oh, God ...*

CHAPTER 25

A Life in
the Balance

"I must confess that I awoke this morning, if you can say that I slept, sick at heart, knowing that I had to plead with you for a human life," Albert Gross said as he began his summation on the morning of Tuesday, February 18. "The Lord giveth and the Lord taketh away."

The horrible events in the Angel Lounge "started twenty-six years ago when this boy, Tommy Trantino, was born," Gross went on. "His father and mother did for him everything that was within their means . . . "

And when Trantino began using drugs, "he became corrupted and defiant and not the master of his own soul. . . . You and I who have no experience with this kind of thing find it extremely difficult, I know, to understand why a boy or a man, intelligent, apparently normal, cannot be the master of his own soul and kick such a habit. . . .

"The inevitable happened," Gross said, referring to the crime that landed Thomas Trantino in Great Meadow. "I don't know, I don't know why prison authorities give these fancy names to prisons because in this 'correctional institution,' instead of preparing this boy for trying to live a normal life, he was permitted to associate with Falco. This is where he met Falco . . . "

Give credit to Trantino for trying to have a normal life when he got out of Great Meadow, Gross said, sliding over his client's inability to live a nine-to-five existence: "It is very difficult, because employers don't want anything to do with prison inmates."

Then the lawyer came to the summer of 1963. "Such is the strange way of fate, while at Coney Island he met that devil incarnate, Falco, and that was the begin-

NIGHT OF THE DEVIL

ning of his end, because while in the first case he had stolen and robbed to feed the heroin, now he became, under Falco's tutelage, a professional criminal ... "

The very last chance for Thomas Trantino to take a different path was on Sunday, August 25, his lawyer suggested. "After the robbery had been committed, Trantino said that he felt depressed. He wanted to go home. You see, however bad we are, the voice of conscience never leaves us alone, and he knew, he knew his conscience told him that he had violated the laws of society.

"But they all decided to go to the Angel Lounge."

By 2:30 in the morning, Gross said, "this boy is loaded, to use the vernacular. He is drunk, he is in a fog." And after drinking enough to have put almost anyone else to sleep, "Trantino was still operating, but operating in a kind of a comatose condition."

In this condition, Gross suggested, the defendant might not have known that Peter Voto and Gary Tedesco were police officers, especially because they wore no uniforms. And if Trantino really had known that two cops were dead, and if he had had a gun when he fled the Angel Lounge, wouldn't he have forced the milkman at gunpoint to drive him far away fast?

"There is only one answer to that," Gross argued. "He didn't have a gun."

The lawyer sought to cast doubt on Pat MacPhail's account. If Trantino had really threatened her with a gun, why didn't she simply stop and get help from a policeman around the George Washington Bridge?

"There is only one answer to that: there was no gun, and there was no threat."

Nor was Pat MacPhail the only woman who should be doubted, Gross said. Speaking of all four women who were at the Angel Lounge that night, he said, "In my life, ladies and gentlemen, in my entire life I have never come in contact with such a coterie of unsavory women."

Sally Vander Fliet, he said, was "nothing but an amateur hustler. This is a girl who couldn't tell the truth if she wanted to tell it."

Pat Falco? "This pitiful thing is seventeen years of age, a lovely girl, but the apple is rotten inside." She was the kind of girl who "picks up a gun with live ammunition in it and holds it on a human being for five minutes and says to him, 'If you move, you're dead.'"

Norma Jaconetta? "I call this a professional hustler. Here is a woman who lived with two men; one wasn't enough for her." She was so in love with Frank Falco, Gross said, that she had tailored her story to protect Falco's memory and blame Trantino for everything.

Finally, Pat MacPhail. "Ladies and gentlemen, I have never seen a cooler, colder customer in my life. This is a first-degree murder trial, and that girl was testifying as though she were taking an examination to drive a car."

The only warmth in Pat MacPhail's heart was toward her two children, Gross said. She was afraid of losing them, which is why she made up the story that Tom Trantino threatened her.

And Nick Kayal. Suppose, just suppose, the bartender had told Peter Voto that the "firecracker" noises the neighbors had complained about were really gunshots. "Just think, Voto and Tedesco might very well be alive today. . . . You can't restore dead men. You can't bring Falco back to life so that he could tell us perhaps what happened."

He begged the jury to spare his client's life: "Cruelty can only breed cruelty, and killing goes on and on and on until this world is nothing but a slaughterhouse, and there seems to be no end despite the Sermon on the Mount, despite the plea of Christ for love, for mercy, for compassion . . . "

Then Gross took a breathtaking gamble. "The courtroom is full, ladies and gentlemen, not because most of the people came here to learn a lesson but because of the scent of blood. That's why most of the people are here, and this is part of the rottenness of human nature. You kneel to Christ and you don't follow him, you don't follow him at all."

Having portrayed the spectators as bloodthirsty, Gross asked the jurors to be nobler, especially since the real villain was beyond earthly punishment. "Falco is the man who shot and killed these policemen. . . . Can there be any doubt of the villain in this tragedy, ladies and gentlemen?"

Anticipating that Guy Calissi would argue that Trantino knew perfectly well what he was doing in the Angel Lounge, Gross said it didn't matter "whether all the psychiatrists in the world take the stand and tell you that this boy is normal.

"This boy is mentally defective," Gross announced, "and when I say mentally defective, he suffers from an emotional disorder which has ruined his entire life. It is the emotional disorder, the insecurity, which drove him to heroin in the first place. . . .

"Can you believe that this was a cool, normal human being who simply got mad, in his right mind, picked up a gun, and proceeded to pistol-whip a police officer and then coldly and coolly gunned them [sic] down as they lay on the floor? That is what you have to find in order to put him in the electric chair."

Bowing to the torrent of sympathy for the victims and their families, Gross told the jurors that Trantino's relatives were also "innocent people who somehow have gotten embroiled in a tragedy not of their own making."

"Which one of you knows when you give birth to a child or you father a child what the future of that child will be? Because no one on this earth, psychiatrists, psychologists, or what have you, knows the seed, the instincts, the forces which compel human beings to do evil. . . .

"Just think what a holiday it will be in Bergen County the day they bring Trantino into the death house and there strap him into an electric chair and turn on the current until the blood boils and the bone and marrow are burned to a crisp. What good can that do? Teach him a lesson? He has had his lesson. He will never get through paying for his lesson."

Gross urged the jurors to take their time deliberating, because a man's life was at stake. He insisted that the state's case was "loaded with doubt," and reminded the jurors that any reasonable doubt had to be resolved in the defendant's favor.

"Don't, I pray you, don't give yourself haunted nights, troubled sleep. I pray to God that he blesses and guides you, ladies and gentlemen, so that your hands will not be stained with blood."

A solemn hush fell on the courtroom. Gross's plea for mercy had been moving and heartfelt. But while no one knew it at the time, it was not Gross's eloquent peroration that would live in memory but rather something he had said a few moments before.

Putting Thomas Trantino to death would accomplish nothing, Gross had said. "Isn't it enough if he should spend the rest of his life behind bars?"

§

After a brief recess, it was Guy Calissi's turn. "This has been quite a burden," he said. "It isn't a pleasant task for a prosecutor, but it is a solemn obligation and, frankly, my nerves are as taut as the E string on a violin."

To people who knew Guy Calissi well, the violin allusion was telling: his parents had made him play the instrument when he was a boy, and he detested it.

"There was no defense," he said. "First, it was a case of lapse of memory, some kind of amnesia, a very convenient kind of loss of memory and a very convenient amnesia."

Calissi said Trantino had lied about taking all those memory-blurring pills. He reminded the jury that Dr. Collins had said anyone who took as many pills as Trantino said he'd taken would have been unconscious if he'd also drunk heavily.

"I don't understand the defense," Calissi went on. "Perhaps you do. You are asked not to stain your hands with blood, and then you are told that this man didn't know anything, didn't see anything, doesn't know anything about this particular case, that Falco is the culprit. Yes, Falco is dead. Convenient to blame it on Falco, and I certainly have no grief for Falco, because he too was in that particular tavern, and he too shot."

Calissi confronted the fact that the bullets fired into Peter Voto's head came from a gun that was never found. "There was another gun," he said, "the gun that Trantino had when he got to MacPhail's house."

The prosecutor knew he would have to address Gross's description of the four young women as tramps on the make. "I don't profess to tell you that they were den mothers," Calissi said, "but the state produced those witnesses who were there when this crime was committed."

In a couple of sentences, Calissi demolished the argument that Trantino didn't know that Peter Voto and Gary Tedesco were police officers. Trantino heard Voto and Tedesco ask everyone in the Angel Lounge for identification, Calissi reminded the jurors.

"But is that important? They were human beings. That's what they were.... Whether they were officers or not, they were human beings and had a right to live."

In order to send Trantino to the electric chair, Calissi had to convince the jurors that he had killed with premeditation, and that premeditation could take place in a matter of moments. So he reminded them that Trantino had marched Peter Voto toward the front of the Angel Lounge, and that witnesses had heard Falco ask, "What are you doing?"

Calissi said there was plenty of time for premeditation—time to change his mind, had he been so inclined—as Trantino held the gun on Peter Voto, then beat him, then fired the shots. "There is only one purpose that a gun ultimately is used for, either against man or beast."

Peter Voto had been slain after giving no resistance. Perhaps he was simply undressing too slowly, Calissi said. Then the prosecutor re-created Gary Tedesco's end: "A bullet in the heart, that shattered the heart, a bullet through the liver that shattered the liver, and he went down.... He moaned and he cried and his body quivered and a bullet, the coup de grâce, silenced him. This is the kind of crime we are talking about."

Calissi virtually sneered at the suggestion that Trantino's early drug addiction and trouble in school ("a life contrary to the mandates of religion and mandates of society") somehow diminished his guilt.

And once again, Calissi alluded to the gun never found, the one Pat MacPhail said she had seen, and the defense's inability to break her on the stand: "She was there like the Rock of Gibraltar, because when you tell the truth, you are like the Rock of Gibraltar, cross-examination or no cross-examination."

He reminded the jurors that Trantino had been seen firing in Gary Tedesco's direction as well as at Peter Voto. "The gruesome details you know about. I am not going to go over them again." Study the autopsy report, he urged them.

Turning to the defendant, Calissi said, "This man in cold blood and premeditation murdered Voto and Gary Tedesco." He asked the jurors to return a conviction for first-degree murder with no recommendation for mercy.

And then Guy Calissi sat down. He had spoken only half as long as Albert Gross and had used far less dramatic language. Calissi was sure he had the truth on his side, and that the real drama, the tragedy, had been acted out on the floor of the Angel Lounge.

§

In his instructions to the jury, Judge Marini said Trantino should be convicted of murder if the panel found he killed both victims, or either one of them. The prosecution did not have to establish a motive.

I will tell you what the law is, the judge said, and it is up to you to decide the facts.

The judge went on for hundreds of words about the defendant's mental and emotional state on the early morning of August 26, 1963. "The law does not require a man to be in full possession of his faculties to subject him to criminal responsibility," Judge Marini said. "Having adopted as the test of responsibility the capacity to distinguish between right and wrong and to comprehend the nature and quality of the act done—there the law stops."

Much of the instruction was technical, subtle, and in legalese, probably necessarily so. But one crucial passage was in plain English:

"The insanity of the accused cannot be inferred from the atrocity of the crime. If such were the case, the more atrocious the crime, the greater the certainty of the defense being sustained and the most atrocious crimes would be attended by immunity from punishment."

But intoxication could be an excuse—up to a point. If the jurors decided that Trantino was so drunk that night that he was incapable of premeditation, then they must not convict him of first-degree murder. But "a person merely inflamed and so forth by alcohol can't use that as an excuse." Nor would voluntary intoxication entitle the defendant to acquittal.

The judge said the jury had to choose from among four possible verdicts: not guilty, guilty of first-degree murder with no recommendation for mercy (a death sentence), guilty of first-degree murder with a recommendation for life imprisonment, or guilty of second-degree murder.

Then the jurors were sent out just before three in the afternoon to weigh the fate of Thomas Trantino.

CHAPTER 26

Kaleidoscope

Guy Calissi had to trust the jurors to sort things out. He knew he didn't have all the pieces of the puzzle, and that some of the pieces he *did* have would not fit. The exact, moment-by-moment "truth" of what had happened in the Angel Lounge would be forever unknown.

Jaded and worldly-wise though they were, the people in the Angel Lounge were caught up in a bloody pandemonium. So the separate memories of that night, while indelible, were kaleidoscopic as well. In that sense, Tom Trantino had described things perfectly.

Nick Kayal didn't see everything; he was crouched behind the bar, eyes closed, saying his prayers during some of the carnage. He and Sally Vander Fliet were the only sober people in the Angel Lounge that night. Sobriety notwithstanding, Sally's memories were perhaps the cloudiest of all.

The four young women had been jailed as material witnesses after being picked up on the morning of Monday, August 26. All were questioned thoroughly by Guy Calissi and his assistants that day, for hours at a time. In the next few days, they went before a grand jury to tell what they had seen and heard. They were nervous and afraid; nothing in their superheated young lives had prepared them for *this*. They were hardly eager to tell everything.

Ambiguities, even outright contradictions, surfaced between what Pat Falco, Pat MacPhail, Norma Jaconetta, and Sally Vander Fliet told the grand jury and what they said in their testimony at the trial half a year later. Some conflicts were brought out by the defense; others simply emerged. Perhaps the women's memories had faded in six months. Or maybe the memories had become sharper as emotions cooled and the women reflected on the big trouble they could be in if they committed perjury.

Norma Jaconetta admitted in court that when she was first questioned, within hours of the shooting, she said as little as she could, and that some of what she did say was not true. "Trantino and Falco were free and they were good to me," she explained. "I tried not to make it harder on them when they did eventually get caught . . . I just tried not to involve them."

Pat Falco was torn apart emotionally. She didn't know her husband's whereabouts when she appeared before the grand jurors. Did she still love him, knowing that Norma Jaconetta had been his mistress? Maybe she felt both love and hate. She must have been afraid she would never see him again, knowing that the police were hunting him down. And she never did see him again.

Asked in her grand jury appearance what she had seen Tom Trantino do, she replied, "I don't know if he shot both of them, or if *I* [emphasis added] just kept shooting on Voto."

At Tom Trantino's trial, the young widow spoke so softly that she had to be reminded repeatedly to speak up. She heaved with sobs as the defense brought out the inconsistencies in her accounts. Of course, she said under cross-examination, she had been mistaken when she seemed to tell the grand jurors that she had shot Peter Voto. She had never meant to say any such thing.

Assuming that Pat Falco was not trying to lie during the trial, the account she gave in the courtroom in February 1964 did not make sense in at least two important respects. She testified initially that a half-hour elapsed between the time Tom Trantino first got the drop on Peter Voto and when the shooting stopped.

But when prodded by Guy Calissi after Judge Marini expressed incredulity that half an hour could have gone by, she backtracked. The whole thing didn't last a half-hour, she said. It probably took only fifteen minutes.

More likely, it was much less than that. Tom Trantino put a hold on Peter Voto just after Gary Tedesco had gone outside to the patrol car. There is no reason to assume that Gary waited in the car for very long before going back inside. From studying the accounts of the witnesses—even allowing for distortion, deliberate or otherwise—it does not seem that enough happened to fill up fifteen minutes.

Gary Tedesco found himself helpless as soon as he reentered the saloon. He was told to take his clothes off. Seeing what was happening to Peter Voto, it is reasonable to assume he undressed as quickly as he could. When one compares the various accounts of the screaming and shoving and frenzy, it seems that no more than a few minutes passed from the time Gary was standing in his underwear until he and Peter Voto were shot. Maybe their agony lasted two minutes, or less.

Pat Falco also testified at the trial that after the shooting she held a gun on Nick Kayal for five minutes after her husband bolted, and that she then went out and got into Norma Jaconetta's car with the other women. But it is simply inconceivable that the others, having rushed out of the Angel Lounge after the screams and the shooting, waited five minutes for Pat Falco before they all drove off. Most likely, the others waited only a few seconds for Pat Falco to come rushing out.

Indeed, determining what happened that evening is a lot easier than figuring out *when*.

Trantino recalled arriving at the Angel Lounge around ten o'clock Sunday night. But Nick Kayal thought Trantino (along with Falco and his wife, Tony Cassarino, and Pat MacPhail) got there between 10:30 and 10:45. And Pat Falco said their party arrived around 11:30.

Kayal's account makes sense, because he also recalled seeing Peter Voto and Gary Tedesco for the first time between 10:30 and 11:00, after the first noise complaint. Could someone besides Trantino, Falco, and their companions have generated that first complaint? The testimony is not explicit on that point—although Kayal said it was a slow night in the Angel Lounge until Trantino and Falco showed up.

But what to make of Sally Vander Fliet's recollection that she and Norma Jaconetta arrived at the Angel Lounge between 9:30 and 10:00, stayed about an hour, and left, not seeing Trantino and Falco and the others until just before midnight, when she and Norma went back to the bar?

And Norma herself had a quite different recollection. She testified that she and Sally got to the Angel Lounge at 10:15 and left around 10:45 to go to the Cottage Inn, where they stayed about a half-hour. Then, Norma said, it was back to the Angel Lounge, where she talked to her friends next to the jukebox around 11:15. She was not pressed on her recollection of time, but it does not seem possible that things could have happened that quickly—the smallness of Lodi notwithstanding.

As for Nick Kayal, he said Sally and Norma arrived between 9:30 and 9:45 and stayed only about ten minutes before going off to the other bar.

The discrepancies about the comings and goings were not resolved at the trial. Nor did it matter. There was plenty of agreement on what really counted.

Yes, Nick Kayal had taken refuge behind the bar, but not before he saw Trantino holding a gun to Voto's head. He was sure of that.

And while Norma Jaconetta's view was partially blocked, she saw Trantino's arm pointing directly at Voto just before she heard shots.

And Sally Vander Fliet and Pat Falco were certain they had seen Trantino shoot Peter Voto.

There was plenty of evidence of Frank Falco's guilt, too, not that it mattered much. Sally Vander Fliet and Nick Kayal both remembered seeing him atop the bar, a gun in each hand. Pat Falco recalled seeing her husband shoot Gary Tedesco (although Guy Calissi might have found it impossible to get her to say that if her husband were still alive).

There remained questions about the three guns found at the scene—and the one that was never found—and about who fired which weapons.

Sally Vander Fliet testified that she saw Trantino shoot Peter Voto with a silver gun. "He had the gun in his hand pointed down at Detective Voto on the floor, and I saw the fire come out of the gun, and I heard the noise and saw the gun in his hand," Sally said.

"Will you describe that gun?" Guy Calissi asked.

"It was the silver gun."

But on cross-examination (and before August Hoppe testified that the silver gun found at the scene hadn't been fired in a long time and didn't work properly), she acknowledged that she could not be sure that the gun Trantino fired at Voto was the silver gun in evidence.

It seems likely that the gun that was never found was also silver. Nick Kayal testified that he saw two silver handguns that night. Shown the hammerless Harrington and Richardson revolver, he said it appeared to be the gun that Peter Voto had found in the towel. "That's the gun that Frank Falco took from him, along with his own pistol," the bartender said.

"Would you describe the gun that you say Trantino had at Sergeant Voto's head?" Calissi asked.

"It looked like a long, shiny silver gun."

But the hammerless silver gun that didn't work was surely not the one that Peter Voto had found in the towel. The gun Nick Kayal wrapped in the towel was in good working order: it had been fired into the dance floor.

Kayal's testimony suggested that the missing gun might have been a semi-automatic pistol instead of a revolver. As Tony Cassarino was taking pot-shots at the chandelier, Kayal said, "I saw two empty shells come at me and hit me in the chest and fall down on the floor by me ... "

One of the big "what ifs" about the case concerns Kayal's conduct. Perhaps things would have turned out differently if he had simply told Voto and Tedesco earlier that there was a loaded gun on the premises instead of hiding it in a towel.

So why didn't he tell? Kayal said he was afraid.

The gun that Trantino beat Voto with must have been the .38-caliber revolver whose hand grip had been broken off. That weapon, found on the floor of the Angel Lounge near the bar, was not only operable, it had been fired three times. However, it does not seem that this could have been the gun that Trantino used to shoot Peter Voto.

It is not disputed that the two bullets recovered from Voto's head came from a .38-caliber weapon that was never found. This missing gun must have been the one that Trantino fired from point-blank range at Voto. Very likely, this was also the gun that Trantino was seen firing at Gary Tedesco, perhaps grazing him in the stomach area.

We know that Trantino had another gun later; at least, we know that if we choose to believe Pat MacPhail.

Voto's own gun must have been the one that Frank Falco used on Gary Tedesco. The evidence showed that one bullet from Voto's gun landed in Tedesco's left shoulder, another in Peter Voto's abdomen. The bullets that ripped through Gary's torso and were never found probably came from Voto's gun, which was found at the curb.

Pat Falco testified that just before getting into Norma's car, she dropped the gun that her husband had given her to hold on Nicholas Kayal. When he was shown Peter Voto's gun in the courtroom, Kayal testified that he thought it was the one that Pat Falco had held on him. Almost surely, it was—which means that Pat Falco frightened the bartender with a weapon that was out of ammunition, not that anyone was counting at the time.

There were other discrepancies about the weapons. Chief Wagenti testified that he noticed two live rounds in the gun with the broken grip; there were actually three, according to August Hoppe. The discrepancy might be attributable to the fact that one live round was situated directly behind the chamber, and was therefore impossible to see. Wagenti also testified that the hammerless silver revolver was empty; it actually held two live rounds.

Other contradictions, minor in themselves, showed that it was impossible to learn exactly what had happened, moment by moment.

Norma Jaconetta testified at the trial that Peter Voto was in his shorts when he was slain. But Officers Robert Oetting and Michael Serpone, who arrived at the bar minutes after the shootings, recalled that Voto was in trousers and T-shirt.

Nick Kayal testified that Gary Tedesco walked out to get a flashlight.

"How do you know that Gary Tedesco went out for a flashlight?" Calissi asked.

"I heard him say he was going out," Kayal replied. "I saw him walk out."

"I see," Calissi said.

Kayal never explained why he thought Tedesco was going to get a flashlight. Peter Voto already had one, and none of the witnesses said anything about Gary coming back into the lounge with a flashlight. The only flashlight found in the Angel Lounge was Peter Voto's. More likely, Gary went out to radio police headquarters, which he did, at ten minutes to three.

Norma Jaconetta testified that Gary was virtually dragged into the bar by Frank Falco upon his return. But Sally Vander Fliet recalled that Gary walked in, took several steps, and turned around in amazement.

Finally, Pat MacPhail testified that after she came out of the Angel Lounge, she sat in her car and saw a police cruiser approach. She said a uniformed officer went up to the entrance of the Angel Lounge.

"He didn't actually go in, just put one foot in the door and turned around and came out and at that time the patrol car left. *To my knowledge, I heard three shots after that* [emphasis added]."

Right afterward, she said, she got out of her car and went to the door of the lounge again—she never did say exactly why—and was met by a straight-arm from Nick Kayal, who told her to go away.

At first reading, Pat MacPhail's account seems to raise a fascinating, and chilling, possibility. If she really did see a police officer drive up to the Angel Lounge, start to go inside, then come out and go away *before* she heard shots, then the lives of Peter Voto and Gary Tedesco might have been saved. Or at least Gary Tedesco might have been saved, if the three shots Pat MacPhail said she heard were those that killed Peter Voto. The saddest inference one could draw from Pat MacPhail's account is that a possible rescuer—a uniformed police officer, who surely had a weapon—had carelessly peeked inside the Angel Lounge, then had driven away.

But it seems far more likely that Pat MacPhail was confused. She testified that, while sitting in her car, she had earlier seen Norma Jaconetta come out of the lounge, then rush back inside. That recollection squares with Norma's account of going back to fetch her good friend Sally Vander Fliet and pull her to safety. So it seems all but certain that the police car Pat MacPhail saw was the one in which Michael Serpone and Robert Oetting had driven up, and that she saw one of them around the door of the bar just before they left in hot pursuit of the car carrying Norma Jaconetta, Pat Falco, and Sally Vander Fliet.

Pat Falco testified that as she was exiting the Angel Lounge while holding a gun by her side, she brushed by two uniformed policemen, saying, "Excuse me." That dovetails with the accounts of Oetting and Serpone.

But Nick Kayal testified that his brief encounter with Pat MacPhail at the doorway, in which he gave her a straight-arm and told her to scram, took place after Pat Falco had left (which, of course, was also after Peter Voto and Gary Tedesco had been shot), and *before* Oetting and Serpone came into the Angel Lounge.

So perhaps Oetting and Serpone, having seen the bodies inside the Angel Lounge, left in pursuit of the car they had just seen on Baldwin Avenue without stopping to question Nick Kayal. That would explain why Pat MacPhail, sitting in her own car, saw a policeman—Serpone or Oetting—standing at the door of the Angel Lounge briefly, then getting in a car and driving away.

The officers' testimony is not crystal clear on the sequence—from the prosecution's standpoint, it did not have to be—but it suggests that they were at the Angel Lounge only very briefly before chasing the car driven by Norma Jaconetta.

Guy Calissi did not try to tie up every loose thread. He knew that unnecessary complexity could be a prosecutor's enemy.

As for the testimony of the two officers, the woman they saw standing by the police car must have been Norma Jaconetta, who had stopped to turn off the headlights in the car used by Voto and Tedesco. She was never asked why she did that, but Norma Jaconetta, the seasoned getaway driver for Tom Trantino and Frank Falco, was probably cool enough to think that a car with its headlights on would attract attention.

Not that it mattered: Oetting and Serpone drove up just then, their car's red dome light whirling and the headlights bathing Norma as she ran to her own car.

The man Serpone and Oetting saw in the Angel Lounge parking lot on his way to the car by the curb was probably Frank Falco. By all accounts, he fled from the Angel Lounge after Trantino did and got to the getaway car soon after.

Guy Calissi did not press Pat MacPhail as to when she had heard the shots. Maybe he didn't want to open the door for the defense to suggest that the state's case was not completely airtight. But Albert Gross and Herbert Koransky did not press her on the timing either. All these years later, it is impossible to know why.

Reading the transcript of a trial from long ago takes one back in time, but not all the way back. A transcript does not reveal if a witness looked eager to please, or heartbroken, or sullen. It tells nothing of the chemistry between witness and questioner, or between witness and jury.

A transcript may contain an occasional on-the-record clue to suggest a witness's emotions—an offer of a glass of water, for instance, or, more tellingly, a tissue. But a transcript cannot preserve, or re-create, the energy that filled the courtroom at a given moment.

Sally Vander Fliet broke down in sobs when she was on the stand; she needed several minutes to pull herself together. She also had to explain away some big, big changes in her story.

Back in August, she had told the grand jury that she had fled the Angel Lounge just before the killing started. But before she and the other women were released from jail on the Friday after the killings, she had second thoughts. In a handwritten statement to Guy Calissi, she acknowledged that she had been in the bar a bit longer—long enough, in fact, that from only a few feet away she saw Tom Trantino shoot Peter Voto.

"I made a mistake then," she explained at the trial. "Everybody is open to mistakes." Conversations with Norma Jaconetta had honed her memory, Sally explained. Besides, she said, "At that time, I just didn't want to believe I had seen it. I was numb. I never experienced so terrible a thing. I was shocked, I felt terrible."

Guy Calissi got what he needed from the bartender and the four women. Enough witnesses saw Tom Trantino pistol-whipping Peter Voto, heard Trantino's threats to kill him, saw the flame leap from the gun Trantino held. Pat MacPhail (and the milkman on whose truck Trantino hitched a useless ride) gave accounts of Trantino's flight, suggesting that no matter how much memory loss he claimed, he was conscious, at the time, of having done something awful.

Significantly, in view of the lore that has persisted through the years, the prosecution never suggested that the victims had been subjected to sexual humiliation. Unless we assume that Guy Calissi held back some of the most horrifying elements of the case even while seeking a murder conviction and the death penalty, we can only conclude that there was no sexual humiliation. None of the witnesses testified to anything like that.

But who told the two men to take off their clothes, and why? Did the killers mean to humiliate them? If so, that seems to have been more Falco's style than Trantino's. At least, Trantino's lawyers have suggested that over the years. In interviews and in a book that he later wrote, Trantino has hinted that before the shooting started he and Falco were thinking about locking Voto and Tedesco in a bathroom, knowing that the pair would surely pause to get dressed once they broke out. By then, Falco, Trantino, and the others would be long gone.

Whatever the truth, Gary Tedesco was stripped of his clothes and his dignity before dying. That has stoked the hatred that Gary's friends and relatives, and almost everyone else in Lodi, feel toward Thomas Trantino.

Another purported "fact" is that both victims were forced to beg on their knees for their lives before being executed. It has been repeated so many times over the years, in newspaper accounts and occasionally even in court documents, that it has become accepted as truth.

Peter Voto was clubbed to his knees by Trantino, but Gary Tedesco was never forced to his knees. At least, no witness testified to anything like that. No witness testified that either victim begged for his life.

Yet there is an allusion from Trantino himself in his book, in a stream-of-consciousness account of the night in the Angel Lounge. Trantino's style is similar to that of e.e. cummings, in that it lacks capitalization and punctuation: "frank leaps onto the bar and goes into a squat with a gun in each hand and the cops are saying dont hurt us please ... "

No one knows exactly what was said, or what went through the minds of Peter Voto and Gary Tedesco. One agonizing question is forever unanswered: How long did they have to endure their terror? Their survivors will ask that question for the rest of their lives.

Everyone agreed that Voto was shot first. Nick Kayal testified that Peter Voto was shot even before Falco turned to Gary Tedesco and asked him if he had a gun. His account suggested that Tedesco's last moments were prolonged and agonizing.

But the victims' relatives could find consolation in the account of Sally Vander Fliet, which seems more plausible than Kayal's in view of the frenzy in the bar that early morning.

"Did Gary Tedesco say anything after the shooting of Voto as you have described it?" Calissi asked her.

"No," she said, "because right after that happened, then there was another boom, a loud boom sound like the ones I had heard before." Sally said she heard him groan. "Then there was another boom, same sound."

Gary Tedesco's survivors can also take comfort in something that Pat MacPhail said. Testifying about meeting Gary Tedesco in the doorway of the Angel Lounge as she was on her way out and he was on his way back in, she recalled that Gary exclaimed, "Oh, my God!" as he saw what was happening inside. Then, she said, he pulled her outside to safety. It was one last professional act by the young policeman.

Guy Calissi was sure that the various memories of that night, disjointed though they were, were enough to damn Thomas Trantino. And in a way, it was fitting that the picture was incomplete. What really happened in the Angel Lounge on the early Monday morning of August 26, 1963, was horrible beyond words.

CHAPTER 27

A Verdict and an "Obituary"

At eight minutes past ten o'clock on the night of Tuesday, February 18, 1964, the jurors sent word that they had made a decision. Fifteen minutes later, they filed into the courtroom.

"Members of the jury, have you reached a verdict?" the court clerk asked.

"Yes, we have," said the forewoman.

"What do you find?"

"We find the defendant, Thomas Trantino, guilty of murder in the first degree with no recommendation for mercy."

Two court officers grabbed Trantino by the arms, in case he fainted. He did not. He merely swallowed hard, twice, and stared glassy-eyed at the jurors.

In the rear of the courtroom, Peter Voto's wife, Connie, sobbed loudly. A moment later, she collapsed and was carried out.

Of course, the defense would want the jurors polled to be sure the decision was unanimous.

"Just a moment," Judge Marini said to Albert Gross and Herbert Koransky. "Just a moment before you poll them."

Looking at the jurors, the judge asked them if they understood that they were asking for a death sentence. "Is that the verdict of the jury?"

"That's right," the forewoman said.

One by one, the jurors were asked if that was indeed what they wanted. Yes, they all said.

"Twelve, Your Honor," the clerk said.

"All right; very well," the judge said. Then he thanked the twelve jurors. "I agree with your verdict, and if I had the power and it was within my power to try the case alone without a jury, the verdict wouldn't have been any different on the basis of the evidence that we have heard in this courtroom."

Shortly afterward, a solemn Guy Calissi spoke to reporters outside. "We have no feeling of pleasure or glory," he said.

Relatives of Peter Voto and Gary Tedesco said they had expected the verdict, and were relieved.

"I'm glad he got a fair trial and good attorneys," Andy Voto said. Minutes earlier, he had squeezed through the crowd, getting as close as he could to the hawk-nosed man who had killed his brother and hissing, "Pete finally got you, you son of a bitch!"

§

The next day, the *Record* ran an obituary of sorts: "The Strip, the one-and-a-quarter miles of nightclubs and taverns along Route 46, is losing one of its charter members." The liquor license of the Angel Lounge was about to be transferred to a little luncheonette in the heart of Lodi. The owners wanted to sell beer.

After reopening in November 1963, the Angel Lounge had never recaptured the spirit of camaraderie and gaiety so vital to a watering hole. The knowledge of what had happened there seemed to be keeping people away.

In mid-December, the Angel Lounge went dark forever.

PART **II**

CHAPTER 28

"May God Have Mercy ..."

Long before he turned twenty-six, he had learned how to jab a dirty needle into his veins and shoot himself full of heroin. But he had never learned how to drive. He had stolen and killed, but he had never held an honest job for very long.

So it was strange, in a way, that Thomas Trantino wore a conservative dark business suit the morning of Friday, February 28, 1964, as he stood before Judge Joseph W. Marini. Two courtroom deputies held Trantino's arms in case he collapsed when he heard the judge say what everyone in the packed courtroom knew he would say.

But first the judge asked him if *he* had anything to say.

"No, sir," Trantino said in a low voice, shaking his head.

Then it was Albert Gross's turn: "Since man has climbed out of primeval slime, there has been punishment motivated by man's appliance of the theory of an eye for an eye and a tooth for a tooth.

"The very salvation of man is based on love, compassion, and understanding. Legalized murder is no better than criminal murder. I hope I may live to see the day when capital punishment is abolished not only in New Jersey but everywhere in the world."

To which Judge Marini replied, "Nothing much you or I can say will change matters."

And that was true; the judge *had* to sentence Thomas Trantino to death. "I think there is much to be said for the death penalty," the judge stated. "I think the reason why public opinion sometimes backs up the death penalty in cases of vicious murders is because life imprisonment frequently does not mean life imprisonment.

"Under existing statutes, life imprisonment can mean parole within twenty-five years. Less credits and good behavior, authorities have estimated a person—*this man*—could get out within fourteen years."

Staring at Gross, the judge said that many people, many jurors, would turn away from the death penalty "if life imprisonment really meant life imprisonment."

Then Judge Marini looked at Guy Calissi. "I take it you have nothing to say?"

"Absolutely nothing," the prosecutor said in a low voice.

Now the judge intoned: "You, Thomas Trantino, will be taken by the sheriff of this county to be delivered to the warden at the state prison at Trenton, there to be placed in close custody and solitary confinement to suffer punishment and the penalty of death in the manner prescribed by law.

"May God have mercy on your soul."

§

Adrienne Peraino watched and listened with disappointment. She had come to the sentencing in hopes that Trantino would go white, perhaps faint, or cry out in terror. He did not.

The execution was set for the week of April 5, but no one really thought it would take place that soon. There would be an appeal by the defense, a process that could drag things out for a long, long time.

Just before the trip to the New Jersey State Prison at Trenton, where the electric chair was housed, Tom Trantino had a visitor at the Bergen County Jail: his wife, Helene. He had not seen her since she had walked out of his life the previous summer. She looked tan and healthy. The conversation was short and strained.

Then Trantino was handcuffed, fitted with a restraining belt, and hustled into the back seat of a police car between two sheriff's deputies. A captain in the sheriff's office drove. The car bearing Thomas Trantino was followed closely by an escort car. The two cars drove south on the New Jersey Turnpike, past refineries and swamps and suburbs and farmland. They arrived at the Trenton prison just after eleven in the morning.

And Trantino entered a new world. "I hope this letter finds you and everyone at home in the best of health," he wrote to his mother. "I arrived in the death house today and just wanted to let you know that all is well ... "

Death row was about a hundred feet long. There were three tiers of nine cells. Each cell had an iron bed, a cold-water sink, and a toilet bowl with no seat.

Day and night, televisions were on. Shouts echoed ceaselessly off the concrete and steel. Some men found it easier to sleep during the day. At no time was everyone awake or everyone asleep. Now and then, the men were allowed out to exercise in the old courtyard. Some lay on the ground and stared at the sky.

Trantino tried to take each day, each moment, one at a time. He knew if he thought too much about what lay ahead, he could go mad.

§

Tucked in a corner of the prison, the electric chair was old, as furniture went. It had been installed in 1907 and had performed reliably 160 times. Yet its use had become sporadic. When Fred Sturdevant, a twenty-seven-year-old from Newark, was put to death on July 4, 1962, for killing his four-year-old step-daughter after having sex with her, it marked the first execution in the Garden State in six years.

The last man to have been shackled against the chair's stiff wooden planking was Ralph J. Hudson. He had been convicted of killing his wife in an Atlantic City restaurant two days after Christmas in 1960. He was forty-three when he was electrocuted on January 22, 1963.

The people who felt a bottomless hatred for Thomas Trantino had every reason to expect that he, too, would sit in the chair. The question was when. On March 30, Trantino's lawyers served official notice that they would appeal the conviction. The move had been expected (appeals in death-penalty cases were mandatory), and it automatically postponed the execution.

And with that, the Angel Lounge case entered a new phase, one that would last for many years. It ceased to be front-page news. The story of Thomas Trantino was now told in bloodless legal briefs, motions, and counter-motions.

One could almost forget how the case had started.

§

On April 12, 1965, the New Jersey Supreme Court upheld the conviction and death sentence. The 7–0 decision rejected the defense's contention that some of Judge Marini's remarks regarding insanity and the law had been prejudicial.

On April 15, Patrick Tedesco sent a telegram to Governor Hughes, asking that he and Andrew Voto be allowed to witness Trantino's execution. Normally, relatives of the condemned and relatives of the victims were not allowed to watch an electrocution. People close to the governor doubted that he would make an exception.

On June 14, the New Jersey Supreme Court rejected the argument that pre-trial publicity had denied Trantino a fair trial. The high court noted that Albert Gross, having initially moved for a change of venue, had withdrawn his request.

So the execution was set for the week of August 22, 1965. At last, the Voto and Tedesco families would get their closure—and how appropriate that it would come around the second anniversary of the crime. Once Trantino was in his grave, the Votos and Tedescos could visit the graves of Peter and Gary with lighter hearts.

And then the grieving families were hurt once again, this time by a friendly man from New Jersey, a man of high intelligence and personal charm. He did not mean to hurt the Voto and Tedesco families; indeed, they would have felt his kindness if they had met him.

The man was William J. Brennan Jr. of the United States Supreme Court, and he was simply following his conscience.

Brennan was a justice on the New Jersey Supreme Court in 1956 when President Dwight Eisenhower named him to the United States Supreme Court. He would serve there for thirty-four years. Throughout his tenure as a Supreme Court justice, he was a staunch foe of capital punishment. Two weeks before Thomas Trantino was to be executed, Justice Brennan granted a stay so the defense could seek a hearing before the full Supreme Court, not due back from recess until October.

Anyone familiar with the U.S. Supreme Court knew it took only a small portion of the cases whose lawyers sought a hearing before it. So if the justices chose not to consider Trantino's appeal, the stay might delay the execution date by only a few months. Did it really matter?

So the second anniversary of the Angel Lounge killings came and went. Thomas Trantino was suspended in time with the others condemned in the limbo of death row. And although he didn't know it, time was on his side.

§

On January 17, 1966, the U.S. Supreme Court declined to review Trantino's case. That seemed to clear the way for the execution, which Judge Marini set for the week of April 24.

But on April 6, the execution was postponed yet again as a federal district court judge agreed to consider arguments by Frances Kahn, hired by the Trantino family to handle the federal appeals, that Judge Marini should have held a pretrial hearing on Trantino's mental state. Her argument was not that Trantino had been insane at the time of the crime, but rather that he had been mentally incapable of assisting in his own defense.

Brought to Newark for a hearing before federal judge Reynier Wortendyke Jr. on June 13, Trantino claimed he had been given barbiturates before being examined by a psychiatrist in his jail cell prior to the trial. By now, the defendant was represented by Leonard Weinglass, a lawyer who would soon be famous for representing anti-war demonstrators.

Judge Wortendyke ruled that Trantino had failed to exhaust all his appeal avenues in the state courts. Weinglass said he would raise the issue of the barbiturates there.

Trantino was scheduled to die in early November, but Judge Marini granted another stay of execution, the fourth in the case. Thomas Trantino's date with the electric chair seemed far off. Executions, once commonplace, were becoming rare in the United States.

And all of a sudden Trantino's claim that his defense had been compromised had to be taken seriously. On December 29, 1966, a former attending physician at the Bergen County Jail acknowledged that he had given tranquilizers to Trantino during the trial. Dr. Michael Sarla said he had recorded the tranquilizer doses in the jail log.

Testifying before Judge Marini on January 3, 1967, Trantino complicated things further. He said that, in addition to the tranquilizers prescribed for him during the trial, he had taken other tranquilizers that were smuggled in to him by another inmate. These bootleg tranquilizers had put him into a lethargic haze during his testimony, he maintained.

It is a bedrock principle of American justice that the accused must be able to assist in his own defense. The people who were eager to see Trantino burn in the electric chair were furious that his own misbehavior had helped to manufacture an issue that might aid him. The jailhouse physician had prescribed tranquilizers because Trantino had shown violent tendencies. And if the defendant's mind had been further clouded because he took pills that had been sneaked into jail—well, whose fault was that?

But the issue was there nonetheless. "I felt as if my mind wasn't balanced that morning," he said of his testimony of February 14, 1964. "I felt as if it was strangled."

Dr. Maximilian Fink, professor of psychiatry at New York Medical College and the author of nearly a hundred articles on the brain's reaction to drugs, backed up Trantino's claims. The drugs the defendant took in jail would have induced loss of memory, a change of mood, a general slowing of the mind, the doctor said.

"I definitely think he would tell a different story under those tranquilizers," Dr. Fink said, noting that one of the drugs Trantino had taken was the powerful Thorazine.

Guy Calissi argued that Trantino knew exactly what he was doing when he testified, and that the defendant's "memory lapses" were meant to mask his guilt. "This was a very sharp and very intelligent man," the prosecutor said.

Leonard Weinglass put Albert Gross on the stand. Trantino's former lawyer said he and his assistants had had difficulty getting access to the four young women. Calissi denied that he or his aides had told anybody not to talk to the defense.

Meanwhile, it was clear that Judge Marini was growing impatient with the defense. "We're all trying to bend over backward and remove barriers to accommodate you," he said to Weinglass at one point. "I don't want to give you a ridiculous reason for an appeal."

Near the end of the hearing, assistant prosecutor Harold Springstead told Judge Marini that a young prisoner named Colin Wagner, who had been on the same cellblock with Trantino, might shed some light on what had happened. He did, and it did not help the prosecution. Yes, Wagner testified, he had given "four or five pills" to Trantino on as many occasions.

Springstead could only hope that Judge Marini, who had certainly not seemed hostile to the prosecution, would consider the testimony of two psychiatrists who had just been called to counter the testimony of Dr. Fink. Dr. Laurence Collins, who had already testified for the state at the trial, and another psychiatrist told the court that Trantino's mind would not necessarily have been as blurred as he said it was.

Springstead also hoped Judge Marini would be swayed by something Colin Wagner had said. Recalling that he offered Trantino some tranquilizers the day he was to take the stand at his trial, Wagner said, "He didn't want any. He said he wanted a clear head."

On January 10, 1967, Judge Marini denied Trantino a new trial. "He was not drowsy, or lethargic, as he claims," the judge said. "He was, to the contrary, quite sharp."

Judge Marini signed an order setting the execution for the week of March 5, 1967, but that was a mere formality. No one expected Thomas Trantino to be strapped into the electric chair any time soon.

CHAPTER 29

From Limbo
to Life

By the spring of 1967, a great debate was being waged across the land about whether capital punishment did any good and, more profoundly, whether it was right.

There were many people who still favored it (especially for heinous crimes like Thomas Trantino's), but there were many others who thought it unworthy of a great people. They pointed out that poor men with dark skin were the most likely to be condemned, and that standards for applying the death penalty varied widely from state to state.

The number of executions had been declining for many years. There were 199 in the United States in 1935, the all-time high. They were still commonplace throughout the 1950s. But with the new decade, the pace dropped dramatically.

To judge by the numbers, the mood of the country (or at least the moods of its courts) was changing from year to year. In 1965, when Thomas Trantino was spared by Justice William Brennan, there were seven executions in the United States. In 1966, there was one. The next year, there were just two.

On June 2, 1967, Luis Jose Monge went to the gas chamber in Colorado for killing his wife and two children. No one knew it then, of course, but his would be the last execution in the United States for nearly a decade.

§

The New Jersey Supreme Court had been agonizing over capital punishment for several years.

Under the rules that were in effect in 1964, the jurors simultaneously deliberated Thomas Trantino's guilt or innocence *and* what sentence he should get if they found him guilty. This circumstance had placed his lawyers in a strategic bind: at what point should they stop trying to convince the jurors that Trantino was not guilty beyond a reasonable doubt and begin trying to persuade them that, *even though he was guilty,* he deserved mercy? It was clear to anyone who had heard or read Albert Gross's eloquent summation that he had had to cross that Rubicon.

In 1964 in New Jersey, a defendant who had been accused of a capital crime could save himself from the possibility of execution by pleading guilty, thereby avoiding a trial by jury but accepting a life sentence. Some criminal-defense lawyers had long argued that that wrinkle effectively deprived the accused of his right to a trial.

In the fall of 1967, the New Jersey Supreme Court ruled that the death penalty had been wrongly pronounced upon two defendants convicted of a shotgun slaying during a robbery at a bus garage in the Bergen County community of Oradell. The court did not order a new trial, but it did set aside the death sentences. It said the trial judge had not responded properly when the jurors asked if they could impose a life sentence without the possibility of parole. "The answer is no," the judge had told them.

The New Jersey high court said the judge should have told the jury not to worry about whether the two killers would ever be paroled; the jurors should simply have decided whether life sentences were appropriate. The implication was that the jury might have voted to send the two defendants to their deaths rather than opt for "life" sentences that would not really keep the killers behind bars forever.

The high court's ruling was subtle, but prosecutors got the message. The state court seemed to be moving toward a separation of the jury's functions in murder cases. Perhaps the court would hold that two juries were necessary in capital cases—one to decide guilt or innocence, the other to decide the rightful penalty.

Or perhaps, if there need be only one jury, the panel should first decide whether the defendant was guilty; then, if the jury convicted the defendant, it should decide whether he should be executed or be sentenced to life in prison.

In 1968, a similar issue came before the United States Supreme Court. The federal law against kidnapping had long given a defendant the chance to save his own life by pleading guilty before a judge rather than take his chances with a jury that might condemn him. In April 1968, the Supreme Court ruled that the law unfairly encouraged defendants to plead guilty.

The parallels between the federal kidnapping law and the New Jersey law on capital punishment were so striking as to virtually invite defense lawyers to challenge the state statute. The first lawyer who did so was Ronald Picinich of Hackensack. His client was one of three suspects in the 1965 shooting death of a young woman in Fair Lawn.

In early July 1968, the New Jersey Supreme Court ruled, five to two, that the April ruling by the highest court in the land on the federal kidnapping law need not be applied to the New Jersey law on murder. The state justices also decreed that state law need not be affected by another recent U.S. Supreme Court ruling, that a prospective juror could not be excluded from a panel because he or she opposed the death penalty as a matter of conscience.

§

On February 3, 1969, five years almost to the day since the start of his trial, the New Jersey Supreme Court took another look at Thomas Trantino's case. Leonard Weinglass again argued that the tranquilizers had caused Trantino to weaken his own defense. He argued, too, that the twelve people who had convicted Trantino in 1964 might not have been questioned enough beforehand about their views on capital punishment.

Around this time, New Jersey lawmakers were trying to balance their consciences with what their constituents wanted, or what they thought their constituents wanted. It wasn't always easy to tell.

In April 1970, the General Assembly held a hearing on a bill to abolish the death penalty. Four people showed up to testify. One lawmaker saw that as a sign that the people didn't support the bill. Others thought the people knew that the death penalty, while still on the books, was for all intents and purposes already dead. By this time, William T. Cahill had succeeded Richard Hughes as governor. Cahill did not believe in the death penalty.

In the fall of 1970, the New Jersey Senate agreed to create a commission to study the possibility of abolishing capital punishment for all but the most heinous crimes.

And in June 1971, the United States Supreme Court saved the lives of thirty-six men on death rows across the country, declaring that jurors with reservations about the death penalty had been wrongly kept off their juries. The Court did not void the convictions, only the sentences.

Other death-penalty cases were making their way inexorably toward the U.S. Supreme Court. Perhaps the Court would one day decide whether the death penalty had any place in America anymore.

In New Jersey, it might not matter. In October 1971, an Essex County Superior Court judge handed down a decision in the case of one Walter Lee White of East Orange. White, accused of killing a man during a holdup in Newark the previous January, was subject to the death penalty if convicted and so sentenced by the jury.

But the judge, citing the 1968 U.S. Supreme Court decision on the federal kidnapping statute, declared that it was likewise unconstitutional in New Jersey for a capital-murder defendant to have to choose between pleading guilty and accepting a life term, or taking his chances with a jury and risking a death sentence. So the judge told the jurors they could not consider sentencing Walter Lee White to death.

Until it was tested on appeal, the Essex County ruling applied to only one case—and perhaps not even to that, if prosecutors could convince the New Jersey Supreme Court otherwise. And the state's highest court, headed by Chief Justice Joseph Weintraub, was considered pretty hard-line on defendants' rights and capital punishment.

Yet the Essex County ruling had to be taken seriously, based as it was on a principle recently articulated by the United States Supreme Court. And not so incidentally, the Essex County judge was a former prosecutor. His name was Brendan T. Byrne, and he would be governor after Cahill.

Who dared predict what Judge Byrne's ruling would mean for the twenty-two men then on New Jersey's death row?

§

While his very name was hated in Lodi, Thomas Trantino had death-row neighbors whose crimes were also horrible. They included a laborer from Newark who had stabbed two young women to death while the two-year-old son of one victim watched from his crib, two Newark brothers who killed a Newark candy store owner in a 1962 holdup that netted about fifty dollars, and three other men who had been sentenced to death for killing police officers. Among the prisoners was one Victor Funicello, whose case was becoming very, very important.

Victor Funicello, who stabbed a Newark car dealer to death in 1965, argued that the law had forced him into an unfair choice: should he go to trial (and risk a death sentence) or plead guilty, thereby escaping the electric chair but subjecting himself to decades in prison? Funicello chose to go to trial, and he was convicted and sentenced to die.

Not fair, the United States Supreme Court declared on June 28, 1971, citing its own 1968 decision on the federal kidnapping law. But the Washington justices were, in the opinion of the New Jersey Supreme Court, exasperatingly terse. The guidance from the highest court in the land was limited to twenty-two words: "Judgment, insofar as it imposes the death sentence, reversed, and case remanded to the Supreme Court of New Jersey for further proceedings."

What did that mean? "We're all trying to figure out just what they mean," Chief Justice Weintraub said.

One lawyer thought he knew. In November 1971, he urged the New Jersey Supreme Court to overturn the state's death-penalty law and resentence the twenty-two men on New Jersey's death row to life in prison. Future defendants convicted of first-degree murder should also be sentenced to life in prison, he argued in a brief.

He zeroed in on the section of the law that permitted a defendant to avoid the death penalty by pleading guilty (or "no defense," as the law technically stated).

"The United States Constitution does not permit the imposition of the death penalty on only those defendants who would assert their right to a trial by jury," the lawyer argued. These were not the words of a long-haired leftist. They were the words of the state's highest law enforcement officer, Attorney General George F. Kugler Jr.

Even before Kugler made his views known, there had been a growing belief among many lawyers that the death penalty in New Jersey had effectively been erased the previous June by the U.S. Supreme Court in the case of Victor Funicello—no matter how terse or vague the New Jersey justices at first found the guidance from Washington.

§

On January 17, 1972, Victor Funicello's name became as important in New Jersey as, say, Ernesto Miranda's had already become throughout the United States. On that day, the New Jersey Supreme Court ruled, six to one, that the state's death penalty was unconstitutional because of what the United States Supreme Court had said the previous June in Funicello's case.

The New Jersey court said it was wrong to force a defendant in a first-degree murder case to choose between pleading guilty or risking the electric chair. Victor Funicello's life had been saved. So had the lives of the other men on the state's death row—including, of course, Thomas Trantino.

§

The very next day, the United States Supreme Court heard arguments on the constitutionality of capital punishment in the nation. It is likely that none of the twenty-two men on death row in Trenton gave a damn.

In June 1972, the nation's highest court ruled, five to four, that capital punishment, as it was then haphazardly administered, was unconstitutional. Some states set about to refashion their death-penalty statutes, in hopes that the Court would one day declare that capital punishment was not unconstitutional *in and of itself.* (In July 1976, the High Court did so declare.)

New Jersey was among the states whose lawmakers rewrote their death-penalty laws to comply with the High Court's standards, although as of this writing, early in 2002, there still has not been an execution in New Jersey since 1963.

But the death penalty could not be imposed retroactively on Thomas Trantino. Events beyond his control, perhaps beyond his comprehension, had swept him through an escape hatch. He would live.

On February 8, 1972, the New Jersey Supreme Court turned down Trantino's last plea for a new trial. Technically, he would be eligible for parole consideration in 1979 or thereabouts. But that was a long way off. Anyway, it was hard to imagine that he could be seriously considered for freedom even then.

CHAPTER 30

Getting Used
to Prison

Like a lot of men at that time, Tom Trantino liked his hair long. In 1970 he balked at getting it cut and lost his exercise-yard privileges for a while. On January 25, 1972, eight days after his life was saved by the New Jersey Supreme Court, he got into trouble again over his hair. He was locked in his cell until he agreed to be shorn.

From early 1967 through early 1972 (while he was on death row and had little to lose), Trantino was involved in one petty incident after another. He swore at corrections officers several times, once hurling a metal bowl in anger. He talked back, and did his time in isolation as punishment.

Shortly after his 1972 reprieve from death, Trantino was transferred from Trenton to the state prison at Rahway, another old-style fortress of brick and stone. He was not an exemplary inmate, nor a particularly troublesome inmate. He was an ordinary one.

§

On November 25, 1973, the *Record* of Hackensack published what was arguably one of the more influential newspaper articles of its time. It did not uncover a scandal, did not throw a light onto a social problem. But it did do something remarkable: it made people loathe Thomas Trantino even more.

"Ten years after the killings, Trantino can talk of being in love for the first time," read the article in the Sunday magazine. "Of discovering care, of dreams of retiring to a farm with his love to paint and write and live in freedom."

The piece was an exhaustive reprise of the Angel Lounge case, and while the writer interviewed Andy Voto and members of the Tedesco family, many readers thought the article way too sympathetic to the killer.

Trantino in love? Painting and writing? Indeed, he had taken up the brush and the pen to help him get through the slow days in his prison cell. His drawings and paintings were described as abstract, often erotic. They attracted attention on the outside, probably more than they would have if they'd been done by a door-to-door salesman instead of a death-row prisoner. A few art critics even called his work "Picasso-like."

Some of his paintings and drawings were displayed in New York art galleries. A few of them were bought. Eventually, Tom Trantino became a minor celebrity.

The article described how a woman named Charlee Ganny had come into his life. Charlee had majored in English at Drew University, where she was an editor on the college newspaper. She got a teaching job at Essex Community College in Newark, took graduate courses, dabbled in leftist politics. She painted as a hobby. Literature, art, politics—these were Charlee Ganny's interests around the time that Tom Trantino and Frank Falco were pulling robberies and Sally Vander Fliet, Norma Jaconetta, and Pat Falco were donning high heels.

Charlee was nineteen at the time of the Angel Lounge killings. She took a slight interest in the case because Sally Vander Fliet had been a high school classmate. That Charlee would one day fall in love with Tom Trantino seemed unimaginable, given who she was.

Charlee's ex-husband, Jeffrey Fogel, was one in a series of lawyers for Trantino. For a time, he headed the New Jersey branch of the American Civil Liberties Union (ACLU). When Fogel inherited the Trantino file from Leonard Weinglass, he and Trantino began exchanging letters. Trantino made tape recordings and shared them with Fogel. And Fogel shared the letters and tapes with Charlee.

"I was down in school when Jeff gave me a tape," she recalled in the interview with the *Record*. "I had never heard his voice, and I put the tape on just before class. I couldn't go to class, I was so struck . . . "

By this time, Charlee and Jeff's relationship had run its course. Charlee was ready for a new love, and she found it. "I had started writing him in the death house," she said. "When I read his things I couldn't help feeling what he was feeling and found myself getting very involved emotionally. I wrote him, and he wrote me, and it didn't take long to decide that we loved each other very deeply. And that was before I even met him."

Without directly saying so, she tried to dispel the notion that there was something sick in her attraction to the Angel Lounge killer, that she had become infatuated with a prisoner because there was something wild or dangerous about him. Before she met him, she steeped herself in his writings and his drawings. "I felt I knew the inner person very, very well," she insisted.

She said that she greatly admired Trantino's writing: "It says people are basically very much alone and searching for something, and it stresses the importance of love in life. Underneath it all is this very deep humor of him laughing at himself at the same time he's feeling all this pain."

She saw him for the first time in February 1972, just after his reprieve. She looked at him through the glass partition at the state prison at Trenton, talked to him by telephone. Though they were only inches apart, they could not touch.

And that, she said later, was that. "We just talked, and it was an incredible feeling," she mused. "I love him very deeply, and he loves me. It's just something you don't expect to happen in your life."

Trantino returned the feelings. In the article that fomented so much hatred against him, he spoke of Charlee's gentleness and intelligence. And he spoke of the dreams they shared. "She has this farm," he said. "We hope to paint and write there and maybe open up a little school. We want a lot of children of our own."

§

Trantino's prison buddies also liked him. They poured out their feelings to the interviewer for the *Record*. "He's the most brilliant man I ever met in my life," said Frank Bisignano. "He's a beautiful person." Bisignano was a death-row survivor who had been involved in a tavern robbery that led to the death of a Newark policeman. (Bisignano's partner had been the actual shooter.)

The photographs accompanying the article showed how Trantino had changed. Gone was the somber, downcast look he'd worn when he was being led in shackles to the courtroom. Tom Trantino in the autumn of 1973 had a sly, self-satisfied smile. His face was framed with the mod hair of the era.

Nothing about him suggested remorse; quite the contrary. He said he didn't remember the night of the killings very well. But one thing he was sure of: "I never did shoot my gun in that f—— Angel Lounge. . . . Those cops were murdered in cold blood. . . . That just wasn't me . . .

"I wasn't living a good life, I was unhappy with my life at the time," he said, pausing to light a cigarette. "I had committed a robbery shortly before the events transpired in the Angel Lounge . . ."

The maddeningly impersonal language infuriated the people of Lodi, as did Trantino's seeming denials that he had triggered the bloody events that "transpired" in the Angel Lounge.

The newspaper was inundated with angry letters to the editor. Days after the article appeared, members of the Bergen County Policemen's Benevolent Association picketed the *Record* building. "Friend of the people it serves," one placard read in parody of the newspaper's motto, "as long as the people are criminals."

Here, I must say what I think. I do so from the viewpoint of middle age, with the memories and impressions of thirty-seven years in journalism, years in which I have made my share of mistakes. The article was well written, interesting, and suspenseful. It was also far too credulous, and the photographs were in awful taste. Trantino and his prison pals look self-satisfied and full of themselves—infuriatingly so, considering their crimes.

I know, as a matter of fact, that the article was written by a talented young journalist. An older editor should have called the writer aside and offered advice: "Try not to forget that Trantino is a killer. Okay? The prisons are full of 'innocent' people."

§

Andy Voto was Lodi's deputy police chief by 1973. He was a man with a lot of friends in Bergen County law enforcement. Many of them remembered his older brother. They were incensed by the account of Trantino's struggle for happiness.

One high-ranking official in the Policemen's Benevolent Association was Warren Carlstedt, a patrolman in the Bergen County city of Englewood. He wrote a long letter to the *Record* about the killings in the Angel Lounge.

"Two policemen were forced to do the most horrifying acts of their lives, then murdered without cause," Carlstedt wrote.

And so in 1973, the dark legend was resurrected and validated. People who knew what had happened—or thought they knew—didn't need to be told what the words meant. For people who hadn't known, who had heard only vague whispers about the Angel Lounge crime, everything was suddenly horribly clear.

Roger Lowenstein, one of Trantino's lawyers, was dismayed. He knew that his client was doing great harm to himself, coming across as "a smirking, arrogant prick," as Lowenstein put it privately.

The lawyer told his client to choose his words carefully, or keep quiet. But it was too late. The damage had been done.

§

Trantino's writing consisted of short verse and longer, stream-of-consciousness reflections. Much of it lacked capitalization and punctuation. Early in 1974, his writings were published by Alfred A. Knopf in a slim volume titled *Lock the Lock*. Charlee had helped him find the publisher.

Here is one of the shortest poems: "i dont know my son/i dont know where all my sperm has gone/i am most people."

Guy Calissi would not have approved.

The book was far from a bestseller. No one knows how many people in Lodi saw it. Those who did were disgusted by the photograph of the frizzy-haired Trantino with bright, friendly eyes and a slight smile. He did not look like a killer.

§

On January 31, 1974, just a few weeks after Trantino's book was published, Jeffrey Fogel and Leonard Weinglass filed a petition in federal court asking for a new trial. The lawyers plowed up some old ground, asserting that Trantino had been hampered in defending himself because of the drugs he'd taken while in jail.

Jeff Fogel had never understood why Albert Gross had dropped his request for a change of venue. Perhaps there were grounds for appeal there, or in the way the young women who had been with Trantino and Falco were questioned.

Jeff Fogel was a man of liberal politics who believed that every defendant deserved a fair shake. Yet he was more than a little bothered that most of the people he defended were guilty as hell. And he thought a lot of them belonged in prison. Years later, his feelings would drive Fogel out of criminal-defense work altogether.

Yet he liked Thomas Trantino, whom he met in 1971 when Trantino was still on death row. Fogel thought that Trantino was truly remorseful, no matter how poorly he expressed it.

§

News of the latest court maneuvers on Trantino's behalf sparked more outrage. So did his poor memory. In mid-1974, he was still insisting that he could not remember the Angel Lounge shootings. What's more, he was claiming "to have been virtually reborn in prison," as one newspaper account put it.

The wife of a police officer wrote a letter to the *Record*. "Too bad that Sergeant Peter Voto cannot be reborn, nor young Patrolman Gary Tedesco," she said. She was against capital punishment "because I could never condone the taking of human life for any reason," and she felt that life imprisonment would be punishment enough if there were no chance for parole.

"However, if this cold-blooded murderer is freed you will find me at the head of a very determined campaign to have the death penalty 'reborn' in this state," she went on. "I have no doubt that there will be many others with me!"

The letter was prophetic. The case of Thomas Trantino would one day cause people both in and outside law enforcement to question their bedrock beliefs about life and death, crime and punishment, revenge and redemption.

§

Trantino's fellow inmates not only liked him, as evidenced by the *Record*'s article, but they also came to view him as a leader.

On Thanksgiving Eve 1971, before Trantino was transferred there, several hundred inmates had seized two wings of the old, fortress-like prison in Rahway and had taken several guards hostage. The prisoners had long complained about overcrowding, lack of privacy, bad food—the same complaints that inmates in many prisons had.

Only two months earlier, inmates at the prison at Attica, in upstate New York, had rebelled over many of the same conditions. By the time that uprising was over, more than forty prisoners and guards were dead. So a sense of dread settled over Rahway, followed by a sense of great relief on Thanksgiving night when the inmates agreed, after being assured that their complaints would be heeded, to end their uprising and free their hostages.

Shortly after his transfer to Rahway, Trantino became a leader of an inmates' council that had been formed after the rebellion to air grievances with corrections officials. The group was not universally liked (corrections officials are wary of any formal organization of prisoners), but it might have saved some lives.

In April 1974, a butcher knife was stolen from the kitchen at Rahway just a few hours after a fight between two inmates, one white and one black. The situation was ominous. The authorities worried that the knife that had vanished from the kitchen would reappear in someone's ribs.

Prison officials began a cell-by-cell search. To their considerable relief, the knife was returned. Leaders of the inmates' council had used the prisoners' grapevine to find it, then had promised the thieves that they would wipe away any fingerprints before turning the weapon in. The council leaders had also managed to cool the feelings of the two prisoners whose fight had begun the trouble.

But if prison officials felt any gratitude, it was soon gone. On the afternoon of April 30, Thomas Trantino and other council leaders held a meeting in a prison recreation yard. It was attended by some two hundred inmates. The fifteen-minute session aired various gripes: prison food, visiting hours, the use of isolation for punishment.

No one ever accused the inmate leaders of trying to foment a riot; the opposite was true. But the authorities saw grave danger in any meeting of that size, and of the emergence of a few recognized leaders among the convict population.

"No matter how noble the purpose, you cannot have a system where any inmates have authority over others," one Rahway official said.

So, late on the night of April 30, several inmate leaders were moved. The two most prominent were transferred to the notorious Vroom Building in Trenton, long used to warehouse the state's most incorrigible prisoners and the criminally insane. One of the two transfers was Rubin "Hurricane" Carter, a former middleweight boxer serving a life sentence for a murder, a crime of which he would ultimately be cleared. The other was Thomas Trantino.

Just before his transfer Trantino had been given the prison equivalent of a promotion, for good behavior: he was elevated from floor-mopper to clerk.

But his book had been published a few months before, putting him in the spot-light, where the authorities didn't think he belonged. He was also remem-bered as the inmate who liked his hair long. And, of course, there was the crime that had put him in prison in the first place.

Trantino would not go quietly into the night. Shortly after his midnight transfer to the Vroom Building, Trantino and three other prisoners filed a suit in federal court. They claimed that they had been moved for flimsy reasons arising from their activities on the so-called People's Council, a group of eigh-teen leaders from the prison population of about 1,100.

The prisoner-plaintiffs had help from the ACLU and the National Confer-ence of Black Lawyers. The suit argued, basically, that prison officials set up an inmate organization for expressing grievances, then dismantled it when it got too strong for comfort.

After a hearing was held in July before federal judge Clarkson Fisher in Trenton, the prisoners won a partial victory. Judge Fisher ruled that correc-tions officials had a right to transfer inmates from one prison to another, but he said prisoners could not be punished without having their side heard. Tran-tino and the others had been denied due process when they were summarily transferred to the Vroom Building, the judge said.

Because of the judge's order, the corrections agency moved Trantino and the others back to the main prison population—but not to the same prison. Trantino went to Bayside State Prison in Leesburg; Rubin Carter, to the prison at Trenton. The inmates' venture into limited self-government had gone too far for the comfort of officialdom.

In October, Trantino's federal court petition for a new trial was denied by Judge Herbert J. Stern in Newark, but not before Judge Stern ordered Fred Galda to submit to questioning. Guy Calissi's former right-hand man was now himself a judge in Bergen County Superior Court.

It was bad enough that Thomas Trantino, who was supposed to have died in the electric chair, was still trying to get out of prison. And Galda, who had helped to put him in prison, had to explain his actions before a federal judge! Had the world turned upside down?

The fact that Trantino was even alive outraged many people. Any talk of his personal growth seemed obscene, given the wreckage he had left in Lodi.

CHAPTER 31

The Other
Victims

Every night, Elaine and Patty Tedesco would hear their mother screaming and crying in Gary's room.

Sadie Tedesco had left her son's things exactly as they were on the last day of his life. The room was a shrine, but the mother drew no comfort from it. None of her prayers would bring her son back from the dead.

When they could no longer bear the sobbing, her daughters would go into the room. Then they would lift her off the bed and take her to her own room, where she would cry herself to sleep.

"The family was destroyed as a unit," Patricia Tedesco said years later, "and we were destroyed as individuals."

Patricia Tedesco is a successful businesswoman who lives in central New Jersey. She is a person of intelligence and self-assurance. But for a long time, there was an emptiness in her life. Years of therapy helped her to understand her problems with men, problems that have not gone away. She began to comprehend that Gary's death, how he was taken away from her forever with no warning, changed the way she looked at life. Loving someone completely, loving too much—that was the path to heartbreak.

§

Elaine Harvey, Patricia Tedesco's older sister, also lives in central New Jersey, but she won't say exactly where. The man who killed her brother might find out. Perhaps that is an unreasonable fear; anyone who has spent any time with the aging Thomas Trantino would think it is. But who has the right to laugh at Elaine Harvey's fears?

Elaine Harvey is good company over a couple of beers, but she guards her personal life. And who can blame her? She loved her strong, gentle big brother as much as anyone could ever love another human being, and Trantino took him away from her.

Elaine has a family, a life. She has been a teacher, has worked with computers. One of the quickest ways to get on her bad side is to suggest that she is a victim.

"It didn't happen to me," she said one day. "It happened to Gary."

Yes, she wishes Trantino had burned in the electric chair. And once in a while, she imagines what her brother's final moments must have been like. "He had to watch Pete be executed," Elaine said. "And he knew that he was next." She hopes it all happened quickly.

Elaine Harvey consoles herself with the knowledge that Gary pulled a young woman out the door to safety before entering the Angel Lounge himself. But the indignity of the way Gary died will trouble her always. "I heard he had garters on when they found him," she said. "You know, I can't remember his voice anymore. It's a blank."

§

For months after the killings, Adrienne Peraino went with her parents to the Tedesco house almost every night. Vito and Bessie Peraino and Patrick and Sadie Tedesco sat around the table for hours. They talked about Gary. They talked about how unbelievable it was, something like that happening in Lodi.

And they talked about what might have been. Maybe Mike Serpone should have rushed to the Angel Lounge after his cousin Gary Tedesco radioed for another car. If Trantino and Falco had heard a siren coming closer, maybe they would have run out of the bar without shooting . . .

Twelve-year-old Patty Tedesco had had enough. Listening to her parents and Adrienne's parents saying the same things over and over and over was driving her crazy.

"I can't do my homework!" she shrieked one night, hurling her books to the floor. The grown-ups stared at her in astonishment.

Finally, Adrienne had had enough too. Gary had been a wonderful chapter in her life, but it was closed. He was gone. Dead. Talking about him every night, especially talking about how things might have been different, was destroying her spirit. She stopped going to the Tedesco house.

Not long before she would have graduated from Montclair State, the school she had chosen so she could be close to Gary, she dropped out. Her parents tried to talk her out of it, but it was no use. Having lost what she had lost, she simply didn't care.

§

In the spring of 1966, the families of Peter Voto and Gary Tedesco settled their lawsuits against the owners of the Angel Lounge and the bartender, Nicholas Kayal. Voto's widow, Connie, got $73,000, plus $6,000 from the Borough of Lodi's insurance carrier.

Gary Tedesco's family got only $25,000; he was only a probationary officer, and he had not been supporting anyone. And because he was not yet a full-fledged member of the police force he was not covered under the borough policy, as Peter Voto had been.

The Tedesco family's lawyer was angry. He said Gary's family also deserved something from the borough; after all, Gary was on duty the night he died. The lawyer also said something that almost had to be said: maybe Gary Tedesco should not have been on real patrol duty. After all, he hadn't had much training. He wasn't even allowed to carry a gun.

Eventually, the Borough Council voted to award the Tedesco family $5,000.

§

Patrick Tedesco couldn't help his wife very much. His own grief was a weight too heavy to bear. He sat in the living room each night, crying and staring into space.

Patrick Tedesco was changing before the eyes of people who knew him. The strong, multidimensional man who was a big wheel in the school district and typed better than most secretaries and coached wrestling and did accounting and wrote poetry—that man seemed to shrivel up. Each week, he seemed older.

From 1963 on, Patrick Tedesco went through his days like a robot. He had one consuming interest: the death penalty. He spoke in favor of it, to public gatherings and to tiny groups, to anyone who would listen.

At dinnertime, he seemed to be gazing into a black pit. Which he was, in a way. Nowadays, the doctors would call it depression. It was destroying him.

Holidays were the worst. Sadie Tedesco wore black. She never stopped mourning the son she loved more than anyone or anything on this earth. Patrick could do nothing to cheer her. Nor could he save himself. Patrick Tedesco died of a heart attack in 1971. No one who knew him doubts that he died before his time.

§

Michael Serpone was no fool. He knew what people were saying: If he'd gotten to the Angel Lounge sooner, Peter Voto and Gary Tedesco might still be alive. A minute, just one minute, might have made a difference.

Or maybe he should have been at the Angel with Pete Voto in the first place. His cousin Gary Tedesco was unarmed and inexperienced. Maybe the arrest at the ice cream store had made Gary overconfident.

Michael Serpone was thirty-three that summer of 1963, old enough and experienced enough not to let his guard down. If *he'd* been with Pete at the Angel, he might have known enough to call for backup right away. He might have reacted more quickly than Gary did, might not have gone through the door when he saw Pete in trouble.

Serpone, after all, carried a gun. He might have fired fast enough to kill both Trantino and Falco. Or he might have killed one of them and made the other give up. Or he might have run back to the patrol car, radioed headquarters, then used the car for cover.

Or maybe he and not his young cousin Gary would have died in the Angel Lounge with Pete Voto. Maybe everyone would have been better off. Serpone thought these things more and more as the months went by.

Michael Serpone had become a policeman not because he liked to wear the uniform or carry the gun, but because he was a man who enjoyed being with people, enjoyed helping them. One look at an old photograph shows that. His smile is wide and friendly, dominating his face.

The picture was taken before August 26, 1963. Afterward, he never smiled the same way again.

He had nightmares about the night at the Angel Lounge. His shoulders sagged. He began to dread going to police headquarters. He was filled with a fear that he would die before his time. His wife, Jennie, was alarmed. She was a nurse, and she knew that her husband could not go on like that.

He spent many hours with psychiatrists. He checked himself into a mental health clinic in Somerset County in 1965. He underwent electric-shock treatments. They did not help.

"Mr. Serpone has been suffering from a nervous disorder consisting of recurring attacks of anxiety, light-headedness, dizziness, periods of fear of loss of consciousness and occasional attacks of inability to breathe," a psychiatrist wrote in 1967.

Once strong and athletic, he grew obese. He suffered from hypertension and diabetes. "He just lost all incentive," his wife recalled later. "He would sit at the dining room table, looking out the window for hours."

He stopped seeing his friends. He was afraid of going out of the house, even to take short walks. He was well short of his fortieth birthday when the New Jersey Police and Fireman's Pension Board granted him early retirement in 1968.

Years went by. Michael Serpone spent them huddled in his bedroom, terrified when his wife ventured outside. He was freed of his dreams and his demons on April 21, 1979. Dead of a heart attack at forty-nine, Michael Serpone was another victim of the Angel Lounge.

CHAPTER **32**

How Can
This Be?

As Michael Serpone was enduring his final months virtually forgotten except by his family and a few friends, an article appeared on the local-news page of the *Record.* "Parole Date Near for 2 Cops' Killer," the headline read on January 25, 1979.

> Thomas Trantino, convicted of murdering two Lodi policemen outside a nightclub 15 years ago, will be eligible for parole in March, the state parole board said yesterday.

The article, accompanied by a photograph of the mod-haired Trantino, went on to say that Trantino had led the two victims outside the bar, forced them to disrobe, then shot them at point-blank range.

In that respect, of course, the article was inaccurate. It implied that Trantino had exercised more cold-blooded, sadistic calculation than he had actually shown (or perhaps even been capable of) on the night of the slayings.

The errors were understandable enough. The earliest accounts of the Angel Lounge killings were available only on microfilm. Besides, the legend of the Angel Lounge had been told and retold so many times that it was hard to separate fact from fiction. One way to do that would have been to read the trial transcript, which, to judge from the coverage, no journalist bothered to do.

§

A "life" sentence did not really mean life behind bars.

That was the bitter message to the people of Lodi in early 1979. The man who should have gone to the electric chair for snuffing out two lives could be considered for parole after serving about fifteen and a half years in prison. Trantino was eligible for time off for good behavior and work credits.

One reason that parole was now a possibility lay in the original charges. There was only one count in the indictment that accused him of killing both Peter Voto and Gary Tedesco. It was not clear, years later, why there was one count and not two separate counts. One explanation is that a condemned prisoner could be executed only once. Another is that Guy Calissi, unsure he could prove that Trantino had killed both Voto and Tedesco, had crafted the indictment to allow for conviction if the jurors thought Trantino had killed *either* Voto or Tedesco, or both men.

It was a technicality, but a crucial one. It precluded the possibility of sentencing Trantino to consecutive life terms, which would have put parole on a more distant horizon.

In Lodi, the Angel Lounge killings seemed like yesterday. Each year on the anniversary of the crime, a wreath was placed on a memorial to Peter Voto and Gary Tedesco in a borough park.

Andy Voto had survived the rough and tumble of local politics and had risen to deputy police chief. He and Matty were happily married. Their children were healthy. Yet the years had not diminished Andy's sense of loss. Try as they would around holiday time, the Voto family—Andy and Matty and Peter's wife and children—could not hide from their sorrow. There was an emptiness at Christmas, at Thanksgiving, on anniversaries and birthdays.

The rift between Andy and his father had narrowed since 1963, when Andy told Genarro that he couldn't take revenge no matter how much he wanted to, but it remained nonetheless. It was there until the moment the father died in 1977.

§

Trantino remained at the state prison at Leesburg, where he had been transferred after the butcher-knife incident at Rahway, until early 1977, when he was moved back to Trenton. In the summer of 1978, he was moved to the prison at Yardville.

The January 1979 *Record* article noted that he had picked up a second nickname. Fellow inmates called him "Natural High" because of his hyperactive personality. There was no hint of remorse.

With little fanfare, Trantino was denied parole that first time. The people in Lodi were relieved. How could the man who had done the unspeakable thing at the Angel Lounge be close to freedom? Less than sixteen years had gone by, for God's sake!

§

Trantino's next parole hearing was set for March 10, 1980. This time around, the people in Lodi wrote letters to the parole board urging that Trantino be kept in prison.

More significantly, the Bergen County prosecutor, Roger W. Breslin Jr., said parole should be denied. Trantino hadn't served enough time, given the heinous nature of the crime, the prosecutor said. The same *Record* article that reported Roger Breslin's stand said this about the fatal night at the Angel Lounge: "Trantino, fearing Voto and Tedesco might connect him to the Brooklyn robbery, led the two outside the nightspot. There the two officers were forced to strip and shot point-blank with a revolver."

Thus, a newspaper account had picked up—and perpetuated—errors from an earlier article. It would not be the last time.

By now, Andy Voto was chief of police. He had many friends in Lodi, of course, and friends among the police throughout Bergen County. "This man was sentenced to death by twelve people," he reminded everyone.

In April 1980, Trantino was denied parole again. The same month, the New Jersey legislature enacted a new criminal code. Responding to the growing power of the movement for victims' rights, the lawmakers decreed that restitution could be set as a condition for parole. Very soon, lawyers and laymen alike would wrestle with the issue of restitution.

Because of this new wrinkle in the law, Trantino was granted a hearing on the issue of restitution. It was scheduled for September 23, 1980, before Superior Court judge Theodore W. Trautwein in Hackensack.

A rally by police was planned for the same day. One of the rally organizers was a police lieutenant from Paramus. His name was Joseph Delaney.

Like all cops, Joe Delaney had seen a lot of terrible things. But as he would tell it later, nothing was as bad as what he experienced as a young patrolman on the early morning of August 26, 1963.

§

Joe Delaney was in a patrol car about five miles away when he picked up a lot of radio traffic about a shooting at the Angel Lounge. He drove there as fast as he could, arriving just after the Lodi cops.

Delaney rushed inside. A smell filled his nose. The floor of the Angel Lounge looked as though someone had spilled a gallon can of bright red paint. He saw the bodies on the floor. The younger, smaller man was in his underwear. How odd . . .

Too late, Delaney realized he should have walked in more carefully, because blood is slippery. His feet went out from under him, but he didn't just fall. His momentum sent him on a long slide across the slick floor. He could feel the blood soaking through his trousers. He had to stop, so he put his hands out in front of him, hoping to grab onto something.

Just then, the big man on the floor managed to sit up. *Oh, he's not dead,* Joe Delaney thought. But Delaney's outstretched hands jammed into Peter Voto's face, causing Voto's head to snap back and strike a table leg with terrible force. *I just killed him,* Delaney thought.

He tried to scream his sorrow, but the scream wouldn't come out right. The sound died in the pillow in the middle of the night.

In his first moments awake, Joe Delaney would lie in the dark, waiting for his heartbeat to slow, trying to sort out what was real and what was dream. It always took him several seconds to get it straight. The slide across the floor was imagination. But he really had seen the bodies on the floor. "I didn't recognize Peter at all, and I *knew* Peter," he said a long time afterward.

But more than the sight stayed with him. "I don't know if you've ever smelled death," he said years later, after the nightmares had finally stopped. "It's a distinct odor. You know it the moment you smell it. It sticks to the hairs of your nose. My mouth gets dry even now, talking about it."

The memory spurred Delaney to start an organization called Police and Civilians Together. Its main purpose was to keep killers who had originally been sentenced to death, or to life in prison, behind bars forever. Not only was Delaney's group able to flood the offices of legislators with letters, but whenever there was a possibility of parole for Thomas Trantino, it was able to marshal hundreds of people for public protests—to great effect.

§

"Kill! Kill! Kill!"

The chant echoed around Roger Lowenstein as he threaded his way through the crowd around the Bergen County Courthouse in Hackensack. He saw police sharpshooters on the courthouse roof. It was the morning of September 23, 1980, and police officers had shown up by the hundreds to vent their hate for Thomas Trantino.

One cop carried a sign that expressed the feelings of all: "The only way Thomas Trantino will be able to make restitution is by dying."

Lowenstein's friend and colleague Leonard Weinglass was otherwise occupied with anti-establishment causes, and Jeffrey Fogel couldn't spend all his time on the Trantino case. So it was Roger's turn.

It was known that the parole board was leaning toward freedom for Trantino, likely by a vote of three to two. The law seemed to call for it, no matter what the public felt. The amount of restitution seemed to be the only thing standing between him and freedom.

Lowenstein noticed that some marchers carried copies of the front page of the *Record* from August 26, 1963, with the headline that would be remembered forever: "Two Policemen Slain in Lodi."

It was strange, the turns that life took. Roger Lowenstein remembered where he was on the day of the Angel Lounge killings. The student-body president at the University of Michigan, he was in Washington for the civil-rights rally that would culminate in a huge gathering in front of the Lincoln Memorial. He tried to persuade some friendly black shoeshine men to join in. The shoeshine men worked at the Capitol of the greatest nation in the free world, in a city that was still very southern. The injustice of it all bothered Roger Lowenstein, who was majoring in English and philosophy and minoring in social protest.

And yet, for all the injustice that Roger Lowenstein saw in the world, the summer of 1963 was a heady time. He had met John F. Kennedy that summer and had invited him on behalf of the student body to speak at commencement in 1964. Lowenstein was thrilled when the president said yes.

On August 28, 1963, Roger Lowenstein heard Martin Luther King Jr.'s "I Have a Dream" speech. He was moved deep in his heart. He had been a witness to history.

On that very day, Frank Falco was shot to death and Thomas Trantino surrendered to the police. And here Lowenstein was, all these years later, sitting in a Hackensack courtroom next to a man in his early forties who had such an unremarkable appearance and was hated so much. How strange . . .

Lowenstein the lawyer was duty-bound to do his best for Thomas Trantino, and he had no ambivalence about that. But Roger Lowenstein the man felt sorry for the survivors of Peter Voto and Gary Tedesco, who had come to court this day to tell what the crime had done to them.

The families told the court how they felt about getting money from the killer. Peter Voto's relatives "would waive any and all compensation if Mr. Trantino could stay just where he is," said a lawyer for the family.

Did the Tedesco family feel the same way? "Absolutely," Gary's sister Elaine said. For years, she had been in therapy, having spent some $14,000 by 1980.

Connie Voto told how she and her husband had built their own home, how he had worked a second job at a funeral home (the one that would bury him) to make ends meet. "He was just the best father in the world," she said.

Patricia Tedesco testified. "I was eleven when Gary died," she said. "I became an adult at the age of eleven. I lost all my childhood."

Patricia's sister, Elaine, told how their father, Patrick, had cried almost every night and had ceased caring about much of anything except revenge and capital punishment in the last eight years of his life.

A young boy when his father died, Jerry Voto was bitter and angry for a time. He had problems in school. Then he had problems fulfilling his dream of becoming a police officer.

Though he finished eighth out of sixty who took a civil-service test for police openings in East Orange, New Jersey, he faced an obstacle. Because of what had happened to his father, East Orange officials told him that "they thought I might be overaggressive." So they were reluctant to hire him, doing so only after he agreed to extensive psychiatric exams to prove his fitness.

By 1980, Jerry's brother, Peter, was living in Florida with his mother. "I was very, very close to my father," he said. "I didn't know what was happening." His childhood had ended in 1963, when instead of going fishing with his father he had stood crying in the light of a new day.

Trantino's was the first murder case in the United States in which restitution was considered as a condition for parole. And as long as restitution was the subject, the lives of Peter Voto and Gary Tedesco had to be weighed in terms of money.

Peter Voto's life was worth more. An actuary testified that Voto's family lost $380,000, based on his age when he died (forty) and the probability that he would have been promoted to lieutenant.

The financial loss to the Tedesco family was placed at $92,571 by the same actuary. Gary was only a probationary patrolman when he died, and Chief Andrew Voto noted that none of the officers who became patrolmen at the time of Gary's impending appointment had been promoted.

To some people, it was unsettling, even repugnant, to evaluate human life in terms of money—although it is done routinely in civil cases. Lowenstein questioned the very legality of making restitution a condition for parole. "No one can bring back the deceased or equate it with dollars," he said. His syntax had swerved off course, but no one disagreed with him.

On December 1, 1980, the parole board voted, three to two, to parole Trantino on the condition that he make restitution. Writing for the majority, Chairman Christopher Dietz conceded that the defendant had committed "the most egregious of crimes," but said he had shown "steady and convincing improvement" in prison.

A dissenter, Gloria Soto, noted unfavorable psychological evaluations. "One cannot help wonder just how much anger is festering inside Mr. Trantino," she wrote, "and when that anger will erupt."

Trantino had been granted his freedom, sort of. But there was a big complication: Judge Trautwein had simply refused to set an amount for restitution. To do so, he had said on October 2, would be "demeaning" to the victims and their families.

Mug shots of Thomas Trantino, taken shortly after the Angel Lounge killings.
Courtesy of the Record

Rahway State Prison.
Courtesy of the Record

A much-changed Thomas Trantino in 1973, when he was interviewed in prison for an article in the Sunday magazine of the *Record*. The article infuriated police officers and many other people in New Jersey, as did Trantino's apparent cockiness. *Courtesy of the* Record

Judge Theodore Trautwein, who refused to set an amount for Trantino to pay as restitution, thus stalling his release from prison.
Courtesy of the Record

Thomas Trantino testifies at his parole hearing in September 1980, declaring that he is penniless.
Courtesy of the Record

Thomas Trantino at the minimum-security Wharton Tract work camp in December 1980. Many people were infuriated by his being allowed to live more as an employee than as an inmate. *Courtesy of the* Record

Judge Sylvia Pressler, who saw something very wrong in the handling of Trantino's case and said so in an eloquent dissent in 1997.
Courtesy of the Record

Thomas Trantino, shown in June 1999 in South Woods State Prison in Cumberland County, New Jersey, reflects on his latest court setback.
Courtesy of the author

Roger Lowenstein argues on behalf of Thomas Trantino before the New Jersey Supreme Court on September 25, 2000.
Courtesy of the Record

On August 22, 2000, four days before the thirty-seventh anniversary of the
Angel Lounge killings, a ceremony was held next to the Lodi municipal building
for the signing of a bill meant to keep murderers in prison for life. The eagle in
the background sits atop a monument to Peter Voto and Gary Tedesco.
Courtesy of the Record

Gary Tedesco's sister, Elaine
Harvey, finds the ceremony
too much to bear.
Courtesy of the Record

Sadie Tedesco, Gary's mother, reacts with dismay in January 2001 to the news that Thomas Trantino will soon be paroled. *Courtesy of the* Record

For Andy Voto, the news of Thomas Trantino's impending parole is a bitter defeat. *Courtesy of the* Record

Out of prison at last, Thomas Trantino prepares to enter a Camden halfway house, the gateway to his eventual freedom.
Courtesy of the Record

A man protests outside the Hope House halfway facility after Thomas Trantino is placed there.
Courtesy of the Record

CHAPTER 33

Held Hostage

In effect, Judge Trautwein was holding Thomas Trantino and the parole board hostage.

The Appellate Division of Superior Court was expected to rule on December 24, 1980, on the parole board's appeal of the judge's refusal to set an amount that Trantino should pay. But would the higher court order Trautwein to set an amount? And what would happen if the judge simply refused, again? This was new legal territory.

"The sooner I am released, the sooner I can be gainfully employed," Trantino wrote to the Appellate Division. As long as he was in prison, he couldn't earn money to make the restitution that Judge Trautwein refused to set and the Voto and Tedesco families didn't want anyway.

Trantino, by this time at a minimum-security work camp at Wharton State Forest, promised, if released, to turn over most of his earnings to the state for forwarding to the Voto and Tedesco families, who could do what they wished with it. He would keep only enough to live on.

"The Tommy Trantino who was sentenced to death was a twenty-five-year-old punk, a drug addict, a person out of control," he said in an affidavit, apparently forgetting that he had turned twenty-six by the time he was sentenced. "That Tommy Trantino is dead. . . . I simply want to leave New Jersey and live my life quietly."

Of course, if the parole board chose to, it could simply order Trantino's release at once and let the courts settle the restitution issue in their own good time. That was what Roger Lowenstein said should happen.

"This situation is especially poignant," Lowenstein argued in a brief. "An indigent inmate expresses a willingness to make restitution if and when a court orders it. There is no purpose being served by Trantino remaining in prison while the courts decide the matter."

The parole board disagreed. It said that freeing Trantino immediately, before the question of restitution was settled, would undermine its authority. The board asserted that restitution was a means to reduce the risk that a released inmate would commit new crimes.

If that logic was hard to follow, so was the entire episode by this time. Lowenstein argued that restitution should be a requirement *after* Trantino was released, not an impossible condition *for* release. Angry and frustrated as the case was heard by three judges from the Appellate Division late in 1980, the lawyer said Trantino was still confined "because people don't like him."

"No," one of the judges shot back. "He's in jail because he murdered two people."

On Christmas Eve, the three-judge panel decreed that Trantino should stay put until the restitution issue was settled. The judges scheduled a hearing for January 28, 1981. Lowenstein asked the New Jersey Supreme Court to release his client in the meantime. No, the high court said.

Trantino's anger boiled over. In a telephone interview, he complained of "Jersey justice." He said he had been "railroaded."

"This is my eighteenth Christmas in prison," he said, "and it's beginning to look like they want me to stay in for another eighteen."

No. Some people wanted him to stay in forever.

§

No politician had to think much in deciding what position to take on the Trantino case.

Early in January 1981, State Senator John Skevin called for an inquiry into whether the parole board's chairman, Christopher Dietz, was "predisposed toward leniency" in voting for Trantino's parole.

Skevin noted that Dietz had served as assistant counsel to Governor Richard J. Hughes, who had granted Trantino several stays of execution. Dietz said he had never discussed the Trantino case with Governor Hughes.

Nor was Hughes soft on crime. In signing stays of execution, he was merely doing what he had to do as appeals dragged on.

No matter. Since Lodi was in John Skevin's district, he could hardly keep quiet about the Trantino case. He knew he would lose no votes by condemning Trantino and anyone who seemed remotely sympathetic to him.

So Skevin asked Attorney General John Degnan to study all the paperwork by Dietz and other state officials during the time (less than two years) Dietz had worked under Governor Hughes. Soon, Skevin asked for a bigger inquiry, into the entire parole operation. (There had been several notorious instances of prisoners' being paroled only to commit new crimes.)

Dietz said the parole board simply followed the guidelines when deciding whether to grant parole—guidelines set by the very lawmakers who were complaining about the parole system.

And Attorney General John Degnan was in an awkward position. In a letter written to the parole board on October 17, 1980, Degnan himself had taken a public stand against parole for Trantino, a highly unusual move for the state's chief law enforcement officer. So how could his office represent and advise the parole board? From now on, Degnan told the board on January 6, 1981, it should get outside counsel.

The Appellate Division hearing, originally set for January 28, was put off until February 11.

§

On February 11 (Trantino's forty-third birthday), the parole board asked a panel of three judges in Trenton to set an amount for restitution and end the impasse. Roger McGlynn, the outside attorney retained by the board, said it might be hard to determine the amount.

If it were, say, a million dollars, it would be beyond Trantino's ability to pay. In that case, regular installments within his reach would be appropriate. "If he hits the sweepstakes or something, that would make a difference," the lawyer said.

But one of Trantino's lawyers, Donald Friedman, who was associated with Lowenstein, Weinglass, et al., argued for immediate release, and never mind restitution. He said Trantino was "a fully rehabilitated artist, author, teacher, and counselor, a man described by a state psychiatrist as a candidate for sainthood."

Reading those words years later, one has to wonder what he was thinking. Had Friedman dared to utter such hyperbole on a street in Lodi, he might have been in physical danger. In a Trenton courtroom, he merely subjected himself to sharp questioning.

It seemed to Judge Morton Greenberg that in ordering restitution as well as release, the parole board had meant to deter Trantino from future crimes. "If you have a guy who won't even acknowledge what he did, how can you show that there's no substantial likelihood of committing a fresh crime?" the judge asked.

Or just suppose Trantino really did believe he wasn't responsible for the horror in the Angel Lounge, the judge went on. "Every time he writes a check, he's going to view it as an act of extortion."

· Just sixteen days after hearing arguments, the three judges issued their decision. They held, unanimously, that the parole board could not make restitution a condition for parole in cases involving death or injury. Relying on previous court interpretations, the judges said restitution was applicable only in cases of *property* damage or loss.

Therefore, the three judges said, Judge Trautwein had been right in refusing to set an amount for restitution. But the judges said the parole board had been correct in finding that Trantino could not be paroled if restitution could not be ordered.

The panel of judges seemed to have erected an insurmountable barrier for Trantino. Perhaps that was their intention. "It is perfectly obvious that Trantino is not entitled to be released at this time," the judges wrote. "If the board had known that the condition [restitution] could not be imposed, it is quite possible it would not have ordered his release ... "

The judges said the parole board should meet yet again to consider whether Trantino should be granted parole. But their ruling made it difficult indeed to figure out just what the defendant would have to do to win his freedom. And it seemed highly unlikely that the parole board would choose on its own to release Trantino, given the intense public pressure and the tone of the judges' decision.

§

About eight weeks later, state corrections commissioner William Fauver defended the controversial parole law before New Jersey legislators during Senator John Skevin's continuing inquiry into the state's parole system. "Some decisions have been made by the board that have become unpopular with the public," he conceded. But overall, he said, the new system was good.

By this time, the furor over Thomas Trantino had called attention to another crucial aspect of the new law: no longer did a prisoner have to prove (as he had under the old system) that he was ready for parole. Rather, a prisoner was supposed to be eligible for parole once he had served a designated minimum sentence—unless the state could show a "substantial likelihood" that he would revert to his unlawful ways.

In other words, the burden of proof had been reversed. It was now up to the state to show that a prisoner should not be paroled. Senator Skevin didn't like this new feature a bit and said he would try to change it.

But some experts on crime and punishment had long argued that consistency and predictability in sentencing were good, that prisoners should be able to know that they would be free in, say, fifteen years, if they behaved. A lot of people, if they thought about it calmly, might agree that it was healthy for convicts to have hope. Without it, anger and despair ruled the cellblocks.

Or rather, a lot of people might concede that *most* prisoners should be able to see something on the horizon. But no one dared say that about Thomas Trantino. "A life sentence must mean life in prison," one witness told Skevin's subcommittee. The speaker was Elaine Harvey, Gary Tedesco's sister.

What's more, two members of the parole board itself attacked the new system, saying that it might make it harder to keep lawbreakers behind bars. "If we look at a man's record or something else and say we'd like to keep him in a little longer, we can't—as long as he has done enough time," Gloria Soto told the Skevin committee. Her words carried extra weight because of her years as a public defender.

And the public mood had changed during Trantino's time in captivity. Executions had resumed in the United States. At first, they were carried out almost exclusively in the deep South, but opinion-pollers found nationwide sentiment supporting the death penalty. To many people in New Jersey, it was a disgrace that Thomas Trantino was alive and eating three square meals a day when a few cents' worth of electric current would have disposed of him years before.

So it was all but inevitable that the state's highest court would hear the case. This, after all, was the first supreme test of the parole board's power to require restitution as a condition for parole.

On June 4, 1981, the New Jersey Supreme Court agreed to hear the case. It was put on the court calendar for mid-December. By the time it was heard, Trantino had infuriated people yet again.

CHAPTER 34

Feeling Close
to Freedom

He loved the outdoors. That much was clear from the way he flexed and strutted in his thermal vest, the way he swung an ax, the way he talked about planting vegetables.

He lived in a spare but comfortable trailer in a work camp. He was a cheerful man as he spoke of "my intellectual spirit and my spiritual growth."

He had embraced life as never before. "There's hope for every man," he said solemnly. This newfound purpose and optimism helped to explain his opposition to capital punishment. "It's murder," he said.

This new, Paul Bunyan-like Trantino was shown to the world by a New York City television station on the night of December 6, 1981, just nine days before the New Jersey Supreme Court was to review his case. His airy musings on life and love were interspersed, to devastating effect, with grainy, black-and-white newsreel footage. There on the old film was Adrienne Peraino, near collapse as Gary Tedesco was about to be lowered into the earth. And there was a younger Andy Voto, barely holding himself together at his brother's funeral.

Some television viewers might have wondered if Thomas Trantino's antipathy to the death penalty was related to his brush with the electric chair. They also may have wondered what the hell Trantino was doing living in a trailer instead of in a prison cell. In fact, his quarters at the Wharton Tract, a minimum-security work camp in the Pine Barrens of South Jersey, were more like a hunting or fishing cabin than a cell.

The Angel Lounge killer had put thoughts of death behind him. He expected to be a free man soon, once the lawyers straightened out that stuff about restitution. And he had so much to look forward to!

"Love came into my life and made my life really blossom," he said.

The woman in Trantino's life was Charlee Irene Ganny, the ex-wife of Jeff Fogel. She had actually been part of Trantino's life for the better part of a decade, as readers of the 1973 article in the *Record* were aware, and had married him in August 1980.

Just as it was not lost on the readers of the *Record* in 1973 that Trantino's heart had more room for his dreams than it did for remorse, many who saw the television broadcast of December 6, 1981, must have come to the same conclusion. If Trantino felt any sorrow for what he had done, he did not express it. For a man who called himself a writer, he seemed to have no idea how he sounded.

Nor could he keep his mouth shut. "My mind is not locked up in prison," he told an interviewer the following March. It was almost spring, and Tom Trantino was looking forward to planting. He boasted of the quarter-acre plot he helped to tend. It supplied Wharton with fresh vegetables. "We also have a terrific flower garden," he said.

He considered himself a nurturer in other ways, too. He counseled inmates with drug and alcohol problems. He had been there himself, after all.

§

A Washington lawyer heard about the true-life love story of the convicted murderer and his former lawyer's former wife. The lawyer had some contacts in the movie business and mentioned the case to them. Nothing came of the idea, but the Washington lawyer's partner, Stuart Pierson, grew interested in the case.

Pierson had been a federal prosecutor in Seattle in the early 1970s, and he had worked in the Justice Department's Civil Rights Division. By the 1980s, he was a criminal-defense lawyer in Washington.

No soft touch, Pierson thought Trantino had done a terrible thing. But as he learned more and more about the details, he realized that what had really happened in the Angel Lounge—horrible though it was—was not as legend had it. So, although white-collar crime was more his staple than barroom killings, Pierson got involved in Trantino's case.

§

"Mr. Trantino has agreed to satisfy any condition within his power," Pierson told the New Jersey Supreme Court on December 15, 1981. He contended that his client was being held illegally and ought to be freed at once until the parole board and the courts could make up their collective mind about restitution.

Roger McGlynn, the parole board's lawyer, asked the justices to ratify the basic concept of restitution. If they chose not to, McGlynn said, perhaps some other requirement could be laid down. Perhaps Trantino could donate some of his free time to charity.

On May 20, 1982, the New Jersey Supreme Court unanimously upheld for the first time the concept of restitution for violent crimes, including Trantino's.

The court specified that the parole board had to apply a two-pronged standard in deciding an applicant's fitness for parole: whether the inmate had been rehabilitated, and whether he was likely to return to crime. The court said the sufficiency of punishment *could not* be considered independently, but only as a component of rehabilitation.

In layman's terms, the court seemed to be saying that the more serious the crime, the more severe the punishment might have to be to reform the prisoner.

The justices called the Angel Lounge crime "cold-bloodedly vicious and wantonly brutal." In view of that, they continued, the parole board had to consider "most scrupulously and conscientiously" whether Trantino had been punished enough for the board "to conclude with confidence that he has been rehabilitated and will not commit future crimes."

Hard as it might be for the citizenry to understand or accept, punishment *for its own sake* was not supposed to be part of the equation. The court went on to say that public outrage over a crime should have no weight in a parole decision.

Trantino continued to deny killing anyone, or to deny that he could remember killing anyone. It was hard to tell which.

The high court cited the lack of contrition and the resentment of authority that had been noted by the parole board's dissenters. Given all that, Justice Alan B. Handler wrote, "it is hard to imagine that Trantino has been sufficiently punished to be considered rehabilitated."

§

In the third week of September 1982, the parole board held a special two-day hearing on the issue of parole for Trantino. On the eve of the first session, held in Hackensack, the acting Bergen County prosecutor, Richard T. Carley, said he opposed parole for Trantino. So did several other Bergen County politicians.

Andy Voto's sense of loss had not diminished. "Trantino is a burglar, a thief and junkie, a career criminal," the Lodi police chief testified. "I am never going to stop trying to keep him in jail."

Gary Tedesco's sister Patricia also appeared. So did Jerry Voto, Peter's son. And Elaine Harvey, Gary's other sister, was there. She spoke not only for her lost brother but for the cause to which she had devoted much of her time and energy since his death. "This case is a big step toward victims' rights," she said. "Maybe we won't get the justice we want, but maybe we'll make it safe for the next family."

The next day's session, at the Yardville prison in Mercer County, was very brief. No one showed up. The full board was to meet again four weeks later at Yardville.

§

The day of the full board meeting, October 21, 1982, was one of the most important in his life, and Tom Trantino dressed for it. He put on a white shirt and brown tweed pants. For four hours, he pleaded his case before the seven people on the parole board, then sat in a waiting room for another three hours while the board deliberated.

Nervously, he pursed his lips. Freedom was close. He could sense it. After all, it was almost two years since the board had told him he could get out if he made restitution . . .

The board voted five to two to deny parole. The majority imposed a "future eligibility term" of ten years, which was not quite as bad as it sounded for Trantino. The jargon meant that, assuming time off for good behavior and work credits, he might be eligible for parole again in six years' time, in 1988.

Shattered, Trantino sank into his chair, shaking his head in disbelief.

The board declined to say who had voted how. Dietz said the board would give a written, detailed explanation for its decision within thirty days. But he felt obliged to make a brief statement immediately. "It would be unfair to say Mr. Trantino has not consciously tried to change," the chairman said. "Obviously, the board felt more time is needed."

But that comment raised an unsettling question. If Trantino had served enough time in 1979 or 1980, when his release seemed imminent, how could he need to do more time by 1982?

The parole board's written explanation in late November declared that there were "psychopathic" elements to his personality and "a serious concern as to Mr. Trantino's ability to deal with the stress of everyday life" in a society from which he had been isolated for a long time.

The explanation did not really clear things up, at least for anyone who could remember two years back. In 1980, board members had cited thorough psychological evaluations in declaring that Trantino was unlikely to commit new crimes if released.

That day in November 1982 produced an extraordinary admission. Christopher Dietz acknowledged regret at how the board had just handled the Trantino case. He said it was "unforgivable" how the board's five-to-two majority had stressed the negative in Trantino's personality while virtually omitting the positive aspects of his psychological evaluation. Dietz's views, which he shared with New Jersey newspapers, showed how he had agonized. In 1980, he had voted to grant parole to Trantino. In 1982, he switched his vote—the only board member to do so.

As 1982 drew to a close, the New Jersey public television network became very interested in the case. The parole board's back-and-forth stance had caught its attention, as had Trantino's predicament of having been "caught in the cracks between the old and new parole laws," as one network official put it.

True enough, Trantino was in a legal limbo of sorts. But in a way, he could take grim comfort from the board's latest decree. In another five years or so, by 1988, he would have done twenty-five. That ought to make him a cinch for parole, under the old code or the new one. Surely the state would run out of reasons to keep him locked up.

Of course, he preferred not to wait that long. On December 2, 1982, Stuart Pierson said he would appeal the denial of parole on grounds that the board had acted unfairly and illegally.

The public television program, scheduled for that very night, was postponed for a week in deference to the Voto family. Peter Voto's widow, Constance, who had suffered a stroke the year before, had died during open-heart surgery. She was fifty-seven. Her funeral was on December 3.

§

The public television program infuriated people in Lodi even before it went on the air. The producers had chosen not to contact the Voto and Tedesco families, prompting the New Jersey General Assembly to pass a resolution expressing its "disappointment."

Nor had Trantino improved his public relations skills. Far from appearing contrite, he asserted that his accomplice, Frank Falco, was unarmed when he was "executed" by the police. He complained that Falco's executioners had never been brought to trial.

The police were apoplectic. Joseph Delaney, by now police chief in Paramus, complained that the show was one-sided. More important for Trantino, Delaney headed a committee of area police officials who were looking into the parole deliberations, particularly Christopher Dietz's remarks.

Law enforcement people had long complained that Trantino had it too easy in the relatively unsupervised Wharton Tract. Corrections officials finally got the message. In December 1982, Trantino was reclassified as a maximum-security inmate. He was taken from the Wharton Tract and sent to the Yardville Correction Center. He was back behind walls and bars, in a real prison.

On April 25, 1983, an appellate court unanimously rejected Trantino's appeal of the previous December.

§

And then it was August again, twenty years since the night at the Angel Lounge.

State Senator Frank Graves, a Democrat from Paterson, proposed a bill aimed at those twenty-two murderers who had escaped the electric chair when the New Jersey Supreme Court overturned the death penalty.

Only nine of the twenty-two were still in prison. Graves's bill was simple: it would keep the reprieved killers in prison until they died. Many legal experts said it would be unconstitutional to round up those who had already been freed and haul them back to prison. Graves wasn't ready to concede that point, and as for the nine men still in prison—well, throw away the key.

The bill died on the vine, but not before reminding people of the nine prisoners who should have gone to the electric chair but didn't. One of the nine, of course, was Thomas Trantino.

§

Three days before Christmas 1983, Trantino took his case to federal court again. He was trying to overturn the 1982 New Jersey Supreme Court decision that had upheld the concept of restitution while instructing the parole board to reconsider whether he had been punished enough. The suit was filed by Stuart Pierson, assisted by the New Jersey branch of the ACLU. The suit asserted that the state court had misinterpreted the new parole law, perhaps intentionally.

Trantino now took responsibility for the Angel Lounge killings, Pierson said, even though "he doesn't remember pulling the trigger, and he doesn't try to remember."

Trantino's lawyers said the parole board had been subjected to great pressure. But Christopher Dietz insisted that "at no point in the board's history has it ever been subjected to outside pressure."

Considering all that had happened, the chairman's statement was astounding. But Frederick B. Lacey, a federal judge, did not think so. On July 11, 1984, he dismissed the suit Trantino had filed with the help of the ACLU. He said it was "absurd" to suggest that hostility toward Trantino pervaded New Jersey's judicial system.

The year ended with another setback for Trantino. Ruling on December 20 in a separate case, the New Jersey Supreme Court unanimously reaffirmed the right of prosecutors to appeal decisions granting parole. Should Trantino ever be freed, he could expect another fight.

CHAPTER 35

A Federal Case

Stuart Pierson was no defeatist. Still, he was pessimistic as he prepared to argue before Judge Frederick B. Lacey in federal court on February 4, 1985, that he ought to be given access to state documents and the right to question Chairman Christopher Dietz about the back-and-forth actions of the parole board.

Lacey was the very judge, after all, who the previous summer had tossed out the suit Pierson had filed with the help of the ACLU. In so doing, Lacey had ridiculed any suggestion that hostility toward Trantino pervaded the state courts.

Pierson did not contend that state officials had misinterpreted parole regulations. Instead, he tried a different tack, arguing for Trantino's release on grounds that he had been unfairly denied credits for good behavior.

The judge appeared skeptical of, even hostile to, that line of argument. And what about this whole restitution thing? "How, after you kill two people, do you make restitution?" the judge asked rhetorically. "How do you make compensation to a son whose father was killed?"

Lacey reserved decision, and Pierson left the courtroom without a lot of hope. He had long felt that defendants started with two strikes against them in federal court. After all, many district court judges had been United States attorneys—prosecutors—before being named to the bench. Pierson thought a lot of them presumed a defendant guilty until proven otherwise. Judge Lacey was a former United States attorney.

By this time, Pierson had become very troubled by the Trantino case. He thought Trantino deserved to pay a terrible price for his terrible deed, but he didn't think he should pay forever. After all, the law was the law, and the law said Trantino was eligible for parole.

As Pierson studied the record, he became convinced that New Jersey officials were bending the law to keep Trantino in prison. Pierson thought this set a terrible example for other convicts. "Unless a man thinks he has *some* chance to get out before he gets old," he asked one day, "why should he try to change?"

§

Roger Lowenstein, who had ceded the federal court aspect of the case to Pierson, winced whenever his client talked in public. He knew that Trantino's talk of a life with Charlee, with children and streams and ponds, just made things worse.

The sad irony was that such talk showed that Trantino was finally acquiring some self-esteem. Many men in prison have never had much of it. Though few politicians dare say it, it is not a bad thing for prisoners to acquire some, along with a respect for honest toil, assuming they are ever to live in the real world again.

§

Glenn Arterbridge was a supervisor at Riverfront State Prison in Camden, where Trantino spent several years beginning in the mid-1980s. "He did anything I asked," Arterbridge said of Trantino. "He was one of the very few inmates I trusted."

Arterbridge is in his fifties now, old enough to remember Trantino's crime. He is no bleeding-heart liberal; he believes in punishment as well as in rehabilitation. Yet he saw good in Tom Trantino. "You work with someone, you get to know him pretty well," he said.

Arterbridge saw Trantino throw his heart and his back into whatever he did—unloading trucks, moving things around the storeroom, digging ditches. But what impressed him more was the self-control Trantino showed as a counselor for other inmates, many younger than he was, some of them full of rage. Trantino took their abuse and came back for more, came back to help.

Was Trantino trying to atone for the great wrong he had done? He never said. Arterbridge never asked. "I could never get inside his head," Arterbridge said.

But Arterbridge was convinced he saw behind the shield well enough to know a few things. "I am positive he would never have allowed me to be hurt by other inmates," he said. "He would have been my wall. I had that confidence in the man." Yes, Arterbridge said, he would feel safe having Tom Trantino as a guest in his home.

And whatever his faults, this prisoner of Italian-Jewish heritage was no bigot, Arterbridge said: "Tom did not care about skin color." Arterbridge is black.

§

In late May 1985, Judge Lacey rejected Trantino's contention that his rights had been violated, and he refused to let Trantino's lawyers go fishing in government files. But, significantly, the judge said Trantino's argument that the parole board had caved in to public pressure was "not totally devoid of merit." If the board had indeed reacted to public pressure, it was wrong, the judge said.

Christopher Dietz again denied that the board had succumbed to pressure, but the judge ordered a hearing. The parole board members would have to explain themselves. And on September 19, they told just how intense the pressure had been. Luis Garcia, a parole board member since 1978, told Judge Lacey he was "taken aback" in 1980 when Attorney General John Degnan publicly urged that Trantino not be let out. What really made Garcia's jaw drop was the sight of a state trooper walking into a parole hearing in the autumn of 1980 to deliver Degnan's four-page letter.

On September 20, Dietz told Judge Lacey that he had been offended by Degnan's action "because it was so inappropriate." But the chairman said the board had not been swayed.

On September 30, Trantino got his say before Judge Lacey. Except for the shackles he wore into court, Trantino could have passed for a shopworker. He wore work clothes. The mod hair was gone, replaced with the trim look of the mid-1980s. He was graying a bit.

Trantino recalled a day in October 1980, when he was meeting with the two board members who had voted to release him, Garcia and Sally Carroll. "I felt it was a positive, good kind of hearing," Trantino testified.

Christopher Dietz was at that session in 1980, and Trantino recalled that the chairman left the room to take a telephone call from the attorney general's office. When Dietz returned, Trantino felt a sudden chill.

"See all these gray hairs on my head?" Dietz said. "They've all got Trantino's name on them." (Gray hairs or not, Dietz was in the three-to-two majority that voted in December 1980 to parole Trantino on the condition that he make restitution. He would reverse himself two years later.)

§

On December 30, 1985, Judge Lacey ruled that the board had not acted unfairly when it reversed the previous decision to parole Trantino. The judge said Trantino had failed to show that the board had buckled to improper influence. It was a crushing blow for the defense.

CHAPTER 36

Andy Voto's Evening

After his brother's death, Andy Voto went to work each day with a pain in his heart. He lived with it. He was a cop, after all, and though Thomas Trantino was an obsession whenever he came up for parole, Andy Voto had work to do.

In 1979, he was named Lodi's police chief. His first big task was a tough one: putting into effect the recommendations of a 1977 state police evaluation that found that the Lodi force needed to be better equipped and reorganized. (There was also the lingering embarrassment of a 1974 grand jury's criticism of Lodi's finest for using borough telephones to make personal calls—including 167 to an exotic dancer.)

By most accounts, Andy Voto did a creditable job of improving the department along the lines of the state police evaluation. And starting in 1980, he was able to do it from a comfortable office in the spanking new police headquarters. The ramshackle old headquarters, where Andy's brother and Gary Tedesco had reported for work so long ago, had been officially condemned before surrendering to the wrecking ball.

In late September 1985, Andy was just sitting down to dinner at his in-laws' house one Sunday afternoon when he got word that a deranged man was threatening the police with two knives outside his home in Wallington. Andy knew the man: a few months earlier, the guy had pulled a similar stunt when he lived in Lodi, and Andy had talked him into surrendering.

So Andy Voto left his Sunday meal and went to help out the police in Wallington. The knife-wielder recognized him at once. "You talked me out of it last time," the man said. "You're not going to this time."

The man had underestimated Andy Voto's powers of persuasion. After fifteen minutes of conversation, he gave up.

The months were running into years, and even the years were rushing by—faster and faster, it seemed. In 1986, Andy Voto turned sixty. He could hardly believe it.

And then it was August 26 again. At the memorial service in front of Borough Hall, Police Chief Andy Voto reflected on the past. The night his brother and Gary Tedesco died sure didn't seem like twenty-three years ago.

"It's yesterday," he said.

§

In the summer of 1989, nineteen of Thomas Trantino's paintings were displayed at a show in Manhattan's East Village. "They show a minor talent at work," one critic wrote.

"We don't need his art," Andy Voto sneered.

On a July night the following summer, Andy was at a rally of some five hundred people in Lodi. Trantino's parole was being discussed once again; it seemed the talk would never end. Many in the crowd wore stickers that said "Murder unspeakable, parole unthinkable."

Andy was pleased at the enthusiasm. He drew energy from it, which was a good thing, because Andy was starting to feel his age. He had suffered a stroke not long before, and he used a cane now.

Andy Voto turned sixty-five in the summer of 1991. He had had a good run, as a cop and as the top cop.

And then his days as a cop were over. His retirement dinner was held at a restaurant in Garfield that summer. About five hundred people came. Many were cops or retired cops. There was steak and pasta aplenty. Wine and good fellowship flowed. So did memories.

It was a wonderful evening for Andy Voto. If there was an edge of sadness, it was because his brother wasn't there.

CHAPTER 37

Too Late to
Be Sorry

The late 1980s were filled with frustration for Andy Voto's archenemy. He seemed no closer to freedom. If anything, he was further away.

Trantino was vice president of the Riverfront State Prison chapter of the Jaycees, and well established as a counselor for troubled youths at the prison in Camden. "I'm like a father to them," he said in 1986. "My life, I think, would've taken a different turn if I had people who would've reached out to me."

Trantino said again that he didn't remember the Angel Lounge crime. But on the twenty-third anniversary he expressed sympathy for the victims' relatives as they marked, in his words, "something that is very serious, and important, and depressing to them."

§

And suddenly, it was 1987. Perhaps Trantino would fare better with a slightly different parole board. Governor Thomas H. Kean, a Republican who had won reelection in a landslide in 1985, had installed a loyal Republican, former Somerset County sheriff Louis Nickolopoulos, as chairman in place of Christopher Dietz.

Trantino dared to hope for release late in the year. But in July, the Bergen County Prosecutor's Office expressed its concern, citing, in the words of first assistant prosecutor Dennis Calo, Trantino's "lack of remorse and refusal to accept responsibility for his crime."

Calo's boss, Bergen County Prosecutor Larry McClure, said, "It is our position that the mere passage of time, in and of itself, is not justification for parole."

Or maybe it was. The new parole law, which contained the restitution clause that had so thwarted Trantino, said a prisoner ought to be paroled if there were no strong indicators, or "substantial likelihood," that he would commit new crimes. So it could be argued that, in the absence of such indicators, the "mere passage of time" *was* justification.

In early November 1987, parole officials rejected two of Trantino's proposals for his life on the outside. Trantino said he and Charlee might live and work in Pennsylvania, where she owned property. No good, said parole officials; Pennsylvania parole authorities had declined to accept responsibility.

Well, then, maybe he could live with relatives in New Jersey. But that idea was no good either. The relatives had moved.

Soon thereafter, Trantino submitted a plan that did seem feasible. Parole officials refused to divulge its details out of concern for Trantino's safety. And on January 28, 1988, it was announced that Thomas Trantino would be paroled. He would walk out of Riverfront State Prison in Camden on March 15 to start a new life.

The parole board made its decision in a fairly routine way. The two members reviewing the case, Sally Carroll and Loren Ranton, had voted to let him go. (Typically, two of the members were assigned to review a case initially and, if they agreed, parole was granted, unless the case was so serious that the entire board wanted to review it. If the two split, a third member would be brought into the process, or the entire board might consider the application. Occasionally, a member would decline to take part in a case, perhaps because of some prior involvement.)

Board members were not required to explain their decisions. But the parole board's executive director, Robert Egles, reminded those who didn't know that the only reason board members could properly deny parole was a belief that there was a "substantial likelihood" that the prisoner would commit new crimes.

The Voto and Tedesco families were furious. Joseph Delaney's group, Police and Civilians Together, began a letter-writing campaign. Delaney himself planned a rally. He had plenty of help from other lawmen—including the Bergen County sheriff, Robert Herb. Speaking of Peter Voto and Gary Tedesco, Herb said, "They were degraded, and that shows an animal-type mentality."

He did not elaborate on what he meant by "degraded." People knew. Or thought they did.

In less sensational cases, two "yes" votes to parole are generally enough. But on February 2, 1988, it was disclosed that two other board members had requested a full review, which meant the entire board had to weigh the case.

The Trantino saga was the subject of Morton Downey Jr.'s talk show on WWOR-TV on Thursday, February 4. More than two hundred people, many of them police officers, crammed into the studio in Secaucus, New Jersey, for the taping. Andy Voto was there. So was Gary Tedesco's sister Elaine Harvey.

So was Joseph Delaney. "I do not understand how rational people can even consider letting him out after they heard the nature of the crime," Delaney said. He did not elaborate. He did not have to.

There was high emotion in the studio, but no argument. "This is the first time that I haven't brought someone in from the other side of an issue," Morton Downey Jr. said, "because there is no other side. They shouldn't let this animal out in the streets."

§

Temperatures fell to the low teens on the night of Friday, February 5. But more than 1,600 people came to the Lodi municipal complex for a rally.

"Trantino will never be paroled because we won't allow it," Congressman Robert Torricelli, a Democrat from Bergen County, said to loud cheering. "Our sense of justice won't allow it."

A few days after the rally, a Republican state senator from Bergen County, Henry P. McNamara, said he would push for a law barring parole for anyone convicted of murdering or attempting to murder a law enforcement officer. Grudgingly, McNamara accepted the reality that such a law could not be applied retroactively to Trantino. Nor could the state's new death-penalty law, enacted in 1982, which called for lethal injection or a minimum of thirty years in prison without parole for convicted murderers.

The parole board was inundated with calls, letters, and petitions. Governor Kean said that he had "very strong feelings" about the Trantino case, but that it would be inappropriate for him to elaborate before the board ruled. No one really doubted what the governor's feelings were.

And then it came out that, at last, Thomas Trantino was sorry for what he had done. Or at least he said he was. Late in February 1988, it was revealed that a psychological report the year before had found that Trantino "shows remorse for his crime and takes responsibility for it, despite an unclear recollection of the offense due to an alcoholic blackout." The same report called the prisoner a "fairly good risk" for parole.

Trantino wrote to the Bergen County prosecutor, Larry McClure, expressing his "complete, unequivocable feelings of remorse and my full acceptance of responsibility for the deaths of Sergeant Peter Voto and Officer Gary Tedesco."

Andy Voto wasn't buying it. "Remorse begins right after the crime," he said, "not when you want parole."

Robert Egles of the parole board said that the depth of Trantino's remorse would be considered, but that remorse was secondary to the question of whether Trantino would commit new crimes.

On March 2, 1988, after a six-hour hearing, the board voted four to three to deny parole. It said Trantino had failed to deal with "deep emotional-personality problems." The board was persuaded by a doctor who said it didn't matter how effectively Trantino had counseled other people to stay away from alcohol and drugs; the point was, he still had not faced up to his own addictions.

The board said the killer would not get another hearing for three years. Trantino took the news "like a gentleman," Chairman Louis Nickolopoulos said.

An article in the *Record* told how the victims had been forced to strip, then had been beaten and shot. "As the officers lay dead on the floor," the article said, "Falco and Trantino danced on the bar and reportedly continued to pump shots into the bodies."

The article angered Trantino. "I'm not trying to minimize that two human beings were murdered," he told a *Record* reporter afterward. "That was horrible enough. But let's deal with the truth."

On this issue, the Bergen County prosecutor, Larry McClure, agreed with Trantino. McClure said he didn't believe the long-running rumors of forced sex. Had Guy Calissi and Fred Galda known of that, McClure said, they would have brought it out at the trial.

But true or not, the sordid story would never die.

§

Over the next year, the case inspired several bills in the New Jersey legislature. Many lawmakers wanted to restrict the parole board, especially by barring parole for anyone convicted of murder and not sentenced to death. In the spring of 1989, the lawmakers settled on a measure to require the full state parole board to decide on the release of convicted killers. The bill was aimed at the procedure under which two of the members reviewed most decisions, as had happened earlier with Trantino. Governor Kean signed the legislation on June 29, 1989.

§

On March 30, 1990, a panel of the Appellate Division ruled that the parole board had been justified in its latest denial. The judges acknowledged the prisoner's "good works and seemingly insightful verbal expressions," but went on, "It is not for us, however, to decide what the truth may be." They said the parole board had been justified in its concern that Trantino might have performed his good works to distract himself and others from his "serious underlying personality problems."

Trantino's good behavior made him eligible for parole only six months later. Unfortunately, 1990 was an election year in Bergen County. As proceedings were about to begin, Assemblyman William "Pat" Schuber of Bogota, a Republican who was running for Bergen County executive, introduced a resolution deploring the idea of release for the Angel Lounge killer.

On July 20, a parole board hearing officer took statements from the victims' families. Sadie Tedesco was able, with her daughter Elaine's help, to hold herself together long enough to tell what her son's murder had done to her.

There was a new Bergen County prosecutor, John J. Fahy, who was every bit as hostile as his predecessors had been. "He was convicted of two murders and sentenced to death," Fahy said. "Just because the New Jersey death-penalty law was overturned doesn't mean he should be free to walk the streets again."

New Jersey had a new governor, too. James J. Florio was a Democrat, less patrician than his Republican predecessor, Thomas Kean, but no more eager than Kean to appear sympathetic to Thomas Trantino.

And just to be sure Florio knew how seriously the police officers felt about the Angel Lounge killer, police lobbyists met with a top aide to the governor, asking that rumors of special treatment for Trantino be investigated by the attorney general's office. Among the rumors was one that Trantino had been granted conjugal visits with his wife. Not true, the corrections department said.

The parole board considered the case at Riverfront State Prison in Camden on August 27, 1990, twenty-seven years and a day after the Angel Lounge killings. On September 25, a two-member parole board panel denied Trantino's latest bid for freedom. On November 21, the full board ratified the decision.

With Trantino's continued good behavior, his name came up yet again a year later, on September 18, 1991. With one of its members abstaining, the board voted to deny release.

CHAPTER **38**

So Much Time

In 1992, people who had not even been born at the time of the Angel Lounge killings had grown up, gotten married, started families, taken out mortgages.

On August 17, Trantino's parole application was weighed yet again, by a two-member panel. A psychological exam of the prisoner, now fifty-four years old, was ordered. On August 19, the Bergen County Board of Freeholders restated its long-standing opposition to parole.

On October 15, the New Jersey General Assembly overwhelmingly approved a bill stating that convicted murderers not subject to the death penalty should spend the rest of their lives in prison. One of the bill's sponsors, Assemblywoman Rose Heck, a Republican from Hasbrouck Heights near Lodi, complained that murderers were getting too many parole hearings. She singled out Thomas Trantino, though he could not be covered under her bill.

Some criminal-justice experts were bothered by the proposal. "It doesn't take into consideration the realities of what it would be like to have a prison full of people who have absolutely nothing to lose," said Karen Spinner of the New Jersey Association on Corrections.

The next stop for the bill was the New Jersey Senate. Two weeks after the General Assembly voted, the Senate's Judiciary Committee held a hearing on the proposal. The site of the hearing—Lodi—virtually guaranteed that no one would express opposition. Andy Voto testified in support, as did other law enforcement people.

Some senators wanted to "grandfather" Trantino into the bill, so he could never again come up for parole. But even prosecutors who backed the bill expressed doubt about the constitutionality of making it retroactive.

The senators thought of another wrinkle: requiring all members of the parole board to hear testimony from relatives of a victim before approving parole for a murderer. The current practice was for two or three members to hear from the relatives.

By the early spring of 1993, the two parole board members assigned to the Trantino case were at an impasse: one recommended parole, one opposed it. A third board member would break the tie, determining what recommendation would go to the full board.

It was another political season. Governor Florio, up for reelection, was reviled by many New Jerseyans for a big tax package he had pushed through the legislature. Ambitious Republicans smelled blood. W. Cary Edwards, a former state attorney general who wanted the Republican nomination for governor, laid out a program that called for more police, stiff sentences for crimes against elderly people, and gun control. And he said that Thomas Trantino's repeated attempts to win his freedom showed the need for stricter limits on parole.

§

Lodi shivered under a cold rain on Thursday, April 22. Only about 150 police and civilians showed up at a rally protesting parole for the Angel Lounge slayer. They cheered Andy Voto when he said, "I want to see him die and rot in jail."

The parole board still had not decided. The thirtieth anniversary of the Angel Lounge murders was approaching. On June 28, Governor Florio signed legislation to bar violent criminals from enjoying furloughs from prison. Furloughs had become an issue since the disclosure that Trantino had been granted three back in 1980. He would get no more. Nor would a lot of other prisoners.

Florio was in a tough reelection race (one he would lose) and insisted that politics had played no part in his decision to sign the legislation. But he could hardly have been unaware of the politics.

§

August came and went. The leaves fell. The weather turned cold. On November 16, 1993, Thomas Trantino was denied parole for the seventh time. The two-member parole board panel, previously deadlocked, had come to agreement after interviewing the prisoner. Assuming good behavior and work credits, Trantino would become eligible again in 1994 or 1995.

In late December 1993, word got out that Trantino might be transferred to another state. New Jersey was among two dozen states that traded prisoners occasionally, usually because the prisoners were problems where they were originally incarcerated.

Assuming Trantino was sent to another state, he would be evaluated to determine when and where he would eventually be placed in a halfway house, the New Jersey Department of Corrections said. The department said it might be better to have him in a halfway house in another state, where hostility was less likely.

But why consider him for a halfway house in the first place? The answer was baffling.

In denying parole in November, the two-member panel had decreed that Trantino would have to be placed in a halfway house to have any possibility of ever being a free man. The board had, in fact, suggested to the Department of Corrections that the prisoner be moved to a halfway house.

If Trantino succeeded in a halfway house, the board reasoned, he could achieve his "full rehabilitative potential." If he did well, he would finish serving the punishment required of him *and* would satisfy the authorities that there was not a "substantial likelihood" that he would commit more crimes when he went free.

So, in recommending that Trantino go to a halfway house, was the board implying that he should be paroled one day?

No, said the board's executive director, Robert Egles. "The board doesn't have a strong feeling one way or the other. If it was their intention to release him, they would have given him a parole date."

Egles explained that the board was simply following a 1982 New Jersey Supreme Court decision requiring it to seek "full rehabilitative potential" for inmates in state prisons. Exactly what that term meant was unclear.

So was the parole board's stance.

CHAPTER **39**

Speaking to
the Wind

It was the first week of January 1994. Christine Todd Whitman, the Republican who had ousted Jim Florio, was just settling in as governor.

The state's acting attorney general, Fred De Vesa, wrote to the Department of Corrections. He said he had never before spoken publicly against a parole or a transfer of an inmate to a halfway house. He was doing so now, he said, because he found it "extraordinary and inappropriate" that Thomas Trantino should have a chance to go to a place that wasn't really a prison. The Angel Lounge crime was so heinous that the man who committed it must surely be a "threat to public safety," De Vesa said.

A couple of days later, the Department of Corrections said it had decided that Trantino should stay in prison. Any notion of sending him to a halfway house was shelved.

§

In late summer 1994, only days after the anniversary of the crime that had made him infamous, prisoner 41608 was entitled to be considered for parole once again. He would be interviewed by two members of the parole board at Riverfront Prison in Camden.

Some lawyers thought the parole board would have to put itself through some fancy contortions to find an excuse to keep Trantino locked up. "The government doesn't have to have a parole system," said Professor Mark Denbeaux of the Seton Hall University School of Law. "If they have one, it does-

173

n't have to be a generous one. But if they have one, they have to follow their own rules."

If one could step back, shut off one's senses and imagination, and momentarily see beyond the terror and death of that long-ago early morning in the Angel Lounge, there were certain facts and questions that were hard to ignore.

Did it really make sense that Trantino had been closer to freedom in 1980, when a parole board majority voted to release him, than he was in 1994?

And was it really fair for Trantino to be told by the parole board that he needed time in a halfway house to reach his "full rehabilitative potential," then to be told by the Department of Corrections that he could not go to a halfway house?

Andy Voto didn't care if state officials went on contradicting themselves. He didn't care if they threw custard pies at one another, as long as his blood enemy was kept in a cage. Andy Voto had spent his life as a cop, not a lawyer. He had seen lawyers bend the law so guilty men could go free, or get off a lot more easily than they deserved to. Now he was using the system to see that a guilty man stayed where he belonged. "Every day I get up, and I think of my brother," the old chief said.

But as long as Trantino continued to behave well in prison, the law required the parole board to reevaluate him continually. He was turned down again on September 1, 1994.

Another year, another reevaluation. On September 14, 1995, he was turned down yet again.

§

In May 1996, the parole board rejected Trantino again. Convinced that his client would never be paroled the normal way, Roger Lowenstein sued the parole board and the Department of Corrections, accusing them of violating Trantino's constitutional rights. Arguments were set for September 17, 1996.

For Trantino, the timing could not have been worse. On September 11, Governor Whitman signed a bill decreeing that cop killers who escaped the death penalty would spend the rest of their lives in prison.

A day after signing the bill, the governor visited Garfield, where many of Gary Tedesco's friends still lived. "We want everyone to know that New Jersey is a great place for cops and a terrible place for killers," she said.

The bill passed by New Jersey lawmakers had been inspired, of course, by the case of Thomas Trantino, who was growing old in prison for a crime he had committed when the future governor, Christine Todd, was a girl of sixteen. The efforts of State Senator Frank Graves and Assemblywoman Rose Heck had paid off. They had gotten a bill that was something like what they had wanted.

Lowenstein said Trantino had clearly been rehabilitated, that political pressure was steering the case, and that it was unfair to punish him under laws passed long after his conviction. The other "heinous offenders" who had been on death row with Trantino in 1972 had all fared better than his client, he pointed out. Lowenstein might as well have been speaking to the wind.

§

It was blustery and rainy on September 17, 1996. No doubt, the weather kept the crowd down. Only about forty people, mostly police officers and politicians, showed up for a thirty-minute rally outside the Bergen County Courthouse in Hackensack, where Trantino's lawyers were arguing for his freedom. Many of the people driving by the courthouse and peering between the swipes of their windshield wipers had no idea what the protesters were there for.

But anyone from Lodi knew. Sitting among the spectators, Sadie Tedesco clutched a picture of her son, taken three months before he was killed. Of Thomas Trantino, she said later, "He destroyed my life."

Andy Voto was there too. "He killed two families," he said. "The town itself was dead for a while because of this."

Roger Lowenstein knew he was fighting a great tide of hate. Political pressures, fear of crime and hatred for criminals, the closeness of Lodi—all these worked against his client. "The parole board will never release Tommy Trantino—never—no matter what the reasons," he told the three judges hearing the case. "The parole board will never let this man go."

Though Lowenstein viewed the Voto and Tedesco families across a great divide, he felt deep compassion for them. But he had come to know Tom Trantino as a man. Was it really so hard to believe that Tom Trantino, having knocked back enough pills and booze to put a lot of people in a coma, could not remember what had happened in the Angel Lounge? Was it really so hard to believe that part of Tom Trantino just couldn't accept that he had done such a thing?

The whole goddamned case has become so politicized, Lowenstein thought. Was there anyone, *anyone,* willing to take an objective look at what had gone on over the years and say that the rule of law was being violated, that something was wrong?

Yes, there was someone. Her name was Sylvia B. Pressler, and she was one of the three Appellate Division members listening to Lowenstein's arguments that day. (The others were Justices Burrell I. Humphreys and Edwin H. Stern.)

Judge Pressler could seem prickly and aloof at first, but no one doubted her intellectual candlepower. For that matter, those who got to know her found Sylvia Pressler a person of warmth and humor as well as intellectual brilliance. She graduated from Boston University in 1955 and from Rutgers University's law school (with high honors) in 1960. At Rutgers, she was managing editor of the law review.

She was active in the Democratic Party. In 1968, she became city solicitor for Englewood. And in 1975, Sylvia Pressler became the first female judge in

Bergen County. She was named to the Bergen County Court, replacing none other than Fred Galda, the former right-hand man for Guy Calissi. Galda had moved up to Superior Court.

Whether they agreed with her or not, lawyers knew they were appearing before someone with a razor-sharp mind who could cut to the heart of an issue in a moment. By the late 1990s, Sylvia Pressler was a justice in the Appellate Division.

§

As the three judges pondered the court record, the Trantino case became, at least for a moment, an issue in national politics. On October 8, the Republican presidential candidate, Bob Dole, campaigned in New Jersey. Andy Voto gave Dole a plug as Dole appeared in the working-class community of Lyndhurst. Dole was grateful. "We're not going to parole anybody," the candidate said. "Nobody's going to get out on parole who commits a crime like the man who murdered your brother. They're going to stay right there. That's where they belong—in jail, in jail, in jail!"

The crowd cheered its approval.

Miles away, unmoved by the crowds, Sylvia Pressler was studying the case, page by page, year by year.

CHAPTER **40**

An Eloquent
Dissent

When an appellate court hands down a ruling that is not unanimous, the memorable words usually belong to the majority. The majority controls, after all. But every once in a while, a dissent is memorable. Perhaps it foresees a change in the law, years or even decades down the road. And occasionally a dissent is memorable for its pure eloquence—as was the case on January 15, 1997.

The two judges in the majority were Edwin H. Stern and Burrell I. Humphreys. They ruled that Thomas Trantino should serve at least three more years before becoming eligible for parole. But, in a partial victory for Lowenstein, they ordered the Department of Corrections to explain why it had repeatedly rejected halfway-house placement.

Judge Stern quoted from a 1993 parole board meeting, after which Andrew Consovoy, the board's chairman at the time, favored parole for Trantino. "This case has never been treated the same way as any other case," Consovoy told Trantino. "You've done all you can do. . . . Tom, it's come to the end. You've done your thirty years. . . . It's got to end."

Some judge should decide the confusion between the Department of Corrections and the parole board, Consovoy told Trantino, "and then you are on the way to get out."

Arthur Jones, a parole board member who had voted against Trantino's release in 1993, apparently did so because the prisoner had not spent time in a halfway house, Judge Stern noted. No fool, Jones knew that political pressure had kept Trantino out of a halfway house. "They're setting you up for failure," Jones had told the prisoner.

In other words, the parole board members were saying that the state was stacking the deck against Trantino, and would continue to do so until the courts ordered an end to it.

Judge Stern noted all of that. But he concluded with the reminder that Trantino was serving a life sentence only because the death penalty had been voided. "He has no right to parole," the judge said. "Trantino can be compelled to serve his sentence for the rest of his life."

Judge Humphreys agreed. "The murders were not a one-time drug-induced act by an otherwise law-abiding citizen," the judge noted. No, Judge Humphreys said, "his record and background are those of a street thug who preys on the weak and helpless." The judge said Trantino was still highly dangerous.

Judge Humphreys was troubled, as so many officials had been before him, by the defendant's claim of amnesia, or whatever one chose to call it, about the night of the crime. "Criminals who have committed much less serious crimes will be spending their entire lives in prison," Judge Humphreys said.

He was alluding to recent changes in the state's sentencing rules, enacted by lawmakers acutely sensitive to the public clamor to be tough on crime. Had Trantino committed his murders after the code revisions, the judge said, "he would likely have received two consecutive life sentences carrying a parole ineligibility of a minimum of sixty years."

There were two things wrong with that statement. First, Trantino had been convicted and sentenced under the old rules, not the new ones. Besides, Judge Humphreys had overlooked a crucial fact: for some reason, Guy Calissi had chosen to indict and try Thomas Trantino on one count of murder—a single count embracing the slayings of both Peter Voto and Gary Tedesco, to be sure, but one count nonetheless. It was a technicality, but an all-important one. Trantino could not have been sentenced to consecutive sentences if he had been found guilty on only one count.

Roger Lowenstein had mixed feelings. Reading between the lines of the majority decision, he said, "They're hoping the Department of Corrections will do the right thing by allowing Trantino to go to a halfway house or out of state, where he won't be such a political controversy."

But what really got his attention was the twenty-seven-page dissent by Sylvia Pressler. "The basis of my disagreement, as difficult as it may have been for me to arrive at, is equally simple for me to explain," she said.

She had concluded that public outcry and political pressure had caused the Department of Corrections and the parole board to mishandle the case. If it were up to her, Judge Pressler said, the corrections department would be ordered to place Trantino in a pre-parole halfway house. And if the corrections department could not, or would not, act swiftly, the parole board should be directed to put the defendant in a halfway house—or parole him outright.

"I am persuaded that the record overwhelmingly demonstrates the arbitrariness and unreasonableness of both the department's denial of halfway house or out-of-state placement and the Parole Board's decision responsive to that denial," she wrote.

The judge understood the heavy responsibilities of parole officials, and the need to give the officials wide latitude. She also understood the suffering Trantino had inflicted, on the Voto and Tedesco families and on Lodi.

"I do not intend to minimize in any way the heinousness of defendant's unspeakable 1963 crime, or to depreciate the irremediable agony of the families of the victims, or to deprecate the still palpable trauma that rocked their hometown communities," she went on. "Nor do I have any doubt of the legitimacy of the cry for vengeance and retribution raised by those who suffered a heart-rending loss in a heart-rending way. Were I one of them, I would, I am sure, join that cry.

"But my obligation is different. My commitment must be to the substantive due process of law and to the integrity of the legal system, which, in the end, is all that ultimately protects us all."

Judge Pressler focused on the 1982 New Jersey Supreme Court decision upholding the parole board's denial of parole. The high court had set down a two-pronged standard the board was obliged to apply to its decision: rehabilitation and the unlikelihood of additional criminal behavior. Punishment was not supposed to be considered independently, but as a component of rehabilitation.

That last was a murky concept—as murky, perhaps, as the parole board's term *full rehabilitative potential*. The quest for clarity was necessitated, in part, by Trantino's unique status: he was the senior prisoner in the New Jersey corrections system, and having been sentenced under old laws, he was being reviewed for parole under new ones.

Judge Pressler appreciated the emotions the case had aroused over the years.

"It is that public outcry—rather than a fair evaluation of relevant facts and psychological opinions—that has accounted for the parole denials," Judge Pressler concluded, noting that for two decades or more Trantino had been "a model prisoner," counseling young inmates, working outside prison walls without incident, even earning college credits.

The judge zeroed in on the 1982 parole board decision to impose a ten-year "future eligibility term," or period (minus credit for good behavior and work) after which Trantino would be up for consideration yet again, assuming no serious misbehavior.

She recalled what Christopher Dietz had told Trantino: "We feel strongly that there should be certainty and hope for any individual who is incarcerated . . . so he can look to the day that he will be released. . . . "

Given the chairman's words in 1982, Judge Pressler asked, how could the parole board justify denying parole again and again in subsequent years?

"The better Trantino does in the institutional setting, the worse he does with the Parole Board," Judge Pressler wrote. "As his own progress towards rehabilitation is acknowledged to have advanced, his opportunity for release has concomitantly declined.

"I cannot rationalize this phenomenon by any standard of reasonableness and fair play that I can envision. It bespeaks to me a decision that is grossly arbitrary and unreasonable.

"I do not believe that defendant can be kept incarcerated indefinitely only because people outside the correctional system insist that he remain there," Judge Pressler wrote. "After all, the entire parole process is predicated on the belief in the potential for rehabilitation and redeemability of all people. Even Thomas Trantino."

CHAPTER 41

What's
to Lose?

Even Thomas Trantino.

At last, Roger Lowenstein thought. At last, someone in public life had dared to say that Trantino was still a member of the human race, and that even considering the great wrong he had done, he was being treated unfairly.

Now he had to try to convince the New Jersey Supreme Court. This would be no easy task; the high court had already reviewed the case, after all. It was rare for the tribunal to look at the same case more than once.

Lowenstein had to decide what tone he would take. He was itching to show his disdain for the state officials who, in his judgment, had simply failed time and again over the years to do the right thing.

And yet, and yet ...

A certain restraint is sometimes called for in dealing with a high court. The jurists who sit in black-robed majesty at the top of the judicial pyramid are worlds removed from the clamor and squalor of lower-level criminal courts, where the daily catch of suspects is paraded in and out of packed rooms. High-court justices deal with weighty issues of statute and court procedure and constitution, issues that sometimes seem strangely abstracted from the flesh-and-blood sufferings that spawn them.

So Lowenstein thought about what tone to take. He thought about it for a few minutes. Then he realized that Judge Pressler had opened the door for him. Her dissent, while even-tempered and eloquent, also expressed indignation. So would Lowenstein.

He had appeared in front of the New Jersey Supreme Court nearly a dozen times before, winning almost every time. (He lost a case when he represented a judge who faced the loss of his robes, and a good deal more, for taking a payoff.) So he was sure the members of the high court respected him as a lawyer.

Besides, Lowenstein had a good deal of confidence in the power of his words. "Most lawyers don't write English," he said later. "They write legalese. I had an advantage, being a writer."

The more he thought about whether to take a sharp tone, the more he asked himself: *What do I have to lose?*

§

"The crime is admittedly a heinous one," Lowenstein said in the introduction to the brief he filed before the state's high court, "but the procedural history described below is a shameful one for any observer trained to respect the rule of law." He went on to blame "terrified bureaucrats" for much that had happened.

Lowenstein deplored the "false mythology" about the case. "There was no evidence of torture, urination on the bodies, humiliation, victims begging for mercy, dances of glee or any of the other myths. . . . The whole panicked incident took less than three minutes."

Lowenstein was pushing the envelope a little: there was no way to prove that the bloody events occurred in less than three minutes, although that estimate seems far more accurate than the purported half-hour that still seeps occasionally into newspaper accounts.

And it was far from clear, despite Lowenstein's assertions, that Falco and not Trantino ordered the two officers to disrobe—although that was Falco's style, as he showed with the hapless printer Robert Munoz in the summer of 1963, ordering Munoz to strip before he shot him and dumped him into the East River.

Finally, while no one who was in the Angel Lounge that night testified that either officer had begged for his life, Trantino himself alluded to something like that in his stream-of-consciousness recollections in his book: "frank leaps onto the bar and goes into a squat with a gun in each hand and the cops are saying dont hurt us please and razor screams like wild horses are slashing kicking in my head . . . "

Lowenstein went on to say that Trantino felt deep remorse for what he had done, despite his inability to peer across the years through a booze-and-drugs haze and recall everything. But the parole board had repeatedly twisted his words, Lowenstein asserted, "so as to imply a lack of contrition, and if the words cannot be twisted, *make them up.*"

That was strong stuff, but Lowenstein made more accusations. He cited a 1995 report by a psychologist, James Bell, who examined Trantino. "Clinically," the doctor wrote, "he impresses as a man who has reached a point of change come about through sincere self-inventory and aspirations to atone for the great wrong he has done in his life." Lowenstein accused the parole board of keeping Trantino in the dark about that report.

Then Lowenstein went back two decades, pointing to a 1975 report by a prison psychologist who concluded that Trantino felt "a deep remorse" for his crime. The doctor said he believed that Trantino had "regenerated himself while incarcerated to a totally new self-image ... and life goals which clinically can be associated with those of mentally healthy, personally and socially well adjusted, law-abiding and in fact contributing members of society."

The lawyer included remarks by Glenn Arterbridge, his client's job supervisor at Riverfront Prison: "Even with all the setbacks he has had over the past several years, setbacks that would have broken the spirit of most, Thomas Trantino continues to be optimistic and my best worker. . . . He has on occasions too numerous to mention gone far beyond the requirements of the job. . . . I tell my staff on their first day of employment that no inmate is a friend and the only inmate they can trust is Thomas Trantino."

Lowenstein portrayed his client as a victim in part of a hardening in the general attitude toward crime; that attitude was "the controlling subtext of this case," as the lawyer put it.

Notwithstanding the fact that Trantino ran afoul of the law because of what he did on August 26, 1963, Lowenstein had a point. Many people believed that they weren't as safe as they had once been from muggers and rapists and burglars. Since the night at the Angel Lounge a bitter joke had made its way into common language, and like many jokes it told a truth: A conservative is a liberal who's been mugged.

So Lowenstein knew the tide was against him and his much-despised client. But to punish a 1963 crime on the basis of 1990s attitudes "is both unfair and unconstitutional," he wrote. "A Parole Board cannot continue to react to a shocking crime by revisiting, on a recurring basis, the same facts, and imposing a continually greater penalty as society grows less tolerant of crime."

The defense lawyer said it was grossly unfair for the parole board to punish Trantino because he said he couldn't remember the night in the Angel Lounge. Lowenstein had no trouble believing his client, who had undeniably downed a lot of alcohol and pills before the killings.

And suppose the memory really was buried. Was it a good thing to dig it up through hypnosis or truth serum in the name of rehabilitation, or "full rehabilitative potential," as it was sometimes put? The only arguments in favor of doing so were "some dime store psychological assumptions on the state's part," Lowenstein wrote.

Send the case back to the parole board, Lowenstein urged the high court. And make the board do the right thing.

The high court heard the case on October 6, 1997. Prosecutors argued that Trantino still had not fully admitted what he had done on that night thirty-four years ago. A statement that the prisoner made to a psychologist in 1995, that it might have been Frank Falco who started the whole thing and actually pulled the trigger, was used against him.

Roger Lowenstein insisted that his client *had* accepted the burden of guilt he would bear for the rest of his life. "He is truly remorseful," the lawyer said. Lowenstein told the justices that the parole board had acted illegally in rejecting his client two years before.

The justices asked many questions. They gave no hint of what they might do, although Justice Alan B. Handler implied that he might be willing to let Trantino stay in prison longer. "You can find, perhaps, some individuals who never were punished enough because they didn't change their behavior," he said.

§

Of course, Andy Voto didn't care if Trantino behaved well or badly. The point was that he should do it in prison until he grew old and senile and died. Having escaped the electric chair, Trantino would never be punished enough on this earth. This was the simple truth for Andy Voto.

On March 11, 1998, the retired police chief appeared before a state panel studying ways to streamline New Jersey's death-penalty procedures. He told the lawyers and lawmakers that he had longed to be his brother's avenger, as their father had commanded. "There were times I could have done it," he said. "But I figured the government would do it for me."

So Andy Voto had kept his cop's oath to uphold the law. And the government he had sworn to defend had let him down. Andy Voto's father had gone to his grave without ever really forgiving his surviving son for not killing his brother's killer. And now there was a chance that Thomas Trantino, whose very living and breathing offended Andy Voto each day, might soon be free. Where was the justice in that?

Voto's appearance before the panel came a month after Trantino's sixtieth birthday. There were fourteen people on death row at the time, but no one had been executed since the state had reenacted capital punishment in 1982. Governor Whitman and many other politicians in both parties thought it was wrong that someone could commit an unspeakable crime, be convicted and sentenced to death, then survive for years, decades, while appeals dragged on. Many voters felt that way too.

On May 15, 1998, the New Jersey Supreme Court ruled unanimously that Thomas Trantino was entitled to a new parole hearing. The justices said the parole board should weigh the prisoner's excellent record in recent years.

The high court said the parole board had erred in requiring that Trantino be "completely rehabilitated." Rather, the justices said, the board should now ask itself whether the prisoner had been rehabilitated *enough* to ensure that he would not commit new crimes. And the justices said the Department of

Corrections had better show good reasons for its refusal to place Trantino in a halfway house.

And Trantino's prospects should not hinge on his having a sharper recollection of the night at the Angel Lounge, Justice Alan Handler wrote for the court. "There is evidence in the record that Trantino's memory loss is consistent, long-standing, and genuine, and, beyond the issue of recollection, his acknowledgement of responsibility is sincere and legitimate," the justice wrote.

§

New Jersey's attorney general, Peter Verniero, said he was "extremely disappointed" that the court had rejected the parole board's insistence on total rehabilitation.

Andy Voto was furious. "They gave him a window to get out," he said, vowing to go to the next parole hearing "if I have to crawl on my belly."

Somewhat ironically, Roger Lowenstein was also troubled by the ruling. While it favored his client in the broadest sense, it also seemed to give the parole board an excuse to close the window on Trantino if it saw a chance that he would revert to crime. Specifically, the justices said, the board could deny parole if the members felt Trantino had not achieved "a sufficient level of rehabilitation that can assure there is no likelihood that he ... will engage in criminal conduct if released on parole."

Lowenstein saw the potential for plenty of official mischief. Still, he assured himself, the parole board would have a heavy burden to show that the gray-haired, sixty-year-old prisoner was a menace to society.

Lowenstein remembered what Judge Sylvia Pressler had written: Trantino couldn't be kept locked up forever just because a lot of people wanted him to be.

Could he?

CHAPTER 42

A Taste of
Tranquility

On August 18, 1998, word got out that Thomas Trantino was being transferred that very day from Riverfront Prison in Camden to a minimum-security rehabilitation center in South Kearny. The rehab center was called Talbot Hall.

The purpose of sending Trantino there was to determine whether he had been rehabilitated enough to be seriously considered, at long last, for parole. In making the transfer so Trantino could be evaluated, the parole board seemed to be doing what the New Jersey Supreme Court had said it should do. Depending on how he fared at Talbot Hall, he could be sent back to prison— or sent to a halfway house, a gateway to parole.

Bergen County Executive William Schuber was incensed at not having been notified of the transfer; the Department of Corrections, after all, was headed by Jack Terhune, a former Bergen County sheriff and Teaneck police officer.

The news sparked a rally outside Lodi Borough Hall. Schuber and the Bergen County prosecutor, William H. Schmidt, vowed to do everything in their power to keep Trantino in a real prison—to make sure, as Schuber put it, that "the criminal known as Trantino never sees the light of day."

§

The four hundred residents of Talbot Hall (they were called residents, not inmates) lived in units named Tranquility, Serenity, and Harmony. Their food was better than prison fare. Their mattresses were thicker. The counselors addressed the residents by their last names, prefaced with "Mister."

As the details of Mister Trantino's new life were coming out in the press, Governor Whitman was returning from vacation. She issued a statement saying she had been "surprised" to learn of the prisoner's transfer. "The brutal murders of two police officers by Mr. Trantino in 1963 still haunt the victims' families and all of the people of our great state," the governor said.

Attorney General Peter Verniero questioned Trantino's fitness to be in Talbot Hall, based on a recent psychological evaluation. Maybe another evaluation was in order, the attorney general said. The corrections commissioner, Jack Terhune, agreed to have a second evaluation done.

Terhune said he had not been involved in the decision to move Trantino to Talbot Hall, that he stayed out of it because he had been in law enforcement in Bergen County. But once the decision was made, Terhune defended it. "Comparatively speaking," he said of Talbot Hall, "it is far more structured than where he came from." The days at Talbot Hall were full of therapy sessions and classes, he said.

The commissioner pointed out that for the past decade Trantino had been living in modular-housing units at Riverfront State Prison in Camden, not exactly the concrete-and-bars setting that most people envisioned when they heard the word *prison.*

By coincidence, Terhune's comments came on the thirty-fifth anniversary of the Angel Lounge murders.

Meanwhile, Roger Lowenstein was upset at the prospect of yet another psychological examination for his client. There had already been dozens of exams over the years, he said, and they all concluded essentially the same thing: "He is a rehabilitated person who is unlikely to commit another crime."

The state hired Dr. Michael Welner, a forensic psychiatrist at New York University School of Medicine, to do a thorough study.

§

Trantino was relaxing in the day room at Talbot Hall on Thursday, November 12, 1998, when a guard beckoned him. There was bright sunshine outside. The temperature was nudging into the fifties. Maybe it would be a mild winter. Maybe by spring—

"The sergeant wants to see you," the guard said.

Before he knew it, Trantino's worldly possessions were crammed into a box and he was hustled onto a southbound bus. The bus did not stop at Camden, for Riverfront Prison, but continued farther south, to the new South Woods State Prison in Cumberland County.

Dr. Welner had summarized his findings in a fifty-two-page report. "Mr. Trantino is a man of noticeable strengths and noticeable weaknesses," the doctor said. "He is a different man from the man who was arrested for this crime and the man who murdered on that night."

The doctor went on to say that "in certain respects he has noticeably matured, but in other respects he still has work to do."

Dr. Welner said he had read all the evaluations of Trantino over the years. He had also interviewed both of Trantino's ex-wives (Charlee had given up hope and reluctantly divorced him the previous year) and dozens of other people. The result was the most extensive evaluation of Trantino's mental and emotional state in three decades.

The corrections commissioner, Jack Terhune, said the Welner report showed "a probability of recidivism" if Trantino were set free and "an inability to assimilate in the community."

Roger Lowenstein had another take. "I never cease to be amazed at the lengths to which they will go to keep him locked up," he said.

PART III

CHAPTER 43

"Sorry Beyond All Measure"

The grass around the house at 56 Christopher Street is parched yellow, like the other lawns in the neighborhood, from the drought. On a hot, bright day in the summer of 1999, Andy Voto is in a good mood as he inspects his yard. He spots a weed, stoops over to pluck it. Then he pulls out another weed. "I can't waste the effort once I bend over," he says.

This little exercise reminds him of Genarro: "My father used to say, 'Don't plant nothing you can't eat.'"

Andy turned seventy-three not many days ago. His hair might be a bit grayer than it was last winter, but he looks stronger.

Relaxing inside, Andy talks about his interview with Ed Bradley for a *60 Minutes* story about the Angel Lounge killings and Thomas Trantino. Andy liked Ed Bradley, liked the give-and-take with him.

Andy knows the *60 Minutes* story probably won't air until the fall, but he can wait. He knows Trantino isn't going anywhere in the meantime. Andy was delighted when his blood enemy was denied parole again in June—delighted, but not surprised. Andy appeared before the parole board, as usual, and he sensed how things were going, not from what the board members said but from what they didn't say. He has become very good at reading the moods of the board members.

"When you've got a very quiet parole board, they're listening," Andy explains.

Inevitably, the talk veers back to 1963. Even after all these years, Andy can't help wondering what might have been: if Nick Kayal had told Pete about the gun in the towel right away, or—

"What day is today?" Andy asks suddenly.

It's Friday, August 6.

Andy's face changes. "Yesterday was Pete's birthday. He would have been seventy-six. We didn't get to grow old together, me and my brother."

§

A hundred miles or so south of Lodi, the rain runs gleaming off the coils of razor wire outside South Woods State Prison.

South Woods has none of the fortress-like ugliness of older prisons. There are no dirty bricks stained with soot and pigeon droppings. South Woods confines its murderers, robbers, and burglars in light-gray buildings with roofs of powder blue.

In popular imagination, New Jersey is defined by the turnpike that cuts through swampland and oil refineries on the way from Big Apple to Brotherly Love. From that perspective, Cumberland County in South Jersey is a world apart, a region of farms and flatlands sloping down toward Delaware Bay. It is hard to believe that the county is in the same state as Newark or Jersey City, or even Lodi. Indeed, Cumberland County lies south of the Mason-Dixon Line.

The opening of South Woods Prison on the outskirts of the quiet little town of Bridgeton in 1997 meant a lot to the county, one of the poorest in the state. The prison brought business and jobs.

The gray-blue motif is continued in the linoleum inside, where a polite corrections official guides me through a metal detector and down a long corridor through steel doors that seem to open by themselves. Finally, there is a big open area leading to other rooms, other corridors.

There are no clangs and echoes. The loudest sound is the hum of a floor-waxer being run by a khaki-clad prisoner. The visiting rooms off the big open area are spacious, well lit, carpeted.

In an odd way, I find the good lighting and the quiet unsettling. Other penal institutions I have visited (the prison in Rahway, New Jersey; state prisons in South Carolina and Texas; even county jails) are noisier, darker. They look and sound like places where bad, dangerous men are kept. Depending on the weather, they may smell that way too.

By comparison, South Woods has an antiseptic quality. If I were directing a movie, I would not choose this setting to introduce the notorious Angel Lounge killer.

But here he is, prisoner 41608, brought in by a couple of guards. *So,* I think, *this is the man Andy Voto hates like no one else who ever lived. This is the man who killed Andy Voto's brother.*

He is a man with a wide, friendly smile. "Nice to know you," he says. His handshake is strong, like a stonemason's. He stands six feet tall. His shoulders and neck are thick from exercise, his torso flat beneath the light-tan uniform.

The guards seat us in a visiting room. They are professional and courteous, yet I think there is something extra in their attitude toward Thomas Trantino. I sense an easygoing respect, and not just because he gives them no trouble.

Perhaps it is because, of some 26,500 inmates in the New Jersey state prison system, he is first in seniority. On this day in the summer of 1999, prisoner 41608 is sixty-one years old. He has been a prisoner since John F. Kennedy was in the White House, since before some of the people guarding him were on this earth.

Although the familiar hawklike nose hasn't lost its shape, there are wrinkles in the neck. The swept-back hair is turning white. Fit or not, he looks his age. In truth, he is a rather ordinary-looking man, neither handsome nor homely.

He sits down. We are alone. His smile goes away. The blue eyes harden as he begins to talk about the latest parole board decision. "That was the most crushing blow ever," he says, shaking his head.

The board denied him parole—again. No one else in New Jersey history has been denied parole so many times. As he reflects on what happened, his face becomes animated and he waves his arms in frustration.

His flamboyant gestures, and the occasional Yiddish expression he tosses into his conversation, are an almost comic reminder of his mixed Italian-Jewish blood and the nickname that was pinned on him so long ago: Tom the Rabbi.

No, he was not really surprised by the parole board's decision. "It was all my prior history," he says. The board members brought up the narcissism and antisocial personality disorder that earlier boards threw at him a long time ago, brought up the fact that he used to hit his first wife—"a cycle of domestic violence," the board said.

"I know I hit her maybe ten times," Trantino says, shaking his head. He says he is not trying to excuse what he did, but he is no longer shamed by it, either. For God's sake, the way he treated his first wife, how he screwed around on her—all that came out at his trial more than thirty-five years ago! He was ashamed of it then, such a long time ago. How much shame is he supposed to carry, and for how long? For the rest of his life?

He knows there are people who want him to suffer until the day he dies. He understands that. He knows there are people who don't believe him when he says, "From my heart and soul, I'm sorry." He says he knows that words aren't enough. Words bring no one back from the dead.

Nor do I feel that *my* words are adequate on this day. I have brought my list of questions, of course, but I soon realize that I won't get very far with them. He tells me he doesn't remember much about that terrible night in 1963, has never been able to remember much.

He knows he was trying to help Frank Falco that night, trying to keep him from getting into trouble again. As for telling the two cops to take their clothes off, Trantino says the idea behind that might have been to lock them in a bathroom. That way, when they got out they'd have to take time to get dressed again. And Falco was probably trying to make sure the cops had no concealed weapons. At least, that was the idea before things went wrong.

But he doesn't remember things very clearly. Never has.

Never will.

How silly of me to ask him about that night, I think. After all, Guy Calissi did not get good answers from Trantino all those years ago. Oh, Calissi got the answers he wanted, all right, but they made no sense, and for Calissi that was the point. Calissi didn't want the jurors to hear good answers; he wanted them to hear bad ones.

§

As I sit in the well-lighted room with the Angel Lounge killer, I realize it was also silly of me to have expected eloquence. This is the man, after all, who talked of "the events that transpired" in the Angel Lounge.

His impersonal language has angered people in the past, but should it count against him now? I remind myself that America's prisons (and its streets and office buildings and schools, for that matter) have lots of people who express themselves no better than Thomas Trantino does. And Trantino may be nervous, trying to make a good impression.

He is vague about Charlee and what hope he still has of being with her. He clearly does not want to talk about dreams of marriage and hearth and children. I get him to talk a little, just a little, about prison life. He says he goes to prayer meetings now and then for the fellowship. Oh, and the salads at South Woods aren't fresh enough.

This is how the talk goes. Maybe he wants to talk about prayer meetings and lettuce instead of what happened in a bar a long time ago. That is his right, I suppose. I share some things about my life; it seems only fair. He nods and smiles. It occurs to me that he may not get many visitors, that he may just want to talk about everyday things with an outsider.

Something else occurs to me as I sit with him. Trantino may not be a true sociopath, a criminal with something missing in his emotional circuitry, incapable of empathy or guilt. But I sense that he is not a man of exquisite sensitivity, either. Maybe he is not a man who carries a burden in his soul every moment. Or maybe the burden is just too heavy to carry all the time.

Or perhaps I have it all wrong. Perhaps he is simply no better than many people at facing his deepest feelings, let alone giving wings to words. He backs away from several chances to speak of emotional turning points, to dwell on remorse about that August night.

His face darkens as he reflects on the ruin of his own life. He touches on the loss of his first wife and the son who doesn't know him. But he doesn't really want to go in that direction.

"I was born with the birthright of freedom," he says. "I gave it away."

And in the closest that Tom the Rabbi can come to an Act of Contrition, he says again how sorry he is—"sorry beyond all measure"—for what he did on the early morning of August 26, 1963.

He doesn't ask people to equate his suffering with the suffering he inflicted. Still, he has paid for his great wrong with almost four decades behind bars. Is it too much to ask that he be a free man at long last, in the quiet evening of his life?

"What is it about my case?" he asks, palms up on the table. "What is it about my case?"

Can it be that he really doesn't know?

The maddening thing, he goes on, is that the parole board had known all the old stuff—the husband-and-wife fights, the personality problems—since the beginning. He thought the board had dealt with all that stuff, just as he had dealt with it.

Again, he lapses into the oddly detached language he sometimes uses. "There are no current behaviors over recent years," he says. "Not for decades."

His mood brightens a little. The CBS correspondent Ed Bradley is coming to visit him tomorrow for a *60 Minutes* report on his case. Maybe network television can help people understand how unfairly the system is treating him.

Back to the parole board. Trantino laughs bitterly. He remembers some state official sitting at the most recent hearing, furiously taking notes, as though already preparing arguments against him. "What the hell do you need to take notes for?" he wonders. "It was recorded electronically."

And he answers his own question. "They were setting this up, to deny me parole."

On this rainy day, it looks like he will have plenty of time to think about the parole board's decision. The chairman, Andrew Consovoy, said it might be three years before Trantino will come up for consideration again.

What really infuriates prisoner 41608, the more he talks about it, is that the board did a switcheroo on him. For many years, Tom Trantino said he just couldn't remember what happened that night so long ago. All right; finally he did admit that he was responsible for what happened, just as the state had said he must if he ever wanted to get out. So now the parole board says the fact that he changed his story means he's a liar, that he still can't face the truth!

The really funny thing, he says, is that in falling all over themselves to find an excuse to keep him behind bars, the members of the board did not go to the heart of the matter, the place and the night it happened.

Isn't it kind of strange, Trantino says. After all was said and done, "They did not revisit what specifically occurred in the Angel Lounge."

§

As I drive away, I should feel relieved, even happy. I have just spent the better part of four hours with the central figure in the story, the man I simply had to talk to, the man around whom everything revolves. Yet I am vaguely disappointed. I don't really know the man.

I wonder if Trantino's answers seem flat because I just don't know him. Or perhaps I already know all there is to know. Or possibly he is simply weary of the subject, tired of all the talk about Lodi and the Angel Lounge. Maybe he just wants to think about things of the present, like lettuce.

No, more than that. He dares to dream of a future. Only he can feel how much guilt he carries in his heart, but it is a safe bet that he would rather carry the burden in the real world than behind bars. I don't blame him for that.

It occurs to me that I have met a thousand men like him, in hardware stores and bars, on construction sites and in the gym. He has no particular charisma, certainly no aura of menace. In truth, he is a fairly pleasant man.

Or have I missed something? Trantino didn't just snap inexplicably that long-ago August; he had been working his way up in crime. Maybe he is the psychopath Andy Voto says he is. Sure, Andy hates him and will always see him as evil, but Andy was a career cop, after all. Cops deal with psychopaths; I don't.

Maybe Trantino is a human chameleon, able to put on a different face for all the faces that he meets. If that is so, where is the real Thomas Trantino? Andy Voto thinks he knows: the real Trantino is the one who showed up at the Angel Lounge all those years ago. Andy would say that Trantino is the same today, only with gray hair.

The questions stay with me. Where is the real Thomas Trantino? *Who* is he? And if he can be many things to many people, what is inside?

Anything?

CHAPTER 44

The Eyebrows
Go Up

The *60 Minutes* report runs on October 17, 1999. The introduction features the words *Cop Killer* splattered with red and superimposed on a picture of a graying Thomas Trantino. The report suggests that Trantino might have been paroled years before if the victims had not been police officers. It suggests that he has changed for the better over the years.

On camera, Andy Voto is bright-eyed and energetic. He looks spiffy in a starched white shirt. "What do I care if Trantino is rehabilitated?" he says, not conceding that he is. "They can't rehabilitate the dead."

Under Ed Bradley's courteous prodding, Andy says he is not by nature a vindictive man. But this time you seem to want a "pound of flesh," Bradley says.

"Oh, a pound and a half!" Andy says. A murderer doesn't just kill a person, he says. "He murders the entire community."

§

Tom Trantino watches the program with some of his prison buddies. There is black-and-white footage of the young Tom Trantino at his 1964 trial, then color film of the prison at Rahway, where he helped to defuse tensions.

"I wanted to make my life an example of positive things," he tells the camera. He says it has been years, *years,* since he did anything that would make him a threat to society.

Two parole officials differ on whether Trantino would be a good risk. One, a former board member, says he wouldn't mind having Trantino for a neighbor. He calls Trantino "bright and well read," and says he has accomplished more in prison than most inmates ever do.

197

But the board's present chairman, Andrew Consovoy, disagrees. "He's a good inmate, a very good inmate," Consovoy says. Still, he says that Trantino would be a bad risk. Why? Because there is overwhelming evidence that Trantino repeatedly struck his first wife, Helene.

"Nonsense!" says Roger Lowenstein. It's absurd and unfair to dredge up long-ago domestic violence and expect a sixty-one-year-old man to defend himself.

Ed Bradley talks about Trantino's criminal record, about the horrible crime in the Angel Lounge. Why should we let someone like that out of prison?

"We let someone like that out of prison because that's what the law requires upon rehabilitation," Lowenstein says. Besides, Trantino is not the man he was all those years ago.

§

Just three days after the *60 Minutes* broadcast, I see Lowenstein in Trenton on a gray, rainy day. In a fifth-floor courtroom of the Richard J. Hughes Justice Complex, he waits to argue before a three-judge panel of the Appellate Division that the state has played fast and loose with psychological evaluations to keep Thomas Trantino from being released.

The complex is named for the former governor and New Jersey chief justice who consoled the Voto and Tedesco families so long ago. Hughes has been dead for seven years now. By an odd coincidence, the courtroom walls and carpet are soft grays and blues, not unlike the motif at South Woods Prison, where Thomas Trantino counts his days. Mandolin music is piped into the courtroom as lawyers and a small audience wait for the judges to appear.

Lowenstein shakes hands with Mary Jacobson, the assistant state attorney general who will oppose him. They smile and exchange pleasantries. There is no personal dispute here.

Yet for Lowenstein the case is more than a myriad of legal questions. Something very wrong is going on, has been for a long time, and it should be stopped — that is what he would shout to the judges, if he thought it would do any good.

His has been an unusual life's journey. He never lost his youthful idealism and anger; he just made a truce with it, for a while. A decade ago, he was pulling down $200,000 a year with his practice. And he found out, as so many lawyers have, that money wasn't everything. There was so much cynicism in the profession, so much personal unhappiness. The endless hours of toil in his Hoboken office helped to ruin his first marriage.

He had always thought he could write — not just cobble well-reasoned legal briefs, but really write. One day in the summer of 1990 he got a call from an old friend in Hollywood. You should come on out, the friend said. The living is fine.

Lowenstein headed west, to write. His timing was good: courtroom dramas were popping up on television, and the TV people needed guidance from real-life lawyers. He signed on as a technical adviser to an ABC program called *Equal Justice* for $300 a week. Pretty soon he was writing scripts for two other shows, *Law and Order* and *The Human Factor.*

In the spring of 1991, he hit the big tinsel. He was one of three lawyers hired to help write episodes of *L.A. Law,* one of the most popular shows on television. He hobnobbed with the show's stars. Lowenstein found, to his amusement, that other lawyers were more impressed than if he had just won an argument before the United States Supreme Court.

The bubble burst that August. There were production problems with *L.A. Law,* and the three lawyer-writers were let go. But Lowenstein was not bitter; he knew that nothing lasts forever, especially in Hollywood. Besides, he had salted away some money.

He stayed in Los Angeles and went back to practicing law. Rather, he went back to representing Thomas Trantino. Why, he is asked. Why does he still defend Trantino, who cannot pay him?

"I finish what I start," he says. So here he is, at fifty-six, defending one of the most reviled people in New Jersey.

§

The music stops, and the judges march in. Calmly, his anger in check for the moment, Lowenstein makes his case.

A crucial issue is whether the state had the authority to send Trantino back to prison after he had been transferred to Talbot Hall as a prelude to being put in a halfway house. After a stay in a halfway house, he presumably would have been ready for parole.

"One would think that would be the end of the question," Lowenstein said.

It wasn't, of course. Trantino's stay in Talbot Hall was cut short when Governor Whitman, several other politicians, and various law enforcement people objected to Trantino's being anywhere but in a place with walls and barbed wire.

"The governor went crazy," Lowenstein tells the judges. "She said, 'Do something about it.'"

Lowenstein says his client should not have been yanked out of Talbot Hall like that—not without a reason, assuming no disciplinary problem or startling new fact, and certainly not because of political pressure.

Lowenstein derides the new and damaging fifty-two-page profile of Trantino done by Dr. Michael Welner, an outside forensic psychiatrist hired by the state. "That's how the Soviet Union dealt with its refuseniks!" he tells the court. He points to a dozen positive evaluations of Trantino conducted over the previous fourteen years.

Lowenstein notes that after Trantino was whisked out of Talbot Hall, he was not returned to Riverfront Prison in Camden but was sent even farther south, to South Woods.

South Woods? One of the judges frowns in puzzlement. "Is that the new prison down there?" he asks.

That's the one, Lowenstein says. "They want him as far away as possible."

It's the state's turn. Mary Jacobson says the corrections department has not yet developed formal guidelines for returning inmates to prison from Talbot Hall, which only opened in April 1998. She says at least ten other inmates have been returned to prison from the rehab center, and that the corrections department has the right to move prisoners.

Perhaps most important, she says Trantino had gained no elevated status when he was sent to Talbot Hall. Ergo, she argues, he was deprived of nothing when he was put back in a cell.

The judges' eyebrows go up a little. There's some confusion about just what Talbot Hall is. It's not a halfway house, the state's lawyer says. But there seems to be no getting around the fact that it's at least a gateway to a halfway house, and that Trantino was closer to halfway-house status in Talbot Hall than he is back behind walls, wire, and bars.

Besides, one judge notes, the state at first said that Trantino was good enough to go to Talbot Hall. "Why isn't the Department of Corrections stuck with that evaluation?"

Another judge wonders about the "new layer of evaluation" to which Trantino seems to have been subjected. Can the state really do that?

Mary Jacobson doesn't get rattled. There was nothing special about Trantino's reevaluation, she insists. The corrections department is a big bureaucracy. Punishment and rehabilitation are serious concerns. Prisoners are reevaluated all the time.

A judge smiles at that. "And each one gets a fifty-two-page psychiatric report?" he asks, eyebrows high.

Lowenstein allows himself a smile.

§

The whole thing takes ninety minutes. Afterward, Roger Lowenstein is pleased. The judges have reserved decision, but no one expected them to rule immediately. Surely, Lowenstein says, surely the judges will see through the state's thin, weak case. Maybe Trantino will have to spend yet another Chanukah in captivity, but the lawyer is willing to bet his client will be with him at a seder come Passover time.

The rain has tapered off to drizzle. It is a cheerless afternoon, made sadder for me because of the legal jargon and arcana. What Trantino said about the parole board is also true of the justices, not that anyone can blame them, I suppose.

It seems strange, somehow, that on this day they never revisited what occurred in the Angel Lounge. Doesn't the suffering of that night deserve a mention, at least? Don't Peter Voto and Gary Tedesco and their kin deserve that much?

CHAPTER 45

Hope for
the Defense

The parole board specifies on November 10, 1999, that Trantino must wait until 2004 to be considered again. It's a year almost to the day since he was yanked out of Talbot Hall and put on a bus to South Woods.

"He can't tell the truth about many, many things," board chairman Andrew Consovoy says. "Despite his getting older, he's essentially the same individual who committed those horrible acts so many years ago. We think he's a serious risk for violence. And we're not going to let him out."

This is the same Andrew Consovoy who encouraged Trantino in 1993 to get a judge to settle the back-and-forth between the parole board and the corrections department, "and then you are on the way to get out."

But by late 1999, after Trantino has had another six years to burnish his rehabilitative potential, Consovoy has done an about-face. The chairman says the decision was based on the board's finding in June that Trantino had a history of domestic violence going back four decades, and that he lied about it. The board has also weighed the fact that Trantino injured a woman in 1956, when he and an accomplice mugged her to steal the dental office payroll—the crime that got Trantino sent to Great Meadow so long ago.

Finally, the board was concerned about his inconsistent accounts of the Angel Lounge shootings over the years. All those factors portrayed a man who might be a danger if he were set free, Consovoy explains at the news conference.

Of course, there is good reason for the board to stress that last point. The New Jersey Supreme Court told the board in 1998 that it shouldn't demand "complete" rehabilitation; rather, it should focus on whether Trantino was *sufficiently* rehabilitated to be released.

Clearly, the parole board is under strain. It is very rare for the board to call a press conference to explain a decision. It did so now, Consovoy says, because with all the publicity, the people have a right to know the board's reasoning.

The Bergen County prosecutor, William H. Schmidt, is pleased. He says he supports "anything that would keep Trantino in jail." And while Guy Calissi is still a revered figure in Bergen County two decades after his death, Schmidt cannot resist a veiled reference to Calissi's decision to fold both slayings into a single count.

"The way we'd do things today, there would have been two indictments," Schmidt explains, "and he would have served a minimum of fourteen and two-thirds years on one, then fourteen and two-thirds on the other. He wouldn't even have been eligible for parole for more than thirty years."

Of course, as Schmidt utters these words late in 1999, it must be noted that nearly thirty-six years have passed since Trantino was convicted and led away to prison.

And even if one thinks that Trantino should have died in the electric chair years ago, or that he should rot in prison, the board's rationale is puzzling. The 1956 mugging and Trantino's mistreatment of his first wife were known many, many years ago, before his trial. To put it another way, what do the parole officials know now that they didn't know two decades ago, when Trantino was actually closer to parole?

And Lowenstein is disgusted by one of the Catch-22s he thinks the state has imposed on his client: For a long time, Trantino said he couldn't have done the unspeakable thing in the Angel Lounge, that he just couldn't remember, that it must have been Falco who did the actual killing—or variations on that theme.

No good, the authorities told him time and again. Unless and until you admit your responsibility, you have no chance of going free. Ever.

So Trantino changed his story, admitting at long last that he was responsible for the two murders. And now the state seems to have used the change in his story as an excuse to call him a liar. Lowenstein thinks a grade-schooler ought to be able to see the unfairness in all that. After the announcement of November 10, 1999, he holds back nothing. The parole board's decision, he says, is "a totally politically corrupt and dishonest exercise by a bunch of cowards who are afraid that the rule of law will cost them their jobs."

§

On June 9, 2000, a three-judge panel of the Appellate Division rules unanimously that Trantino's time for freedom is at hand. The court tells the parole board to release him in thirty days. It tells the corrections department to transfer him to a halfway house so he can prepare to return to society.

To no one's surprise, Governor Whitman says her administration will appeal to the New Jersey Supreme Court. In Lodi, a few dozen police officers gather outside the municipal building next to the eagle-topped memorial to Peter Voto and Gary Tedesco, in their graves nearly thirty-seven years.

Andy Voto has to lean on his cane. He says, "I want a message delivered to Trantino: I hate your guts, and I'll follow you to the grave, no matter how crippled I am."

The three appellate judges agree to delay Trantino's transfer to a halfway house to give the state time to appeal. Still, Trantino has won a major victory. The three jurists—Michael P. King, John E. Wallace, and Robert A. Fall—have found a "sense of wrongness" in the board's actions. They say parole officials paid too little heed to "substantial and positive" factors in the prisoner's attempts to win freedom.

Moreover, the three judges strongly suggest that they accept a basic thrust of Lowenstein's arguments: that the state has put Trantino in an untenable position. The judges note that the parole board cited Trantino's divorce from the despairing Charlee as a reason for denying parole, "yet by Trantino's undisputed testimony it was the apparent hopelessness of parole that caused Charlee to seek a divorce."

No matter how one feels about Trantino, one statement expressed by the three judges is unassailable: "It would be virtually impossible for any inmate to win parole release if his past life were allowed to override successful efforts at rehabilitation."

Theoretically, the New Jersey Supreme Court could simply let the Appellate Division ruling stand—in which case Trantino would soon walk out of prison. But it would be surprising if the high court did not give the state a hearing.

Lowenstein is quietly confident. Privately, he puts his chances at much better than fifty-fifty if the case goes to the high court.

§

On June 16, 2000, the New Jersey Supreme Court sets aside the Appellate Division's release order for the time being. The justices schedule a conference for July 5 on Attorney General John J. Farmer's petition that it hear the state's appeal.

Only three of the six high-court justices, Gary S. Stein, James H. Coleman Jr., and Virginia Long, take part in the June 16 proceedings. The three others have had to stand aside: Justices Deborah Poritz and Peter Verniero both served as attorney general, and both opposed parole for Thomas Trantino. And Justice Jaynee LaVecchia had to recuse herself because she formerly was a high-ranking member of the attorney general's office. Two judges from the Appellate Division, James M. Havey and David S. Baime, are temporarily seated on the high court to give it the quorum of five.

As expected, the court agrees in early July to hear the state's appeal. The session is set for September 25 in Trenton. So Thomas Trantino will spend another summer behind bars.

The summer becomes a hot one for Andrew Consovoy. He comes under scrutiny on accusations that he underestimated the backlog of cases. Some inmates file a federal suit claiming that a prisoner has to wait months for a parole hearing that is his right soon after he becomes eligible for consideration.

More embarrassing for Consovoy personally is the revelation that state investigators are looking into his alleged friendship with an ex-convict who is friendly with mobsters. Consovoy meets with the governor's top aides, and a week later, on July 28, he resigns. His replacement is Mario Paparozzi, a former assistant corrections commissioner who teaches law at the College of New Jersey.

CHAPTER 46

Halfway to Freedom

"This case is about one thing, and that is protecting the public safety," Deputy Attorney General Harold McCoach tells the New Jersey Supreme Court on September 25, 2000.

Beneath his charming veneer, McCoach says, Trantino is what he has always been: a dangerous man with a "borderline personality disorder" and an inability to handle normal stress.

Not at all, Roger Lowenstein says. He says there is no evidence that his client poses an unacceptable risk of committing another crime. What the case is really about, Lowenstein says, is the parole board's refusal to face the facts and do the right thing.

Lowenstein is encouraged by the questions that the justices hurl at Mc-Coach: Why were some psychological tests considered reliable and others not? Shouldn't Trantino's good prison record for the past three decades count for something?

Peter Voto's son Jerry is in the audience. So is Jerry's younger brother, Peter, who came all the way from Florida. As a boy, Peter went to bed dreaming of going fishing with his father and woke to learn that his father was dead.

Elaine Tedesco Harvey is there, too. She cares not a whit whether Trantino is rehabilitated, as his lawyer says. "I really don't care if he becomes Jesus Christ," she says. "My brother will always be dead."

Andy Voto is not there. He had another stroke several weeks ago, then took a nasty fall in his home, shattering his hip. After hip-replacement surgery, he spent days in a rehabilitation center. He was cheered by throngs of visitors and a stream of get-well cards. But he was annoyed by the leotard-like stockings he had to wear to help his circulation. His face showed the pain and the years.

The Supreme Court argument is the second event Andy has had to miss. On August 22, outside the Lodi municipal building and near the monument to Peter Voto and Gary Tedesco, the president of the state senate, Donald DiFrancesco, signed a bill to keep murderers who escape the death penalty behind bars for the rest of their lives. The law was inspired, of course, by Thomas Trantino.

On top of everything else, Andy's mother-in-law has died after a long illness. All in all, the summer was Andy's worst since 1963.

Autumn crosses into winter.

§

News travels fast in a prison. On the afternoon of Wednesday, January 17, 2001, the inmates of South Woods Prison learn that the New Jersey Supreme Court will rule the next morning in the case of their senior comrade, Thomas Trantino.

Prisoner 41608 goes to bed nervous but hopeful. When he wakes with the early light, he cannot stand the wait until it is ten o'clock. As the hour draws near, he wonders if he will be disappointed yet again.

The court rules, four to one, in Trantino's favor. But the victory is not total. The justices say he cannot go out into the world immediately. He must spend a year in a halfway house first. If he does all right there, he will be a free man in twelve months. There will be no stalling or dithering this time: the high court says he must be transferred to a halfway house within thirty days.

Trantino feels relief, not euphoria. Nor does Lowenstein exult. The road has been too long for that, and he feels for the Voto and Tedesco families as well as for his client. Still, he cannot resist hurling a dart.

"It's always been a cheap shot for the Bergen County politicians," he says. "They wave the flag—Trantino, Trantino!—to get the votes.... At every turn, the governor, the attorney general, corrections and parole officials violated their own oath, subverting the rule of law."

§

Justice Gary Stein has written for the majority. What he calls "the critical and controlling question" is whether the parole board was justified in determining that there was a "substantial likelihood" that Trantino would commit another crime if released.

Stripped to its essentials, the ruling holds that the board was not justified in so determining, that indeed it had ignored or given too little credence to evidence that Trantino was a fairly good parole risk.

"The court does not underestimate the pain and anguish its disposition is likely to cause to families and friends of the victims of the Lodi murders," the ruling says. "The court is also aware that the disposition will not be readily understood by members of the public who will find it incomprehensible that the law requires parole release of an inmate who was responsible for the murder of two police officers."

If the same kind of crime were committed today, Justice Stein writes, parole would be impossible. And though the jurist doesn't put it this way, Trantino was lucky in some ways; had he committed his crime a few years earlier, he almost surely would have gone to the electric chair.

In any event, like it or not, once Trantino escaped the electric chair he eventually became eligible for parole, barring proof by the state that he was very likely to return to crime. "It is the absence of that proof that entitles Trantino to parole, not sympathy or compassion for him," the ruling says.

"We previously have expressed our abhorrence of Trantino's crimes," the court goes on, noting that the horror of that night "is seared not only in the memories of the victims' families and friends but also in the consciousness of society. From the standpoint of retribution, perhaps no prison sentence, whatever its length, is sufficiently severe."

Acknowledging the public outcry over the possibility of parole over the years, the court says that "agencies of government cannot ignore the law in special cases. At its core, this case is more about the rule of law than it is about Thomas Trantino."

§

Justice Stein is right about one thing: the public does not really understand why the Angel Lounge killer should go free. After all, some people have never really understood why he didn't go to the electric chair.

Bergen County Executive William "Pat" Schuber, in Washington for the inauguration of President George W. Bush, says the state should appeal the high court's ruling, which he says "strikes at the heart of the people of Bergen County."

Newspaper reports add to the outrage. In an article on reaction to the ruling, the *Record* of Hackensack says that "Trantino was convicted in February 1964 of forcing Sgt. Peter Voto and provisional Officer Gary Tedesco to take off their clothes at gunpoint, then shooting them as they pleaded for their lives. Some Trantino critics have asserted that the officers were subjected to prolonged torture or sexual assault. Trantino's lawyer, Robert [*sic*] Lowenstein, said nothing like that happened, but such stories have become legend among police officers, fueling an anti-Trantino furor."

But some of the reaction is hard to ignore. First of all, there is the dissenter, Judge David Baime of the Appellate Division, who had been temporarily assigned to the New Jersey Supreme Court to hear the case. He thinks the parole board was justified in concluding that Trantino poses a big risk.

"The stakes are high," the dissenter writes. "If the Appellate Division is correct, Trantino deserves his freedom and is entitled to parole. But if the Parole Board is right, the consequences of Trantino's release will be felt, not by some pain-free public entity, nor by some penitent psychologist, social worker or public official, but by tomorrow's next victim for whose protection and welfare we hold office.

"In my view, the Parole Board's denial of release is supported by substantial credible evidence in the record. I would not wager the safety of the public on the odds that Trantino is a changed man."

The judge zeroes in on the findings of the parole board's chief psychologist, Dr. Glenn Ferguson, who ultimately concluded that Trantino did pose a substantial risk if released. But Judge Baime recalls Dr. Ferguson's earlier, opposite findings, in which the doctor concluded after a 1995 examination that Trantino's crime was "so contrary to his moral character" that it might have been motivated by "a drug-induced psychotic state."

The judge is clearly flabbergasted and cannot resist addressing what he calls "the aura of unreality that surrounds this enigmatic statement."

"It is undisputed that at the time the crimes were committed Trantino was a philandering wife abuser who was harboring two wanted killers and who had committed a string of burglaries and robberies," Judge Baime writes, referring to Frank Falco and Anthony Cassarino. "In light of these circumstances, Ferguson's statement that Trantino's crimes were 'so contrary to his moral character' is utterly confounding."

In any event, Dr. Ferguson changed his mind in 1998, opining that Trantino was indeed a risk for committing new crimes. The judge thinks the doctor was right in the end, and thinks that the parole board was reasonable in finding "that Trantino is manipulative, deceptive and explosive, and that these traits make him a poor candidate for parole."

The judge makes his own "diagnosis" of Thomas Trantino, finding that he has suffered from "convenient amnesia" about that night in August 1963. And some of Trantino's overdone language (such as "the events that transpired in the Angel Lounge") strikes the judge as a grudging and belated admission of guilt, an admission that is "abstract, obtuse and convoluted."

Judge Baime looks back to the early days of the case and the trial of 1964, when the jury "viewed Trantino's claim of a drug-induced psychotic episode, and saw nothing but the heart of darkness."

The dissenter knows his judicial colleagues share his deep concern for the rule of law and the parole system, as well as for the safety of the people. He and they have simply come to very different conclusions.

"The story of sin and redemption is as old as humankind," Judge Baime concludes. "It is all too easy to succumb to the chimeric vision that good ultimately triumphs over evil in the human soul. But reality bites, and too often the truth lies elsewhere. The Parole Board viewed Trantino's claims of rehabilitation with a healthy dose of skepticism. So do I."

And what of Trantino's excellent behavior record in prison for at least two decades? Some criminal-justice experts believe that the way an inmate lives his life behind bars, in a controlled situation free of the choices, burdens, and temptations that make up everyday life on the outside, doesn't count for much in the end. They say that a prisoner's conduct is no real indicator of how he will be in the real world.

The prospect of Trantino's release raises another question for Brendan Byrne, the former governor, judge, and prosecutor who would like to see the death penalty abolished and replaced by life in prison without parole. "When you get a guy who's a model prisoner, as apparently this fellow has been, then you're going to get people who say stay with the death penalty because life may not mean life," Byrne says. "If someone's a model prisoner, then somebody might let him out."

§

But Thomas Trantino is to become a free man, whether anyone else likes it or not. Roger Lowenstein says his client doesn't want much: "Give him some fresh air, toilet paper, and toothpaste and he'll be happy."

No doubt, just being able to come and go as he pleases is what the gray-haired Trantino wants most. But he also hopes to rekindle the relationship he had with Charlee, who waited for him so long, only to lose hope in the late 1990s.

First, though, Trantino has to behave himself for a year in a halfway house. But where? The New Jersey Supreme Court has said it should be in the Camden–Cherry Hill area of South Jersey. There are three such halfway houses in the region, run by Volunteers in Service to America under contract with the state. But the agency wants nothing to do with the notorious Angel Lounge killer, fearing that someone might try to kill him and thus put other residents or staff members in danger.

Corrections officials wonder about housing Trantino in Trenton. They call James Hemm, who runs a halfway house there, for advice. "I told them to send Trantino out of state," Hemm says. "I think he would be in jeopardy in any program in the state."

Lowenstein says he is open to suggestions, as long as there is no thought given to putting Trantino in North Jersey. "It would be too hurtful to the victims' families," the lawyer says. It would probably be dangerous to Trantino, as well.

The Department of Corrections mulls over the situation. Technically, the operators of the halfway houses don't have the right to refuse someone, the department says. Not if they want to keep doing business with the state, for $57 a day per inmate. The department would rather not have to force a house to accept Trantino, but it can if it has to.

Maybe New York should take him, some official says. After all, he was on parole from New York State in 1963 when he started it all. And Trantino's brother, Richard, lives on Staten Island.

But no one can force Richard Trantino to take in his brother. And what if he won't? Maybe the only thing to do is to open a halfway house just for Thomas Trantino. Nothing about this case is typical.

§

Sunday, February 11, 2001. Although he doesn't know it when he wakes, this is the day Thomas Trantino will take his first steps back to the real world. As afternoon turns to evening, his keepers at South Woods order him to put his clothes into a duffel bag. Almost before he knows it, he is out of the prison, riding in a red Buick with two plainclothes officers, heading almost due north on a good hour's drive, to Camden.

Remarkably, it is his sixty-third birthday. He has been given the gift of freedom.

"Why are they going to bring him here?" a Camden resident asks. "Camden's got enough problems."

No one could dispute that. For years—decades, really—Camden has been an urban basket case, its business and industry long gone. Its 80,000 or so residents are older, poorer, and sadder than people in most other cities. There are no restaurants, no shopping centers. There is no reason to go to Camden, and many reasons to want to leave. City government has been ineffective or downright corrupt. Some residents would leave if they could afford to; others know nothing else, and so what they know best is despair.

"If New Jersey needed an enema," a cruel joke goes, "then Camden is where they'd put the hose."

Trantino's destination is a halfway house on Fairview Street in one of the grittiest of Camden's mostly rundown neighborhoods. Abandoned houses sag forlornly on the streets nearby. With no irony intended, the halfway facility is called Hope House.

Trantino arrives just before midnight. Reporters have gotten wind of the transfer, and the plainclothes officers must shove their way past them. Despite the chill, Trantino is clad in a short-sleeved prison jumpsuit.

Normally, the people running a halfway house are given three days' notice before an inmate arrives. This time, the state has given no notice. Trantino is brought to Hope House and signed in before anyone can protest or plead to lawmakers to put him somewhere else. Anywhere else.

Hope House, meant to accommodate 125 inmates on two floors, is the most modern building in the neighborhood. The cinder-block structure is surrounded by an eight-foot-high chain-link fence, but it is not locked. It is not a prison, after all.

Yet it feels like one, at least to Thomas Trantino. By Monday morning, city officials and the people who live around Hope House feel the presence of the man who has been foisted upon them like a poor relation.

"I am vehemently opposed to the placement of Thomas Trantino in my city," says Mayor Gwendolyn Faison.

State Senator Wayne Bryant, a Democrat who represents Camden, is just as furious. "The state of New Jersey has taken the usual approach that what it doesn't want, it decides Camden needs," he fumes.

Why, Bryant wonders aloud, doesn't Bergen County take Trantino? After all, the crime was committed there. Bergen has no halfway house, it turns out. But there is one in neighboring Passaic County.

The hatred for Thomas Trantino is almost palpable on the grim streets of Camden. He is ordered to stay inside Hope House. Only his lawyer is allowed in to see him. For the moment, Trantino's life is just as it was in South Woods, except that the prison was in a more cheerful setting.

Trantino understands at once: he cannot stay in Camden. He calls Lowenstein collect in Los Angeles and tells him so. Lowenstein calls the state attorney general's office and says he will prepare an application to move Trantino to another state. He even expects the support of William Schuber, the Bergen County executive. "For the first time, we are all on the same page," Lowenstein says.

Lowenstein is asked where Trantino will go. "Anywhere that's never heard of him," he says.

CHAPTER 47

Winter
in Lodi

The reporters who seek out Andy Voto are friendly and respectful, whether they reach him by phone or come to his house in Lodi. But their queries get to be a strain on Andy and his wife, Matty, after the New Jersey Supreme Court's ruling.

Over and over, Andy has to tell the same story, say the same things—the things he has been saying for years. "They have no respect for the victims," he tells one reporter. "You can't trust the justice system. You can't trust the penal system."

Andy is exhausted. He's not a hundred percent better from the hip surgery, either. And it's not like he's a kid anymore. Andy will be seventy-five in the summer of 2001.

About two weeks after the court ruling, Andy wakes in the middle of the night. He doesn't feel well at all. He's having trouble breathing. No, it's worse than that. After a few moments, he has this terrible feeling in his chest and realizes he can hardly breathe at all ... can hardly breathe ...

He rouses Matty, who calls an ambulance. Within minutes, Andy is in Hackensack Medical Center, a few miles from his home. The doctors and nurses give him something to calm him, then give him oxygen. Now that he can breathe, his panic subsides.

He's still in the hospital on a bitter-cold day in early February 2001, holding court with relatives and friends but unable to hide his black mood. "I don't think I'll make it to my seventy-fifth birthday," he says.

His visitors steer him away from talk like that, but no one can blame him for worrying. Yet Andy still likes to banter, and his eyes light up over a good argument. And nothing energizes him like the mere mention of his mortal enemy, Thomas Trantino.

"Scumbag," Andy mutters. "Puke . . . " In truth, no words are adequate to convey the depths of his hatred.

A few days later, the doctors determine that Andy has come down with a virus that weakened his heart. The condition is treatable, but he has to be careful. He starts looking forward to his seventy-fifth birthday.

§

On a cold winter day, a wreath leans against the sand-colored stone over the ground where Peter Voto is buried in St. Nicholas Cemetery in Lodi. Many of the nearby gravestones carry Italian names. Some have photographs from long ago, pictures of stern-faced men in dark suits and women in plain dresses. Some of the men and women are from the old country, or the old Lodi. They are from a time long gone.

Gary Tedesco's grave is a couple hundred yards from Peter Voto's. Gary lies next to his father, just inside the fence that separates a busy street from the place of the dead. Gary's marker bears the familiar photograph of the serious young man with the crew cut and thin tie from another time. *Died in the line of duty,* an inscription says.

And so he did, but for what? Not to save a life or stop a crime. He died because he and his partner went to see about a ruckus in a saloon.

The monument outside the municipal building calls Peter Voto and Gary Tedesco "two heroes." Yet if Trantino and Falco had decided just to leave the two cops tied up, then had driven off in the police car with Peter Voto's gun, the Angel Lounge episode would have been an embarrassment, a fiasco, grist for editorials and inquiries, rather than the stuff of legend.

There would have been sharper questions in public about whether a veteran police sergeant was alert enough, or whether it was folly to allow an untrained, unarmed rookie to ride on regular patrol and be in harm's way. In light of what did happen, the questions seem almost obscene, but they are there nonetheless.

At the trial in 1964, Chief Phillip Wagenti related how new cops prepared for duty in Lodi: "I told [them] to come around and get acquainted. . . . I told the superiors these new men would be around the headquarters and teach them some of the routine police work." The veteran cops, he said, took the rookies along and "showed them the boxes and streets and showed them the places of the town."

An illusion died with Peter Voto and Gary Tedesco. It had to do with the nature of police work, even in a small, friendly community. Police work is dangerous, whether an officer is chasing a speeder, arresting a wife-beater, or breaking up a bar ruckus.

Peter Voto may have been in danger a hundred times before the last night of his life. A hundred times he prevailed because of his strength and size and savvy. How was he to know that two of the men in the Angel Lounge that night were not run-of-the-mill barflies but gun-toting hoodlums?

All we know is that he let his guard down for a moment, with terrible consequences.

Things might have been different if he had had a seasoned partner. One can even imagine that things might have been different if Gary Tedesco's first collar, in the burglary at the ice cream store, had not been so easy. If, instead of giving up peacefully, a burglar had rushed him in the dark, flashed a knife, knocked him to the ground, and run away, Gary Tedesco might not have gotten a commendation. He might have picked up some bruises, needed some stitches, worn a knife scar as a reminder. He might have learned a lesson that would save his life not many days later.

The Bergen County Police Academy was started a couple of years after the Angel Lounge killings. Prospective police officers get some seven hundred hours of training, much of it running through the various life-and-death scenarios that can come up in police work. Ron Calissi, the prosecutor's son who became head of the academy, said the Angel Lounge killings are often cited as a lesson.

Guy Calissi died in 1980. His son said the prosecutor never had second thoughts about seeking the death penalty against Trantino. And once the killer escaped the electric chair, Guy Calissi thought he should stay behind bars. Forever.

§

The cemetery where Andy Voto and his big brother earned pocket change watering the plants a long, long time ago summons so many thoughts of life and death on a cold winter day.

Judge Theodore Trautwein, whose refusal to set an amount for restitution two decades ago was pivotal in keeping Thomas Trantino in prison, died in a retirement home in Hollywood, Florida, on August 17, 2000. He was eighty.

Albert Gross, who represented Thomas Trantino at the 1964 trial, became a successful sculptor on the eve of retirement. His metal works sold for thousands of dollars. He had everything a man could want.

On the early morning of September 17, 1997, one of his three sons, Nelson, was abducted by three teenage boys outside a restaurant he owned in Edgewater, New Jersey. They forced him to withdraw $20,000 from a bank and then drive them around.

One of the three kidnappers grew fearful that Gross would recognize him as one of his former busboys. So, in a desolate spot near the George Washington Bridge in Manhattan, the ex-busboy stabbed Nelson Gross and smashed his head in with a rock. The three youths were soon caught and pleaded guilty to charges that made them liable to thirty years in prison without the chance of parole.

Old age was kind to Albert Gross: he couldn't grasp the details of his son's death. His other sons, Michael and Paul, spared him the worst.

Albert Gross died in 1998 at the age of ninety-one.

Some months ago, I reached one of the four women who were at the Angel Lounge with Thomas Trantino and Frank Falco. She said she has never really recovered from that night and asked me to leave her alone.

§

To get to Sadie Tedesco's house on Harrison Street, one drives up a hill from downtown Lodi. The house is the one she has lived in all these years. It is a cluttered storehouse of memories. There are pictures of Gary, not just the serious young man of the crew cut and thin tie but the little boy Gary, in the cowboy costume or sailor suit. So long ago.

Sadie Tedesco doesn't hear very well. She tires easily. All this talk about parole for the man who took her boy away upsets her. She says Trantino never should have been paroled the first time, from Great Meadow. "If they'd kept him in prison, maybe Gary would still be alive," Sadie says.

She loves her boy as much now as she did when he was young. The thick hair would be gray by now, like his father's. "He was one fine boy," she says. "And not just because he died that way."

The Tedesco family was no more perfect than any other family, and there are hints that Gary's death deepened fault lines, perhaps between the sisters, or between mother and daughters. Patricia Tedesco's words come to mind: "The family was destroyed as a unit, and we were destroyed as individuals."

Sadie Tedesco is vague about her age, though simple math puts her in her mid-eighties. She enjoys friends, chocolates, a little wine now and then. But she never learned to "get on with her life" after her son was taken from her. Maybe the pain she feels keeps Gary alive, in a way.

Over the kitchen table hangs a photograph of the teenage Gary on a sunny day, leaning against a gleaming red '32 Ford he restored. Sadie gazes at it and frowns. "I'll have to get it done over," she says. "It's fading."

§

The former Adrienne Peraino has many pictures from long ago. She shows them without tears but with a faraway look in her eyes. She tries not to waste time wondering how things might have been different if Gary had been a little less confident or . . .

Ah, what's the use. "He lives on as a twenty-two-year-old," she says with awe. "I have a son who's older."

Adrienne got engaged at Christmastime in 1965, to one of Gary's friends. With a little hesitation, she went to see Patrick and Sadie Tedesco to tell them face to face. They brightened for a moment and wished her well.

She didn't invite them to the wedding the following summer. Her heart was just too full of too many emotions. But when she and her new husband emerged from the church, she saw Patrick and Sadie standing across the street, waving at her. "They wanted to be there for me," Adrienne says wistfully.

The marriage to Gary's friend lasted quite a few years, then fell apart. But now she has a new husband, with a big smile and a friendly way. He understands why she keeps the old pictures.

Here's one of Gary and her, sitting at the Tedesco family table for a Sunday dinner. And here's one from Patty's confirmation that spring of 1963, just a few months before everything changed.

And here is her favorite. Yes, it's the color photo of Gary when he was seventeen or eighteen, leaning on a sunshine-filled day against the shiny red '32 Ford he had restored so lovingly. It's the picture Sadie Tedesco loves so much. Gary's expression is proud and serious.

Years after Gary's death, Adrienne went back to school and got her degree. She lives in central New Jersey now. She speaks French and teaches computer science to junior-high students. She wonders about the life she and Gary might have lived, the children they might have had.

Might have had. "Would we have gotten married? Who knows?"

It's the not-knowing that bothers her. She has no doubt that Gary would have finished college; he was too focused and mature, too *good,* to leave something undone. She knows he would have been good as a Lodi cop or, more likely, a state or federal lawman.

But would they have married? They might have, or they might have grown apart. Adrienne knows that. She is sad that the relationship ended the way it did, when they were still growing together. Her feelings about the man who ended the life of her first love are simple: "Let him continue to pay until the day he dies."

She doesn't get back to Lodi much anymore. "It's all so different there now," she says. "We lived in a different world then."

But if you are from Lodi, *of* Lodi, you never really get away, not that you want to. Adrienne takes a ring from her finger and holds it up for display. Her father bought it for her mother years ago, and her mom gave it to Adrienne just before she died.

"You know where he bought it? Tony Grasso's jewelry store."

Tony Grasso. Once a co-owner of the Angel Lounge, now owner of a jewelry store located practically across the street from the Lodi police station. Such is the smallness of Lodi.

§

Tony Grasso's daughter Deborah is running the store on a Saturday afternoon in winter. Her father, now in his late seventies, has left early and doesn't care to talk about the long-ago. But Deborah Grasso, a friendly woman who teaches remedial math at a community college, doesn't mind. "Sin Strip?" she says incredulously. "Oh, please!"

We all have our selective memories, and in Deborah Grasso's the Angel Lounge was a place where bands played and people went to drink and to eat simple food. She went to the bar herself as a child, during the daytime, when her father was cleaning up or seeing to one thing or another.

"It was just a fun place to hang out," she says of the Angel Lounge. How about gambling? No, she says. Or prostitution? No, she says, a little steel in her voice now. "He had too much respect for my mother." A poster on the wall sums up Tony Grasso's values: "There's no better lesson in how individuals can come together for the greater good than the American family."

Tony Grasso met Frances Pinto, the woman who would become his wife, at Palisades Amusement Park many years ago. Apartment buildings now stand where, once upon a time, people took thrill rides and ate cotton candy on summer days, where Norma Jaconetta and Sally Vander Fliet spent a lazy Sunday afternoon in 1963 before heading for the Angel Lounge and the rendezvous that would change so many lives.

Deborah Grasso loves her father, and proudly shows pictures of him as a smiling young man in his army uniform, with jet-black hair. Here's an old black-and-white photo of Tony Grasso and his good friend Anthony Perillo, wearing silly hats and silly grins at some holiday party from way back, when so much of their lives lay ahead and they were dreaming of prosperity in their new bar on Route 46.

So why did the terrible thing of August 26, 1963, happen in the Angel Lounge and not somewhere else?

There is no good answer to that, Deborah says. "It was just a bad set of circumstances."

The other Tony agrees. "We never had trouble there," Anthony Perillo says in a telephone interview from his winter home in Florida.

He, too, is in his late seventies. He chuckles for a moment as he lets himself remember the Angel Lounge as it was before the awful night. "It was sort of a dump," he admits. But a friendly dump, he says. "It could have happened anyplace. Whoever comes through the door, I don't know who they are."

So, he is asked, who are these people who suggest that the Angel Lounge was some cesspool? "People who never went there," he replies. You have to remember some things, Perillo says. For one thing, the bars on Route 46 were already there by the time he and Tony Grasso came back from the war.

Anthony Perillo knew about death; one of his cousins was killed in the Battle of the Bulge. But Perillo can never forget driving to his bar that summer night and seeing the bodies on the floor: "I turned my head away."

Perillo's wife, Margaret, is Nick Kayal's sister. Perillo says he feels bad all these years later for his brother-in-law, who served underage girls and two hoodlums that night in 1963 and wrapped a gun in a towel, an action that helped to bring death into the place. Nick Kayal never quite got over what happened, his brother-in-law says.

Anthony Perillo's voice softens as he recalls the days of unbearable sadness after the killings, especially when he went to Peter Voto's wake. He had known Peter Voto, after all. Hell, he knew the Tedescos, too. Gary's dad was his accountant and had tried to get Gary a job tending bar in the Angel Lounge, for God's sake . . .

After the killings, Anthony Perillo got out of the saloon business. He sold Italian foodstuffs to restaurants and pizza places for a while, then retired. He goes back to Lodi in the warm weather. He has friends there still. Anthony Perillo is from Lodi, *of* Lodi.

§

The two Tonys came home from the war with a dream. They wanted to sell booze and make money. What was so bad about that, really?

The Tonys were family men. They and their wives raised a mathematician, a sales executive for a tea company, a restaurant owner, a chiropractor, and an accountant.

The Tonys wanted to sell booze and fun. They meant no harm. How did Anthony Perillo put it? *"Whoever comes through the door, I don't know who they are."*

True enough. But there are different kinds of bars, and they attract different kinds of people. For a long time, the word was out that if you wanted to stay up late drinking and not be hassled for it, then Lodi was the place to go.

Bars that stay open until five in the morning, as the Route 46 joints did for a while, draw rough people. By the time Lodi decided the places should close earlier, the tone had been set. Three o'clock is still a late closing time for Sunday night (or Monday morning). A bar that keeps those hours can expect to draw more than its share of low-life drunks. This isn't moralizing; it's simple common sense.

The Angel Lounge of the two Tonys may have been no worse than the other bars along the strip. Maybe the two Tonys ran a *better* place. But the freewheeling ways set the stage for the horror of August 26, 1963. Many years ago, Guy Calissi said the apathy of ordinary citizens allowed the bars to flourish. He was right. The notion that the bars were just a nuisance was another thing that died with Peter Voto and Gary Tedesco.

CHAPTER 48

Rip Van Winkle

It is February 11, 2002, Thomas Trantino's sixty-fourth birthday. He walks out of a Camden halfway house, where he has lived quietly for a year, into sunshine and freedom. It turns out he never moved far away, despite the resentment in Camden.

He has saved $1,800 from working in a Camden pizzeria on a work-release program. Quickly, he goes to a drugstore and buys cologne and hair dye. The hair is all gray now; he looks his age.

He carries a black bag holding a new portable computer, a gift from his brother. He is eager to learn how to send e-mail. He wants to get a cell phone. He wants to have a social life, but the world has changed so much. Trantino feels like a latter-day Rip Van Winkle.

Trantino says again how sorry he is for what he did. He dares to ask for forgiveness, and says he wants to move on with his life.

The Voto and Tedesco families cannot stand to hear him. "He can say he's sorry, but he can't be as sorry as we are," Andy Voto says. "He can change, but for the families what remains is pain, anguish, and frustration."

Thomas Trantino says he remembers a vow he made to himself in prison a long time ago, something to hold onto in case he ever got out: "That I would do no harm."

He wants to live with his father, now eighty-nine, on Staten Island. But that idea falls through when the father's landlord threatens to evict the old man. The landlord doesn't want a killer around.

Roger Lowenstein says the New Jersey parole authorities may be trying to sabotage Trantino, hoping he'll mess up enough on the outside that he can be returned to prison, thus satisfying the Voto and Tedesco families.

Not so, parole officials insist. They say they're trying to help Trantino find housing and employment.

Lowenstein says he would feel safe with Thomas Trantino in his home. Defense lawyers don't feel that way about all their clients, not by a long shot. But Lowenstein says Trantino is a changed man, nothing like the hoodlum who triggered the bloodbath in the Angel Lounge. He says the Thomas Trantino of 1963 is long dead. In his place stands a gray-haired man in his sixties.

Let us hope that Andy Voto is wrong about the man who killed his brother. Let us hope that Trantino is not a liar, a manipulator, a man cold as ice on the inside. Let us hope that Judge David Baime's worry, so eloquently expressed in dissent, is unfounded and that Thomas Trantino simply wants to fade away, to live the evening of his life quietly.

As I close this book, I feel that I don't know Thomas Trantino well enough. Perhaps that is because I spent only one long morning with him. Or perhaps there is just not that much to know. I think that what makes Trantino unusual, the only thing that makes him unusual despite his dabbling with brush and pen, is the one terrible wrong that he cannot undo, the deed of an early summer morning a long time ago.

Having asked so many people to share their thoughts and memories with me, I feel obligated to say what I think. I believe that Trantino is not an evil man now, even though he did an evil thing a long time ago. I believe him, I *choose* to believe him, when he says he is sorry and wishes he could go back in time to call back the evil moment.

I recall a television interview with one of Charles Manson's women. She was in Sharon Tate's house that night in 1969 when the actress and several other people were killed. She was a joyous participant in the butchery.

Now, this former Manson acolyte is a middle-aged woman of better than average intelligence. On television, she looked like someone you would see at the supermarket or the shopping mall, or even the country club.

She hopes to get out of prison one day, to live quietly and anonymously. Maybe even do some good in the world. But she will always be a captive. Each morning when she opens her eyes to the new day, she has the same thought: *"I am the bringer of death. And I deserve to carry that burden because of what I did."*

Thomas Trantino has not expressed himself that way. Maybe he can't. Too much has been made of the slim book he wrote years ago. It simply does not matter that he chose, for a time, to write and paint instead of building model airplanes or birdhouses. And truth to tell, he seldom gives wings to words.

Or maybe he just is not an exquisitely sensitive man. Maybe he feels as sorry as he is able to feel.

Not all killers are alike, after all.

I remember my visit to South Carolina's death row years ago. I met a simpleton who had crushed a friend's head with a board after an argument over whiskey, then had gone home to hide in his own attic. The police found him easily enough, since his feet protruded from under the floorboards.

A few cells down was a man whose stare froze me. I spoke not a word to him, nor he to me, yet I feared and loathed him. There was nothing in his eyes, just nothing. Later, I learned that he had kidnapped a businessman for ransom, then had done away with him to avoid loose ends. The victim's body was never found.

When this killer's eyes locked on mine, he was safely behind bars. I had nothing to fear from what he might do. The chill I felt was from what he was. I felt the presence of pure evil.

Tom Trantino is no simpleton; far from it. Nor, I think, is he like the empty-eyed killer, whose crime was far more calculating and devious. Trantino is what he has been for many years: a man who did a horrific thing that no power on earth can undo.

And as horrible as it was, it was not as it has so often been depicted in print and on television. Mistakes in journalism, as elsewhere in life, are so easy to see in retrospect. There was a crying need years ago for some reporter *somewhere* to go back to the beginning, to do a thorough reprise of what happened, and what did not. The coverage of the Angel Lounge case over the years generated much more heat than light, regardless of how one feels about Trantino and the parole system and the law in general.

I know a number of lawyers who defend people on death row. They say that capital punishment is wrong and imposed unfairly, and that it does no good. Yet it must be said that the lives of Andy Voto and his father would have been better had Thomas Trantino gone to the electric chair. So would the lives of Patrick and Sadie Tedesco and their daughters, and the lives of the children of Peter Voto. So, perhaps, would the life of Adrienne Peraino.

All those people would have suffered less if the Angel Lounge killer had been executed. They could have visited the graves of Peter Voto and Gary Tedesco with something like peace in their hearts. But as one who has witnessed an execution, I can say that watching Thomas Trantino die might have given them nightmares after the sweet rush of revenge.

So the law didn't give those people the vengeance they wanted. The law cannot make things better for them now, not that it ever really could. The sad truth is that the law is not always just. If it were, Charles Manson would not be alive in prison at this writing, and Richard Speck, who killed eight nurses in Chicago in 1966, would not have died a natural death behind bars, years after his unspeakable crime.

§

But while he escaped the electric chair, Thomas Trantino has been doubly punished, in a sense. More than two decades ago, he thought he was close to freedom. He had visions of raising children with his wife, Charlee, amid streams and ponds in the country. This was to be his second chance for the straight life, the good life he had squandered before.

The state nurtured those dreams. The state led him to believe—incredibly—that he could go free after serving a mere sixteen or seventeen years for killing two men. Then the state killed his dreams, day by day, year by year. Trantino lost his wife, his visions of a new family, what was left of his youth.

In view of what he did on August 26, 1963, not many people sympathize with him. But the way the state handled the case over the years, through its various agencies and changing lineups of officials and for whatever reasons, amounts to a terrible way to run a criminal-justice system. Maybe parole never should have been dangled before Trantino two decades ago. Maybe *that* was the irreversible error.

Andy Voto and his kin and the parents and sisters of Gary Tedesco had every right to do what they did. If defense lawyers can use the system to help guilty people go free (and not always in the name of some higher, constitutional ideal), surely the families of victims can use it to try to keep criminals in prison.

To spend time with Andy Voto—good cop, good son, good brother—is to wish peace for his spirit. He fought the brave fight against his enemy. For more than two decades, since talk of parole first came up, Andy won a victory each day Trantino spent in prison. Each day. I am told by the Department of Corrections that Thomas Trantino spent more time in prison than anyone in New Jersey *ever* has.

Thomas Trantino has paid an awesome price. For what he did on that long-ago summer night, he gave up a great piece of his life, from young manhood through middle age, years when he might have been raising a family, wrestling with choices, and savoring love, friendship, and laughter.

Now that he is free, I wish him a peaceful life, for everyone's sake. I wish him a long life, too, because he has much to atone for.

§

The bars along Route 46 in Lodi are long gone, replaced by used-car lots and fast-food places. The site of the terrible crime is only a few minutes' drive from Andy Voto's house. Such is the smallness of Lodi.

A tile-and-marble shop sits where the Angel Lounge used to be. How many people who come in to ask about kitchen and bathroom fixtures know what happened on this ground?

It was so long ago. Yesterday.

INDEX

Alesso Funeral Home, 50–51, 63
Angel Lounge, xi, 10, 21, 34–36, 217
  closing of, 117
  lawsuits against, 52, 54, 141
  liquor license suspension of, 55–56
Angel Lounge murders
  different memories of, 108–115
  mythology of, 53, 61, 135, 168, 182, 207
  Trantino's memory of, 193–194
  trial of, 62–115
Appeals, 123–126
Appellate Division hearings, 198–203
Arterbridge, Glenn, 161, 183
Attica prison riot, 137
Autopsies, 63–64

Babagnoli, Matilda, 30
Baime, David S., 203, 207–208, 220
Bayside State Prison, 139
Bell, James, 182–183
Belli, Frank, 29, 52
Bello, J. *See* Falco, Frank
Benedetto, Rocco, 21, 22, 25–26, 46, 52, 72
Bennett, Tony, 53
Bergen County, New Jersey, x–xi, 6
Bergen County Jail, 55
Bergen County Policemen's Benevolent
  Association, 134, 135
Bisignano, Frank, 134
Bradley, Ed, 191, 195, 197, 198
Brennan, William J., Jr., 124, 127
Breslin, Roger W., Jr., 145
Brill, Frank, 48–49

Brooklyn burglary, 32–34, 76
Bryant, Wayne, 211
Byrne, Brendan T., 130, 209

Cahill, William T., 129
Calissi, Ethel, 57
Calissi, Guy W., 108–109, 111–115, 117,
  122, 125, 144, 168, 178, 194, 202, 214
  cross-examining Trantino, 87–92
  prosecuting Trantino, 45, 46, 49, 52,
  57–59, 60–61, 62–64, 66, 69, 72, 75,
  77, 94–99
  summation of, 105–106
Calissi, Ron, 59
Calo, Dennis, 165–166
Camden, 210–211, 219
Carley, Richard T., 156
Carlstedt, Warren, 135
Carroll, Sally, 162, 166
Carter, Rubin "Hurricane," 137–138
Cassarino, Anthony "Tony Winks,"
  26–27, 32–35, 37, 45–46, 52, 69–70,
  73, 75, 76, 78, 88, 89, 91, 93–94, 111,
  208
  at Angel Lounge, 79–81
Children's Village, 17
Coleman, James H., Jr., 203
Collins, Dr. Laurence M., 97–98, 105, 126
Consovoy, Andrew, 177, 195, 198,
  201–202, 204
Cook, Daniel, 7
Cop-killer legislation, 174
Cottage Inn, 79

De Vesa, Fred, 173
Death penalty, 121–122, 127–131
Death row, 122–123, 130
Defense lawyers, 55–56, 59–60
Defense witnesses, 74–101
Degnan, John, 150–151, 162
Delaney, Joseph, 145–146, 158, 166
Denbeaux, Mark, 173–174
Dietz, Christopher, 148, 150–151,
    157–158, 159, 160, 162, 179
DiFrancesco, Donald, 206
Dole, Bob, 176
Downey, Morton, Jr., 166–167

Edwards, W. Cary, 171
Egles, Robert, 166, 167, 172
Equal Justice, 199
Essex County ruling, 129–130
Executions, 127

Facella, Robert, 63, 64
Fahy, John J., 169
Fairview Street halfway house, 210
Faison, Gwendolyn, 211
Falco, Frank, 16–17, 25–27, 32–34, 35,
    37–39, 75–78, 88, 89, 92, 93, 94,
    102–105, 110, 114–115, 182, 184,
    193–194, 208
  at Angel Lounge, 79–85
  death of, 47–48, 59, 147, 158
  friendship with Thomas Trantino,
    20–22
  in Gary Tedesco's murder, 111–112
  at Great Meadow State Prison, 18
  hunt for, 45–47
  Munoz murder by, 69–70
Falco, Patricia, 20, 21–22, 25, 26, 27, 33,
    34, 38, 45–46, 67, 85, 94, 103
  at Angel Lounge, 78–85
  testimony of, 108–110, 112, 113
Fall, Robert A., 203
Farmer, John J., 203
Fauver, William, 152
Ferguson, Dr. Glenn, 208
Ferraro, Frank. *See* Falco, Frank
Fink, Dr. Maximilian, 125

Fisher, Clarkson, 138
Florio, James J., 169, 171
Fogel, Jeffrey, 133, 136, 146
Fordham Law School, 60
Four Seasons, 53
Friedman, Donald, 151
"Full rehabilitative potential," 172, 179
Funicello, Victor, 130–131
Fusco, Frank, 45–46

Galda, Fred, 46, 48, 49, 52, 54, 60, 71–72,
    138, 168, 176
Ganny, Charlee Irene, 133–134, 155, 161,
    166, 188, 194, 203, 209
Garcia, Luis, 162
Gerling, Enid, 48–49, 52–53, 54
Gilady, Dr. Raphael, 63–65
Grand jury hearing, 108
Grasso, Deborah, 216–217
Grasso, Tony, 9–10, 51, 55–56, 216, 217
Graves, Frank, 158–159, 174
Great Meadow State Prison, 15, 17,
    18–19, 75, 102–103
Greenberg, Judge Morton, 151
Gross, Albert, 55, 56, 59–60, 72, 74,
    75–76, 94–96, 98–99, 114, 116, 121,
    123, 125, 128, 136, 214
  summation of, 102–105
Gross, Michael, 55
Gross, Nelson, 214
Guns
  confusion about, 110–112
  testimony on, 71–72

Hackensack Hospital, 68
Hale, William, 45
Halfway house, 209
  recommendation for, 171–172, 173,
    177–179
  transfer to, 210–211
Handler, Alan B., 156, 184, 185
Harvey, Elaine. *See* Tedesco Harvey,
    Elaine
Havey, James M., 203
Heck, Rose, 170, 174
Heights Inn, 9

Hemm, James, 209
Herb, Robert, 166
Hi-De-Ho Club, 9
Hope House, 210–211
Hoppe, August O., 71–72, 111, 112
Hotel Manhattan, 47
Hudson, Ralph J., 123
Hughes, Richard J., 50–51, 52, 123, 150
The Human Factor, 199
Humphreys, Burrell I., 175, 177–178

Jacobson, Mary, 198, 200
Jaconetta, Norma, 21–22, 26, 34, 37–38,
    45–46, 75, 76, 94, 103, 108–109, 110,
    113, 217
    at Angel Lounge, 78–85
    testimony of, 112, 113
Jones, Arthur, 177
Jury
    in murder cases, 128
    selection of, 60

Kahn, Frances, 124
Kallen, Kitty, 53
Kayal, Nicholas, 34–35, 46, 51, 52, 54, 67,
    73, 76, 108, 109
    lawsuits against, 141
    testimony of, 78–86, 104, 110–112, 113,
    115
Kean, Thomas H., 165, 167, 168
Kesselman, Samuel R., 93–94
Kidnapping, federal law on, 128–129
King, Michael P., 203
Koransky, Herbert, 55, 56, 63, 73, 114,
    116
Kugler, George F., Jr., 131

L.A. Law, 199
Lacey, Frederick B., 159, 160–162
Lafayette, Marquis de, 6–7
LaVecchia, Jaynee, 203
Law and Order, 199
Life magazine, "Requiem for a Punk,"
    48
Lock the Lock, 135–136

Lodi, ix, x–xi, 3, 6–10
    after Trantino's release, 212–218
Lodi Borough Council, 55–56
Long, Virginia, 203
Lowenstein, Roger, 135, 146–148,
    149–150, 161, 174–175, 178, 181–185,
    187, 188, 198–200, 219–220
    appealing parole board decision,
    202–203, 205–206, 209, 211

MacPhail, Patricia, 22, 25, 26–27, 32, 37,
    39–40, 45, 46, 75, 81, 85–86, 89, 90,
    92–94, 108
    at Angel Lounge, 77, 78–85
    testimony of, 100–101, 103, 106,
    112–115
Major, James A., Sr., 55
Manhunt, 45–49
Manson, Charles, 221
Marciano, Rocky, 3, 4
Marini, Judge Joseph W., 54, 59–60, 69,
    73, 74, 87, 91, 94–95, 97, 98–99,
    106–107, 109, 116–117
    appeals and, 123, 124, 125–126
    sentencing of Trantino, 121–122
McClure, Larry, 166, 167–168
McCoach, Harold, 205
McGlynn, Roger, 151, 155
McNamara, Henry P., 167
Meyner, Robert, 57, 58
Monge, Luis Jose, 127
Mount Virgin Church, 52
Munoz, Robert, murder of, 20, 26, 45,
    69–70, 81, 182

New Jersey Association on Corrections, 170
New Jersey General Assembly, 170
New Jersey Supreme Court
    capital punishment rulings of, 127–131
    restitution hearings of, 154–159
    ruling for Trantino release, 206–209
    second hearing before, 181–185
Nickolopoulos, Louis, 165, 168

Oetting, Robert W., 66–68, 85, 112, 113

Paparozzi, Mario, 204
Parenti, Frank, 40
Parole
    denials of, 161–162, 165–169, 179, 193, 195, 206–209
    laws regulating, 170–171
    restitution requirement for, 149–153, 166
Parole board
    Appellate Division ruling on, 201–203
    hearings of, 144–148
    political pressure on, 178–179
    restrictions on, 168, 170–171
    unfairness of, 177–180
Patronage jobs, 8
Paul, Les, 53
Peraino, Adrienne, 23–24, 29–30, 34–35, 42–43, 122, 140, 154, 215–216, 221
Peraino, Bessie, 140
Peraino, Joseph, 35
Peraino, Vito, 23, 43, 140
Perillo, Anthony, 9–10, 34, 51, 55–56, 86, 217–218
Picinich, Ronald, 128
Pierson, Stuart, 155, 158, 159, 160–161
Pinto, Frances, 217
Police and Civilians Together, 146
    letter-writing campaign of, 166
Poritz, Deborah, 203
Pressler, Sylvia B., 175–176, 181, 185
    dissenting opinion of, 178–180
Prosecution witnesses, 63–72
Prosecutors, 57–59, 61
Psychiatric testimony, 93–99

Quinn, Thomas, 47–48

Rahway inmates' council, 137–138
Rahway state prison, 132, 137, 197
Ranton, Loren, 166
Record articles, 132–135, 168, 207
Rennie, James, 7
Rennie, Robert, 7
Restitution requirement, 145–148, 166
    Appellate Division hearings on, 149–152
    testing of, 149–153

Riverfront State Prison, 161, 183
Riverfront State Prison Jaycees, 165
Rockefeller, Nelson A., 52
Route 46 bars, 8–10, 52. See also Angel Lounge

St. Nicholas Cemetery, 52
Saint Joseph's Church, 52
Santangelo Funeral Home, 50–51, 63
Sarla, Dr. Michael, 125
Schmidt, William H., 186, 202
Schuber, William "Pat," 168, 186, 207, 211
Schwartz, Joseph, 69
Sentencing, 121–126
Serpone, Joseph, 24
Serpone, Michael, 30, 46, 66–68, 112, 113, 140–142
Sin Strip, 8–10, 52
60 Minutes story, 191, 195, 197–198
Skevin, John, 150, 152–153
Smith, Edgar, 57
Soto, Gloria, 148, 153
South Bergen County Licensed Beverage Association, fundraising show, 53
South Woods State Prison, 187, 192, 199, 206
Speck, Richard, 221
Spinner, Karen, 170
Springstead, Harold, 126
Stays of execution, 123–126
Stein, Gary S., 203, 206–207
Stern, Edwin H., 175, 177–178
Stern, Herbert J., 138
Sturdevant, Fred, 123
Supreme Court, U.S., 124, 128
    capital punishment rulings of, 129, 131

Takvorian, Ted, 55
Talbot Hall, 186–187, 199–200
Tedesco, Gary, 5, 23–24, 29–31, 34–36, 61, 66, 92, 105–106
    at Angel Lounge, 79–85
    funeral of, 50–52
    memory of, 213–214
    murder of, 43, 59, 64–65, 67–68, 91, 108–115, 140

Tedesco, Patricia, 28, 29, 43, 139, 140, 147, 156, 215, 221
Tedesco, Patrick, 23, 24, 28–29, 34, 43, 52, 123, 140, 141
Tedesco, Sadie, 24, 28–29, 139, 140, 141, 169, 175, 215, 216, 221
Tedesco family, 50, 139–142
Tedesco Harvey, Elaine, 24, 31, 42–43, 139–140, 147, 152, 156, 167, 169, 205
Terhune, Jack, 186, 187, 188
Torricelli, Robert, 167
Trantino, Barbara, 49
Trantino, Blanche Stein, 11–12, 53, 73, 99
Trantino, Helene Pierra, 19, 20, 22, 25, 27, 75, 122, 198
Trantino, Nat, 11–13
Trantino, Richard, 53, 209–210
Trantino, Thomas, xi, 25–27, 32–34, 40
 at Angel Lounge, 78, 80–85
 appeals and stays of execution for, 123–126
 arraignment of, 52, 55
 book of, 115, 135–136
 conflicting testimony about, 108–115
 cross-examination of, 87–92
 on death row, 122–123
 early life of, 11–15
 flight of, 37–39
 Frank Falco and, 20–22
 at Great Meadow State Prison, 18–19
 hunt for, 45–49
 interview of, 192–196
 lack of remorse of, 182–183
 marriage of, 19
 memory failure of, 178, 185
 mental state of, 93–99, 107
 New Jersey extradition of, 52–53, 54
 New Jersey Supreme Court review of, 127–131
 painting exhibit of, 164
 parole denials to, 143–148, 157–159, 165–169, 171–172
 at Pat MacPhail's, 100–101
 personality and behavior record of, 196, 208–209
 prison life of, 132–138
 psychiatric evaluation of, 182–183, 187–188
 release of, 219–222

 restitution requirement for, 149–156
 ruling for release of, 206–209
 second marriage of, 155
 sentencing of, 15, 121–122
 60 Minutes interview of, 195
 surrender of, 48–49, 51
 testimony of, 74–77
 transfer to Talbot Hall, 186–187
 transfer to Vroom Building, 137–138
 trial of, 56, 62–117
 writing and drawings of, 132–134
Trantino case politics, 173–176
Trautwein, Judge Theodore W., 145, 148, 149, 152
Trial summations, 102–107
Trial verdict, 116–117
Two Tonys Incorporated, 9–10

United Piece Dye Works, 7–8

Vander Fliet, Sarah Jane (Sally), 26, 34, 35, 37–38, 45–46, 76, 78, 79–80, 81–82, 84, 103, 108, 113, 133, 217
 testimony of, 110, 111, 112, 114, 115
Verniero, Peter, 185, 187, 203
Victims' rights movement, 145
Vivere Lounge, 20, 45, 75
Voto, Andrew, 3–5, 41–42, 51, 117, 123, 135, 144, 145, 148, 154, 156, 163–164, 167, 170, 171, 175, 176, 185, 196, 203, 205–206, 219, 221, 222
 interview of, 191–192
 at New Jersey Supreme Court hearing, 184
 on release of Trantino, 212–213
 on *60 Minutes,* 197
Voto, Carolyn, 44
Voto, Constance, 44, 51, 116, 147
 death of, 158
Voto, Genarro (Jerry), 42, 44, 51, 144, 191
Voto, Jerry, Jr., 147, 156, 205
Voto, Mary, 51
Voto, Maryanne, 41
Voto, Matilda, 41, 212
Voto, Peter, 4–5, 30–31, 34–36, 44, 66, 92, 147–148, 205

at Angel Lounge, 79–85
discrepancies about murder of,
   108–115
funeral of, 50–52
memory of, 213
murder of, 41–42, 59, 61, 64, 67–68, 72,
   90–91, 105–106
Voto, Peter, Jr., 44
Voto family, 50

Wagenti, Chief Phillip, 65, 112, 213
Wagner, Colin, 126
Wallace, John E., 203

Weinglass, Leonard, 124, 125, 129, 136, 146
Weintraub, Joseph, 130
Welner, Dr. Michael, 187–188, 199
Wharton State Forest, 149, 154–155
Wharton Tract, 158
White, Walter Lee, 129–130
Whitman, Christine Todd, 173, 174, 187,
   199, 202–203
Winchell, Walter, 53
Wortendyke, Reynier, Jr., 124

Yardville Correction Center, 144, 158
   parole board meeting at, 156–157